A Diary of the Public Correspondenc Hope of Craighall, 1633-1645 • Sir T

Publisher's Note

The book descriptions we ask booksellers to display prominently warn that this is an historic book with numerous typos or missing text; it is not indexed or illustrated.

The book was created using optical character recognition software. The software is 99 percent accurate if the book is in good condition. However, we do understand that even one percent can be an annoying number of typos! And sometimes all or part of a page may be missing from our copy of the book. Or the paper may be so discolored from age that it is difficult to read. We apologize and gratefully acknowledge Google's assistance.

After we re-typeset and design a book, the page numbers change so the old index and table of contents no longer work. Therefore, we often remove them.

Our books sell so few copies that you would have to pay hundreds of dollars to cover the cost of our proof reading and fixing the typos, missing text and index. Instead we usually let our customers download a free copy of the original typo-free scanned book. Simply enter the barcode number from the back cover of the paperback in the Free Book form at www.general-books.net. You may also qualify for a free trial membership in our book club to download up to four books for free. Simply enter the barcode number from the back cover onto the membership form on our home page. The book club entitles you to select from more than a million books at no additional charge. Simply enter the title or subject onto the search form to find the books.

If you have any questions, could you please be so kind as to consult our Frequently Asked Questions page at www.general-books.net/faqs.cfm? You are also welcome to contact us there.

General Books LLC™, Memphis, USA, 2012.

ఇం ఇం ఇం ఇం ఇం ఇం ఇం ఇం

At a Meeting of the Committee of the Bannatyne Club, held on Monday the 20th of November 1841,

A Manuscript in the handwriting of Sir Thomas Hope, Lord Advocate of Scotland, in the reign of King Charles the First, entitled "Nott of the Pacquettis and Letteris sent and ressavit from Court," from the year 1633 to the year 1645, having been placed for publication at the disposal of the Club;

Resolved, That it be printed for the use of the Members, under the title of "A Diary of the Public Correspondence of Sir Thomas Hope of Craighall, Baronet," &c.

DAVID LAING, *Secretary.* THE BANNATYNE CLUB. MARCH, M.DCCC.XLIII.
THOMAS THOMSON, ESQ. PRESIDENT.
THE EARL OF ABERDEEN.
THE VISCOUNT ACHESON.
VICE-ADMIRAL SIR CHARLES ADAM.
THE EARL OF ASHBURNIIAM.
LORD BELHAVEN AND HAMILTON.
WILLIAM BLAIR, ESQ.
JOHN BORTHWICK, ESQ.
BERIAH BOTFIELD, ESQ.
10 THE MARQUESS OF BREADALBANE.
SIR THOMAS MAKDOUGALL BRISBANE, BART. GEORGE BRODIE, ESQ. CHARLES DASHWOOD BRUCE, ESQ.
O. TYNDALL BRUCE, ESQ.
THE DUKE OF BUCCLEUCH AND QUEENSBERRY.
THE DUKE OF BUCKINGHAM AND CHANDOS.
THE MARQUESS OF BUTE.
THE REV. RICHARD BUTLER.
JAMES CAMPBELL, ESQ.
20 DAVID CARNEGY, ESQ.
THE BANNATYNE CLUB. SIR GEORGE CLERK, BART.
WILLIAM CLERK, ESQ.
HON. H. COCKBURN, LORD COCK BURN, (*VICE-PRESIDENT.)*
DAVID CONSTABLE, ESQ.
ANDREW COVENTRY, ESQ.
JAMES T. GIBSON CRAIG, ESQ., *TREASURER.)* WILLIAM GIBSON CRAIG, ESQ.
GEORGE CRANSTOUN, ESQ. JAMES DENNISTOUN, ESQ. 30 GEORGE DUNDAS, ESQ. RIGHT HON. WILLIAM DUNDAS, LORD CLERK-REGISTER. WILLIAM PITT DUNDAS, ESQ. LORD FRANCIS EGERTON. JOSEPH WALTER K. EYTON, ESQ. SIR CHARLES DALRYMPLE FERGUSSON, BART. COUNT MERCER DE FLAHAULT. WILLIAM GOTT, ESQ. ROBERT GRAHAM, ESQ. RIGHT HON. THOMAS GRENVILLE. *40* THE EARL OF HADDINGTON. THE DUKE OF HAMILTON AND BRANDON. EDWARD W. DRUMMOND HAY, ESQ. SIR THOMAS BUCHAN HEPBURN, BART. JAMES MAITLAND HOG, ESQ. HON. JOHN HOPE, LORD JUSTICE-CLERK. COSMO INNES, ESQ. DAVID IRVING, LL.D. THE BANNATYNE CLUB. HON. JAMES IVORY, LORD IVORY.
SIR HENRY JARDINE.
50 HON. FRANCIS JEFFREY, LORD JEFFREY.
THE EARL OF KINNOULL.
DAVID LAING, ESQ., *(SECRETARY.)*
SIR THOMAS DICK LAUDER, BART.
THE EARL OF LAUDERDALE.
VERY REVEREND PRINCIPAL JOHN LEE, D.D.,
LORD LINDSAY.
JAMES LOCH, ESQ.
LORD LOVAT.
ALEXANDER MACDONALD, ESQ.
60 HON. J. H. MACKENZIE, LORD MACKENZIE
JAMES MACKENZIE, ESQ.
JOHN WHITEFOORD MACKENZIE, ESQ.
WILLIAM FORBES MACKENZIE, ESQ.
JAMES MAIDMENT, ESQ.
THOMAS MAITLAND, ESQ.
HON. A. MACONOCHIE, LOHD MEADOWBANK.
THE VISCOUNT MELVILLE.
THE HON. WILLIAM LESLIE MELVILLE.
WILLIAM HENRY MILLER, ESQ.
70 THE EARL OF MINTO.
HON. SIR J. W. MONCREIFF, BART., LORD MONCREIFK.
JAMES PATRICK MUIRHEAD, ESQ.
HON. SIR JOHN A. MURRAY, LORD MUR-

RAY.
WILLIAM MURRAY, ESQ.
b THE BANNATYNE CLUB. MACVEY NAPIER, ESQ.
ROBERT NASMYTH, ESQ.
SIR FRANCIS PALGRAVE.
LORD PANMURE.
SIR THOMAS PHILLIPPS, BART.
80 EDWARD PIPER, ESQ.
ROBERT PITCAIRN, ESQ.
ALEXANDER PRINGLE, ESQ.
JOHN RICHARDSON, ESQ.
THE EARL OF ROSEBERY.
THE DUKE OF ROXBURGHE.
ANDREW RUTHERFURD, ESQ.
THE EARL OF SELKIRK.
JAMES SKENE, ESQ.
WILLIAM SMYTHE, ESQ.
90 THE EARL SPENCER.
JOHN SPOTTISWOODE, ESQ.
EDWARD STANLEY, ESQ.
THE HON. CHARLES FRANCIS STUART.
THE DUKE OF SUTHERLAND.
ARCHIBALD SWINTON, ESQ.
ALEXANDER THOMSON, ESQ.
WALTER CALVERLEY TREVELYAN, ESQ.
DAWSON TURNER, ESQ.
ADAM URQUHART, ESQ.
100 RIGHT HON. SIR GEORGE WARRENDER, BART.

Sib Thomas Hope, the progenitor and founder of the family of that name in all its Scottish branches, was a person of too great celebrity and distinction in his own age, to make it necessary, in this place, to give any account of his life or character, either as a lawyer or a statesman. The following pages, to which the title of a "Diary" has been affixed, may perhaps be supposed to exhibit but a slender claim to public notice. The greater part of the volume is occupied with little more than minute chronological memoranda of his official, as well as private correspondence, during the last twelve years of his life, when he held a very important place in the service of the State, as Lord Advocate of Scotland; but it derives a considerable degree of interest and value from the numerous allusions incidentally introduced to the passing occurrences of the day, during a very critical period of our national history; and still more, perhaps, from the scattered lights that are thrown on the personal character of one of the most remarkable men of his own age, as well as on the political characters and connexions of some of his distinguished contemporaries. The overflowing sweetness and tenderness of his domestic habits and feelings are pleasingly conspicuous: the depth and sincerity of his religious impressions, degraded as they are by strange and humiliating indications of weakness and credulity, are unequivocally manifest: his veneration for the ancient monarchy and his anxiety for its preservation, his grateful affection for the person of the King and his anxious regards for his welfare, appear to have been put to severe trials by his conscientious zeal and unflinching attachment to that frame of ecclesiastical polity for which his countrymen were then contending; but the sincerity of his professions cannot fairly be questioned, and becomes the more conspicuous by occasional misgivings of himself, and by the distrust he sometimes betrays of the wisdom and safety of the measures which, in the perilous conflict of parties, he felt himself compelled to advocate and maintain. The honest simplicity of the disclosures in this record of his secret thoughts, will certainly do him no discredit, (with those at least who have not discarded all pretensions to candour,) how much soever opinions may be at variance as to the steadiness of his course on the troubled tide of public affairs during the last years of his life.

A collection of the letters of this distinguished person would probably afford additional illustrations of his own character, as well as of the momentous events of his own time. Very few of these are at present known to exist; but the two following, printed from the originals, seem to be consonant with the view here taken of his political conduct at the most important crisis of his life. The first is addressed to William Earl of Morton, one of the most zealous adherents of the King; the other to the Earl of Rothes, one of the most ardent leaders of the Covenant.

TO THE RYCHT NOBILL ERLL, MY LORD THE ERL OF MORTOUN.

Pleas Your Lo.,

I am glaid from my hart of your Lordlhip's tender and pious expreffioun, tuiching the greiffis of the subjectis in the matter of religioun, and I am not ignorant how thair procedingis is taxt of seditioun; but as I am not to justisie any of ther es, sua I wische from my hart that the too narrow refpect to the forme prejudge not the caus. It wer ane notabill testimonie of his Majestys love to religioun and justice, first to purge and try the errores of theis novatiounes, and to see them rectisied; but if theis be neglectit, and a courfe takin in the first place of the transgreffe of forme, (quhilk yit the nobilmen and barones affirmes not to be done, but legallie and according to the warrand of preceding lawis,) it wil be counted a hard measur. And I am effrayit to think of the seirsull consequence of it, quhilk can be no less nor the lose and ruyne of this poor countrey; and then the greter loss to our Sacred Soverane, quho sal lose a number of the maist loyall and saythsull subjectis that ever a prince had. The Lord divert this seirful calamitie, and strenthen your L. to do theis dewties in a matter so important, quhilkis ar proper to your L. as a Peer of the land, and come of ane nobill hous quhom God made the protectoris and begineris of his bliffit truth thairin at the first Beformatioun. So humblie kissing your L. handis, I rest,

Your L. humbill and bund servitor,
Sa Thomas Hope.
Edinburgh, 21 Merche 1C38.

VI

To The Right Nobill Erll, Mt Lord The Erll Of Rothese.

Pleass Your Lordship,

This inclofit will gif your Lordship satisfaction of quhat your Lordship commandis, and the beirar will cleir any doubt therein. He hes told me of the resolutioun takin for hindering the Subscriptioun; and I find your Lordship's letter inclyne that way, quhilk makis me almost stupeseit; for if I had not both conceivit and cleirlie seine it to be the gretest good that ever happenit to Godis Kirke since the Reformatioun, trewlie I sould haif bene lothe so quicklie to haif embracit it. But quhen your Lordship, (and utheris quhom God hes blifftt with that honour to be insirumentis to bring his Kirk to this happie estait wherein it is now, and to the sull persectioun quhairof thair is nothing inlaiking but that quhilk, on 2 Merche 1580, wes, be Actis of Kirk and Parliament, establischit for the governement of Godis Kirk in this kingdome,) dois sey me to oppugne it, I am brocht to suiche a perplexitie that I know not quhair to fix my mynd; for I dar not deny obedience to my Souerane quhair he commandis that quhilk is lausull, and aggreabill to Godis word, and quhilk 3e both think to be so, and hes interpret so in your particulars expreffit in that quhilk 3e haif suorne; and, on the vther part, I can not find in my hart to think or construct ill quhat theis (quhome God hes so mercisully and wonderfully blifftt in the beginning of this work) seymes to inclyne to. But I may and will say, I find ane good warrand for myself to do quhat I did, and prayis to the Lord that thairs may haif als good success as in hart I wische; onlie I feir that the courfe of oppositioun takin sall not produce to them according to thair pious intentionis; and I cannot say that intentiouns ar a good warrand ather to resuse quhat is good, or to do that quhilk is contraire. The Lord direct 30W all, and if 3¢ wald eschew the feir of diuisioun, chok it in the entrie, be commanding ane absolut vnioun, quhilk is very eafie if 3e sall gif ordor to all to subscryve this, as one in substance with the other. Pardoun me, my Lord, if I haif exceidit the bounds of my an suer, VII for the buffines and the feir of the event of it breckis my hart; but go quhat it will, 1 trust in God to haif both my lyffe and foule for a pray. So committing 30ur Lordsliip to Godis grace, I rest,

Your Lordsliips humbill seruitor, SB Thomas Hope.

Craighall, 2d October 1638.

The original manuscript of this volume, entirely in the handwriting of Sir Thomas Hope, has been preserved in the family of his lineal heir-male and representative, Sir John Hope of Craighall, Bart. The writing, from its minute and abbreviated form, (of which a small portion is given in facsimile,) is in many cases scarcely legible, and it is not wonderful, that in some previous attempts to decipher certain parts of it, very palpable errors should have been committed. Its transcription was one of the last labours of the late Mr William Whytock, whose skill and patience as a copyist had in other instances been most usefully employed in the service of the Club, and to whose modest worth this tribute is justly due. In its subsequent correction for the press, some mistakes may, in all probability, have been fallen into; but in general, where an intelligible reading could not be ascertained, it has been deemed safer to leave an entire blank.

March 1, 1843. *N.B.*—On page 4, and *passim*, for "Lord Panmuir," read "Laird of Panmuir." SIE THOMAS HOPE'S MAEY OF HIS PUBLIC COEEESPONDENCE, WITH OCCASIONAL NOTICES. 1633—1646. NOTT OF THE PACQUETTS AND LETTERIS SENT AND RESAUIT FROM COURT.

His Maiestie return it from Bervick to Londoun on Weddinsday the 17 July 1633.

29 July 1633, Mononday.

Sent ane pacquet of letteris to the Erll Stirling Secretar, quharin to him and to James Levingstoun, and to my brother James, and within it one to Doctor Dauidfoun from my fone Sir Thomas. Item, letteris from L. Sandsurd to Mr. Levinstoun.

Thir delyuerit be me to Mr. James Gordoun, quha promisit to send the samyn with Patrick Dickfoun servitor to the Marquess of Douglas. This slippit be Mr. James Gordoun his negligence, and he delyuerit my pacquet to Mr. Robert Barclay servitor to the Lord Lorn.

Item, delyuerit to the said Mr. Robert Barclay from my self, a letter to the Erll of Stirling, quhairin advertisement anent the continuatioun of his Maiesties letter to the seffioun vntil November. Item, of the Lord Tra-Erl Traquhair. quhair his outrage at Exchekker on 27 July. Item, of the Haying of the signator of Nova Scotia. Item, off the act of allowance to the chamrlans, with reservatioun to his Maiestie, quhilk wes contradictit with clamor, and be the Lord Traquhair refusit.

6 August 1633.

John Meldrum, his Memorandum.— Writ a letter to the Erl Stirling, quhilk wes to go with Mr. James Law, anent the convictioun of John Meldrum, and within it a letter from John Macmorran to Mr. Levingstoun; quhilk letter wes delyuerit to Mr. James Law on 3 August. But Mr. James went not and thairfoir I delyuerit it to Mr. James Gordoun, and with it an other to my Lord Stirling, more ample fpeiking of the buffines of Frendraucht; and within it one to Doctor Chalmers anent that and Cragyvar, quhilk went with Charles Mowatt, servitor to the Erl of Buchan, this 6 August 1633.

Item, the Lord Carnok went to toun this day, and sent with him a letter to James Levinstoun, anent Coldenknows, and als anent the convictioun of John Meldrum.

8 August 1633.

Sent with Captain Maxwell ane letter to the Lord Stirling, defyring him to send the contract and signator of Tilliculty hither, quhilk was sent to bun a 3eir since.

12 August 1633, Mononday. Delyuerit to Dauid Muirheid my letters to Lord Stirling, Erll Ancrum, and James Levingstoun, and in the Lord Stirling's, the signator of Perstoun for Sir William Murray, and cravis ansuer for Anna Lyoun and Sir William Steuarts.

Item, writtin to them anent the Countess of Airth her coming to Court.

16 November 1633. Pacquet sent by my Lord Register, and in it sent two pacquets, one to the Erl of Stirling, and the other to the Lord of Panmuir; and within it letters from John Pilmur. Item, another pacquet contening two letters, one to ather of tham; and in them written anent the letter to the Commiffion, for proceiding first in termes of erectioun, and for appointing the day of sitting.

23 November 1633, Setterday. Pacquet sent be myself to the Secretar, quhairin a letter from the Commiisioun to his Maiestie, anent discumng of the valour of the tithes of erectioun; followit ane

anent the third day of the week. Item, to the Lord Panmuir, with John Pilmur his letter to Mr. Andro Ramsay. Item, to Erll of Ancrum. Item, to Dean of Winchester. Item, to my Lord Alexander. Item, to Mr. Walter Neische. 27 November, Weddinsday.

Delyuerit to Mr. James Gordoun, a pacquet to be sent by an servand off Monsieur Briott, quhairin to my brother William, letters to the Erll of Erl Portland Portland, Thesaurer, and Sir William Balfour. Item, to the Erll Stirling, Ij"ltm f Ing" with the Master of Worlds signator, and to Lord Panmuir.

This day Alexander Alexander cam post with the gift off ward and marriage of the Erl of Buccleugh, quho deceffit at Londoun off the apo-(Erl Buccleugh) deplexie on fryday the 22 of November 1633; and returnit bak on Sounday, ce8slt1 December 1633.

11 December 1633, Weddinsday. This nicht at 8 hours at evin, a pacquet sent be me, quhairin a letter to Lord Tanmuir, and within it the forme of my warrand for the Marquess of Hamiltoun, anent my 2000 lib. sterling. Item, to William Murray, with an signator of Inchaffray to Patrik Murray. 14 December 1633, Setterday. Letters delyuerit to Mr. James Gordoun, directit to the Erll Stirling, quhairin to the Lord Panmuir, with the Marquess of Hamilton his letter in my favours. 21 December 1633, Setterday. Lord Marquess de-This day Sir James Lockart went to Court, and sent with him a gret ereit of proper wad- Tib» 11 1

RettiS. pacquet ot writtis; quhairin to Lord Panmuir, with a letter anent the

Marques his proceiding, and anent the decreit of proper wedsettis gevin 18 December 1633. Item, to the Erl Stirling with James Levinstoun his signator of Coldinknows, dockettit be me. Item, letteris to Mungo Murray from the Erl of Anandaill. Item, letteris to my brother James, and within them 2 to Robert Hope.

27 December 1633.
My fone Alexander went to Court, and gevin him 60lb. sterling.

9 January 1634, Thursday.
Sent letteris by pacquet direct to my Lord Traquhair, quhairin one to Erl Stirling, one to Lord Panmuir, and within it one to him from

Item, to my fone Mr. Alexander, my own to the Erl of Ancrum for Bishop Caithness.

17 January 1634, Fryday.
Sent ane gret pacquet to the Erl of Stirling, quhairin the Erl of Lothian his signator, the Bishop of Edinburgh his gift, with an letter to the Marques of Hamiltoun, 2 to the Erl Stirling, 2 to Lord Panmuir, and within them on from John Pilmuir. Item, an letter to Lord Alexander, one to Sir

G. Flescher, one to the Erl of Ancrum, one to Sir Robert Gordoun, one to my brother, and within it one to James and another to Harry. Item, my letter to my fone Mr. Alexander, and within it one from James Hope to him, quhilk cam from Rouen efter he wes gone for Court.

23 January 1634, Thursday.
Delyuerit a pacquet to Mr. James Gordoun to go vnder cover in Sir Archibald Atcheson his poll pacquet; quhairin to the Secretar anent James Levinstoun signator, quhilk he bids me reffaue, but sent not; and one to Lord Panmuir, quhairin the copy of the contract betwix the Marques and him. Item, one to my sone Mr. Alexander.

25 January 1634.
Sent letteris my (by) Doctor Bailie to Lord Panmuir, quhairin to himself, to the Marques, to Earl Stirling, and to my sone Mr. Alexander, and within his one from Alexander Lowis to Hary Hope.

29 January 1634.
This day Alexander Pirrie went to court, and sent with him letteris to the Erl of Stirling, quhairin one to the Lord of Panmuir and ane other to my sone.

4 February, Twysday, 1634. Reffauit letteris from my sone Mr. Alexander, of dait 23 Januar, acquainting me with the deceso of my deir brother James Hope. My brother departit on 22 Januar 1634, being Weddinsday, at 4 in the morning.

8 February 1634, Setterday. Pacquet sent to the Erl Stirling, quhairin 2 to his Maiestie, ane anent Home, with the extract of the process and informatioun, 2 anent his Maiestie's affaires; sent with the Erl of Traquhair. Item, letteris to the Lord Duik, Erl Traquhair went, Lord Marques, Erl Stirling, Erl Ancrum, Lord Panmuir, Sir James uFeb" Lokhart, Lord Alexander, my sone, and to William Murray of the bedchalmer. 12 February 1634, Weddinsday.

This day reffauit an pacquet direct to me, quhairin wes his Maiestie's letter to me, geving me libertie to compeir for the aires of Home. Item, an letter from the Marques of Hamiltoun.

Item, this famyn day sent an pacquet be me to the Secretar, quhairin letteris to the Lord Marques, to Lord Panmuir, my sone J...

Item, sent a letter to my Lord Traqukair anent Mr. James Ahany his signator; and anent the gentilmen of Kylismuir.

20 Feb. 1634, Thursday. This day about 8 hours at evin, reffauit from Anthonie Alexander letteris from the Erl Stirling, Lord Alexander, and my fone. 21 February 1634, Fryday. This day a pacquet sent with a servand of Patrick Wod, quho raid post this nicht at 4 afternoone; quhairin to the Erl Stirling, Lord Traquhair, Lord Panmuir, and my fone.

22 February, Setterday, 1634. Letteris sent by the Erl of Laderdaill, quhairin to his Maiestie, to the Marques, Panmuir, and my fone, with the copies of his Maiestie's letter, His Maiestie's pre- and informatioun anent his Maiestie's prerogative royall in the cognoscing rogative royall. fafa og Lor(j8 Item, to the Erl Stirling and Erll of Traquhair.

22 February 1634. This day delyuerit an pacquet to the Erl of Annandaill, quhairin wes one to the Erl of Stirling, schewing of the acting of his Maiestie's letter in exchekker, anent the impost of 6s. sterling on the coall transports beyond sea. Item, one to Lord Panmuir, schewing the reffait and paffing of Sir George Flescher his signator of pensioun of 200fly sterling, and of the affise hering for his lyftyme for ij00 merks of tak deuty. Item, one to my fone. And thais the Erl of Annandaill promisit to send with John Steuart's son, quho wes going post. 1 Merche 1634, Setterday. This day a pacquet delyverit be me to Mr. James Gordoun, to go under his

cover, quhilk is direct to the Erl Stirling, and thairin to him, signifying the finding of the charter of Ladop being Mariage. Item, acquainting him with the signator of his escheit quhen it sal pass. Item, within the pacquet, on to my sone, and with it on to the Marquess of Hamiltoun, with the copie of the sumonds and depositiouns aganis Dauid Beatfoun of Cardon. Item, on to Lord Panmuir anent my Lord Bahnerinoch. Item, on to the Erl of Traquhair. Item, on to Allan Lockart.

4 Merche 1634, Twysday. Sent letteris with James Steuart to my sone, and within letter to Lord Panmuir, with John Pilmuirs to Mr. Patrik Lyndsay, and an accompt of Bame. our treattie with the Lord Balmerinoch anent Barrie. 6 Marche, Thursday.

Letters sent to my sone, and to the Lord Panmuir, with the informatioun Decreit, James of the caus of Home, efter the decreit quhilk wes gevin 4 Merche 1634. pоTM6 & Lady 13 Merche 1634.

Memorandum.—His Maieltie's letter to the Seffioun, anent his Maiestie's Prerogative, prerogative, wes presentit be my Lord Doun on Twysday the xj Marche 1634; and the Lords gaue thair ansuer, and sent it up be Sir Robert Spottifwode, president, on Thursday, 13 Marche 1634.

Item, at this samyn tyme I sent vp an pacquet to my sone be the Erll of His Maiestie's preLauderdaill, quhairin on to, his Maiestie, and within 7 articles anent the rogatlve / prerogative. Item, on letter to the Marques of Hamiltoun. Item, letter to Lord Panmuir, and within it my declaratioun and insormatioun. Item, to my sone, with the copies of both. Item, to Erl Stirling, Lord Alexander, and Mr. W. Neische.

Memorandum. This day Alexander Narn of Sandsurd went to court, Mr. Alexander, and sent with him to my sone Mr. Alexander xxv 12Ib peices and 10 singel 30Ib-8terling 22 Marche, Setterday, 1634. This day an pacquet gevin to Mr. James Gordoun, quhairin on to the Brechin to Lord Erl of Stirling, with the signator to the Mr. of Work. Item, on to Lord PanmurePanmuir, and thairin Erl of Rothes anent Brechin.

This went not quhil 28 Merche, being Fryday, at 10 hours at evin; at quhilk tyme I sent an pacquet to the Erl of Stirling, and thairin letters to the Erll, with the twa signators of Ralistoun, and new gift of the forrestis of Tillicultry dockettit be me, viz. Ralistoun to John Lord Colvill, and the gift to Erl of Stirling and Lord Alexander his son, for thair lystymes. Item, letters to Lord Panmuir, with advertifment anent the signator of Soap. Item, to Erll Ancrum. Item, to Sir James Lokhart. Item, to Doctor Chalmer. Item, to my sone Mr. Alexander, with a number of letters to him.

Last Merche, Mononday, 1634.

The clerk of Register went to court; and sent with him an pacquet to Lord Stirling, quhairin to Lord Panmuir and my son, anent thair ansuers to his Maiestie's letter for pleading in Seffioun, and anent foolilh Mr. R. Crag.

1 Apryll, Twisday, 1634. Sent a letter to the Marques of Hamiltoun, with the fignator of commiffion for compounding anent extraordinar taxatioun, with consent of the exchekker, or any fyve, the chancellor, thesaurer, and deput being one. Countess of Home. Item, this day about 6 at nycht the Countess of Home, with the Erl of Erl Lauderdaui, and Lauderdaill, the Lord Doun, and Lord Maitland, with his lady, cam to my 2oolbrmi8e f chamber, 3II(1 ther first tne Countess apart in the window, and then scho, the Erl Lauderdaill and Lord Doun, promisit to me, if thai get any tHing be the process, to gif me two thoufand merkis. The Countess called it pundis. *Item, this promise renewit be hir and the Erl of Murray, and Lord Doun, on Weddinsday the 6 of August, 1634, at 5 hors at nycht* 23 April 1634.

Pacquet sent from Craighall, quhairin the letters to Lord Panmuir, anent the words allegit fpokin in exchekker to Sir John Hay concerning Home. 7 May 1634.

Pacquet sent from Edinburgh, quhairin to Erl Stirling, with the letter anent the Commiffion for the Borders. Item, the Laird of Ludquharn his letter, with myne to the Secretar in his favors.

Item, my letters to Lord Panmuir, with the rentall, and ansuer off Brechin.

Item, my letter to Robert Hope anent Hiltarvet.

13 Junij 1634, Fryday. Berar sent be my Lord Traquhair from the Commiffion to his Maiestie, Lord Balmerinach. anent Mr. William Haig and the Lord Balmerinach. Item, to Lord Panmuir anent Soap and Barrie. Item, from my fone to Robert Hope, with the account for xxiiij'1$0^n$ merks. Item, to Mr. Alexander anent the fewar. Item, to Erl Stirling, to Sir James Carmichaell. Item, to Andro Pitcairn, with his rycht from Arthor his brother. 23 Junij 1634.

Andro Hay went post, and sent with him letters to the Lord of Pan-Erl Traquhair. muir, quhairin to him with the grevances aganis Lord Traquhair; (1) of my precept of 2000 1b, (2) of my. ... of Advocat, (3) of removing from exchekker tabill, (-4) of my exceptioun of Kynninmonth. Item, warrand Kynninmonth. to pass the Kings hands, allowing Kynninmonth to except it from the surrander. Item, letter to Mr. Alexander, with an other to Lord Duik for the exceptioun of Kynninmonth.

25 Junij, Weddinsday. Allan Lockart post with the dockettit contract betuix his Maiestie and the Marques of Hamiltoun, anent the difpositioun to him of the hail taxatioun. 3 Julij 1634. Allan Lockart returnit from court. 5 Julij 1634, Setterday. Delyuerit to Charles Mowat my pacquet to the Erll of Buchan, quhairin Erl Mar, his sig-letters to my sone, and within it letters to his Maiestie, with the Erll of natorofDrybrugh.Mar, signator of Cardrose. Item, letters to James Maxwell for that purpose anent Dirltoun. Item, letters to Sir James Carmichaell, to Hary Alexander, to Mr. William Nesche. Item, sent vp be John the band to Hiltarvett. Robert Hope of 2400 merkis, for the pryce of Hiltarvett. pensioun. 8 Julij 1634, Twysday. Erl Airth, his sus Mr. Hary Drummond went to court, and sent with him a letter to his Maiestie anent the suspension betwix the Erl of Airth and his creditors. Item, an letter to Lord Panmuir, with one to my fone, with the informatioun for ansuer to the Erl of Traquhair his calumnie anent the sur-

render of Sanctandrois, delyuerit to the Archbilhop of Sanctandrois. 12 July 1634, Setterday. Memorandum. This man went nott, in refpect G. Home cam from court with a letter to me anent the submiffioun of Home. 3 August 1634. The Lord Alexander went to court, and sent with him ane pacquet to my sone, quhairin ane to the Erl of Ancrum, with the affignatioun off the tak of the teindis of Coldinknowis to be subscryvit be him, with a letter from the Erl of Lothian his son and Mark Case to that effect. Item, ane letter to Sir James Carmichaell, ane to Dean of Winchester, and within it a letter reffauit from Hew Scrimgeor. Item, a letter to Hary Alexander; and at this tyme I wret none to Lord Panmuir, becaus he wes on his journey to Scotland.

8 August, Fryday, 1634. This day at vj hours at evin, the Lord Panmuir came to Edinburgh from Londoun. 18 August 1634, Mononday. Exchekker comptis. This day the vnhappie chekker compts subscryvit; and the Lord Alexander went to court, and with him sent ane pacquet to my son, with William Murray his signator. 19 August 1634, Tuesday.

This day the Erl of Roxburgh told me that his Maiestic knew perfytlie that Erl Roxburgh the Erle of Airth wes trewlie come of Dauid, and that Malice wes son to anent Erl of Airth Eupham and Patrik; and a glance of this I had from Erl of Airth on 13 August, and from the Lord Marques on 18 Auguft the efternoon, quhilk wes efter the greit blast. God mak me thanksull:—Non semper timidis servare vexatum procellis equor.

Item, this day delyuerit to the Bischop off Ross by his brother, ane pacquet to my sone Mr. Alexander, and within it a letter to his Maiestie, and ane other to the Bischop Canterbury, in savors of the Bischop of Ross, and thairin to the Bischop for my son Mr. Alexander.

26 August 1634, Twysday.

This day at 4 efternone the Marques of Hamiltoun returnit to court; Marques of Hamiland went to Ledingtoun and delyuerit to his Lordship ane letter to his juesanent the Maiestie, with certain articles anent the comptis and exchekker. comptis.

Item, delyuerit to Thomas Dalmahoy, in presence of Doctor Baillie and My sone Mr. Alex Mr. George Noruell, an pacquet to Mr. Alexander, quhairin is 50 Bb sterling an er 50 b sterling of gold. Item, a letter to him, and an other from his brother Sir Thomas; and one from me to James Levingstoun, quhairin I defyre him to reid the last part of my letter to his Maiestie, in quhilk I declare that I haif sent my letter to his Maiestie with certain articles, and defyris his Maiestie that thai come in the hands of none but his Maiestie and the Marques of Hamiltons; or if in otheris, in James Levingstoun's awin hands; and expreffed quhat sufferings I sustein for his Maiestie's seruice, but that I intend not to leiue for the frownings of any man; being so resoluit out of the fyer of Strathern not to boudge for the refpect of any, and bleffing God that now his Maiestie hes gottin the trewth of that buffines.

Item, sent with the Marques an pacquet to my sone Mr. Alexander, anent my ansuer to his Majestie tuicheing submiffioun of Home, quhairin is the submiffioun with the doubill of thair ansuers; and this sent to Ledingtoun with ane boy off the Erl of Lauderdaill's. 27 August 1634, Weddinsday. Delyuerit to the Erl Stirling, in his awin hous in Alexander Clerk's lodging, the new Soap signator dockettit be me, with the old figned be his Maiestie, with the signator of Brichen and Navar to Lord Panmuir, and an other of Balmakelly to him and his sone Hary, with informatioun how to vse the samyn.

Vicount of Stor Item, delyuerit to the Erl Stirling ane nott anent Vicount Stormonth, Lord Quhythil, and Sir James Steuart. month. 1 November 1634, Setterday. This nycht about 9 at nycht, sent ane pacquet to the Erl Stirling, quhairin 1 pacquet to him self, another to his sone from Mr. James Gordoun, and within his two from me. Item, to my sone Mr. Alexander, quhairin to Lord Panmuir from me, and tua from James Murray. Item, from me to Erl Annandaill, with a pacquet from Thomas Maxwell. Item, to Erl Ancrum, and within a packett from Erll of Lothian. Item, from me to James Livingstoun, to Sir James Carmichaell, to L. Sandsurd, to Exceptioun of Babethan. Item, a pacquet to Patrik Wodd. Memorandum. In my from lhminder letters to Lord Panmuir I haif sent a gift of non entry of Carloingie. of Sanctandrois. Item, my warrand for exceptioun of Kynninmonth from the surrander of Sanctandrois. 9 November 1634. Sent letters with Doctor Baillie to my sone Mr. Alexander, quhairin from my self, Sir John, and Sir Thomas, to him, with ane band to Robert Hope of 200 merkis. Item, to Erl Stirling, to Lord Alexander, to Erl Ancrum, thanks; and anent Erl Traquhair his fpleen. Item, to Erl Annandaill anent the Thesaurer's and the of my pensioun. Item, to Dean Winchester. Item, to Lord Panmuir and to Alexander Narn. Item, to the Marques of Sone borne to my Hamiltoun, congratulatioun for his new born fone, and defyring ane ansuer mUtouTM f anent the articles and my precept. 12 November 1634, Weddinsday. This day Mr. Nathaniel Vdward went to Court, and sent with him a letter to Mr. Alexander, and within it a letter to Erl Annandaill, in ansuer of his reffauit 11 November, and another to James Levingstoun anent Sir James Baillie his offer for Nuck. 13 November 1634, Thursday. This day a letter sent to the Erl Roxburgh to Broxmouth, and within Ditta, Lord it the ditta aganis Lord Balmerinach, to be schawin to his Maiestie. Item, a letter to Mr. Alexander, and within it one to James Levingstoun anent Sir James Baillie. 14 November 1634.

This day a pacquet gevin to William Douglas, seruitor to the Erl of Mem. —In this I Mortoun, quho went post, quhairin to Erl Stirling anent Lord Balmeri-nVanenTuie" noch's dyet and ditta. Item, to Lord Panmuir about it, and within Ms bying of his anletter the ditta to be schawin to his Maiestie. Item, letter to Sir James Carmichael for the samyn. Item, letter to my fone Mr. Alexander.

27 November 1634, Thursday. This day

sent with the Erl of Lothian, a letter to the Erl of Ancrum his sather, with a pacquet to my fone Mr. Alexander, quhairin to himself, with a nott of the Bishop Roffe his outragious speeches; commanding him to keip quyet, except the Bishop Roffe move any questioun or challenge aganis me; with a letter to the Archbilhop Canterbury. Item, a letter to the Erl Stirling, to Lord Alexander, to Sir James Carmichael, to Sir William ElpMnstoun, to Erl of Annandaill, to Lord Panmuir, and within it a letter from Mr. David Falconer to him, with Patrick Strachan his writtis. 29 November 1634, Setterday. Sent with Sir James Lockart to Sir Robert Gordoun, the Dean of Winchester, inclosit in one to my sone.

Last November 1634, Sounday. Justice Court and This nycht about 6 at nycht, Sir James Carmichaell, Justice Clerk, cam Balmennach. from Qourt to attend the criminal dyet aganis my Lord Balmarinoch, quhilk is on Weddinsday nixt 3 December.

1 December 1634, Mononday. This day letters sent to Erl Stirling by a servand of Anthonie Alexander, Mr. Wark deecssit. quho went with his signator of Mr. Wark, vacant be decese of Sir James Murray, quho deceffit on Setterday.

Item, sent thairin to Lord Panmuir with Mr. Patrick Lyndsay's letters. Item, to my sone Mr. Alexander.

8 December 1634, Mononday. Pacquet sent to the Erl Stirling, quhairin from Mr James Gordoun, Justice Clerk, L. Thorntoun. Item, from my self to Erl Stirling, to Lord Alexander, to Lord Panmuir, to my sone, and in it a nott tuiching the criminal proces, and off the plott for laying the blayme on me if it miscarry. My Pacquett stop-This stoppit be Erl Traquhair all Twysday till nycht, and it went on plt-Twysday at 10 hours at nycht.

Item, the Erl of Traquhair sent a pacquett, quhilk went on Thursday 11 December, and in it one from me to the Lord of Panmuir, anent the Bischop of Brichen his ansuer.

12 December 1634, Fryday. Lord Chancellor Being at the Justice Court aganis the Lord Balmerinoch, pacquet cam seiknes at n oun. Traquhair, quhairin letters to me from Erl Stirling, Lord Panmuir, and my sone, of 3 December, advertising me off the Chancellar's deidlie My sone Mr. Alex-palsey and the Erl Mortoun's seiknes. Item, that my sone at Windsoir wes ander extraordinar r i -»yr. n.., j« n sworn be his Maienie m extraordinar Larver. Carver.

15 December 1634, Mononday. ✝ Anthonie Alexander went post, and sent with him a pacquet to the Erll of Stirling his sather, quhairin to himself, the Lord Alexander, Haiy Alexander. Item, a pacquet to my sone, quhairin to Lord Panmuir, to Marques of Hamiltoun, to Erll Roxburgh, to Erl of Annandaill, to James Levingstoun, with-ArthorNesmyth's letters,to Sandsurd,to Babethan,and to myfone himself,

Item, sent a letter from James Narn to his brother the L. Sandsurd, quhilk cam to me efter the closing of my pacquet.

Item, thairefter I drew vp ane breviat off the proceidingis m the Justice Lord Balmerinach. Court aganis the Lord Bahnerinoch, and inclosit in ane letter to the Lord Panmuir, to be schawin to his Majestie; and another letter to the Erl Stirling, defyring him to sie it in Lord Panmuir's hands; and I defyrit the Lord Panmuir to communicat the samyn to the Marques, to Erl Roxburgh, and to 12 December 1634, the Erl Stirling, and wret to the Erl StirHng anent the deceiss of the Erl ofErU decessit. Mar, quho deceiffit 12 December 1634, on Fryday, at one efter midnicht.

Item, Erl Traquhair sent a servand to Court this day, but told me nothing thairoff.

19 December 1634. This day Robert Allan, servitor to James Levingstoun, returnit to Court, with quhom I wret to him. 23 December 1634, Twysday. This day Mr. James Ferquharfoun went post to Court, and sent with Lord Balmerinach. him a pacquet vnder the cover of Mr. James Gordoun, direct to Erll of Stirling, quhairin to Erl Stirling, to Lord Panmuir, and within his the breviat of the criminal proces aganis Balmerinoch, from 16 December to 20 inclusive, at quhilk tyme it wes continewit to xj of Februar. Item, ane nott of the priuat procedings in that buffines with the Justice his affeffors and the Bischoppis. Item, to him in the samyn letter a draucht of my precept of 20008) sterling. Item, a letter to Marques of Hamiltoun. Item, to Erl Roxburgh, to Lord Alexander, to Hary Alexander, to Erl of Annandaill, all anent the criminal process. Item, sent to my c sone Mr. Alexander a letter, and within it a doubil of my precept, to be drawin vpon the thesaurer but prejudice of my former preceptis. Item, from my sones Sir John and Sir Thomas to Mr. Alexander. Item, from James Hope, my nephew, to him.

Memorandum. Mr. James Ferquharfoun went not quhil Fryday the 26 December, and I sent with him the former, togither with another pacquet direct to the Erl of Stirling, quhairin one to himself, with a nott of the Clerk Register. Clerk of Register's abuses to me. Item, one to Lord Panmuir, quhairin wer the lyk nott, with a nott of the calumnies laid on me in this process aganis my Lord Balmerinach.

Item, one to my sone, quhairin the samyn nott, and als within his, one to the Marques of Hamiltoun, Erl Roxburgh, Erl Ancrum, Erl of Annandaill, L. Sandsurd. Item, one to Sir James Hamiltoun from the L. Lyndsay. 25 December 1634, Thursday. This nycht, about 5 hours at nycht, a pacquet cam to me from Erl of Stirling, quhilk I opened in presence of the post maister's sone, and delyuerit Lord Chancellor to him al the letteris except thois that wes to myself. By this I wes adverbs mi!6 DTMm"tisit that the Lord Chancellar deciffit on 16 December 1634.

Item, immediately I wret an ansuer to Erl Stirling and Lord Panmuir, and delyuerit it to Mr. James Gordoun, to put it in his pacquet with Mr. James Ferquharfoun.

27 December 1634, Setterday. The Erl Traquhair went post, and sent with him letters to Lord Panmuir, Earl Stirling, Earl Ancrum, and my son, for retractatioun of the Erl Traquhair's promiffes of sauor. 29 December, 1634, Mononday. This day I directit a pacquet to the Erl Stirling, quhairin wes thrie or four pack-

uettis from Mr. James Gordoun. Item, letters to the Erl Traquhair from me, and with them the conjunct Commiffioun of the borders. Item, letter to Sir James Hamiltoun, quhairin his signator of Alderstoun, quhilk held of auld of Torphechen. Item, letters to Erl Stirling, Lord Alexander, and Lord Panmuir, and to my fone. 3 Januar 1635, Setterday.

Sent letters with Mr. Hary Drummond and Capitan Graham, my letters for the Erl Stirling in ansuer of thais reffavit last December. Item, to Lord Panmuir, and within it the letter returnit quhilk he sent to Erl Traquhair. Item, the letter from his Maiestie to Bischop Brichen (now Edinburgh) anent Moneky. Item, letters to my fone from myself, my sone, and his mother. Item, a letter from me to George Hope, thanking him for his kyndnes to Mr. Alexander.

Item, gevin to him, 4 Januar, being Sounday, ane letter to Erl Stirling, Archbishop of within it the signator of the Chancellary to the Archbischop of Sanctandrois. chœlkr.13 4 Januar 1635, Weddinsday. Sent with Sir Robert Ramsay letters to Erl Stirling, to my fone, quhairin to Erl Annandaill, and within his to the Countess his lady, to James Levingstoun and his lady, to L. Sandsurd, and one to Sir David Cunyngham from his mother.

29 Januar 1635, Thursday. Sent letters with the Lord Lorn, and thairin to my fone Mr. Alexander, Mr. Alexander 45 doubill angells and ane half, and 9 tuelf pund pieces and ane half,60 1b-sterling quhilk is in haul 60lb sterling, therof 50lb sterling to himself and 10fl) sterling for his sister Marie. Item, to Lord Panmuir, with the procutory of Bahnakelly. Item, one to Archbischop of Canterbury. Item, to Erl Annandaill, to Erl Ancrum, to Erl Stirling, to Sir James Lockart. 12 Februar 1635, Thursday. This day John Hamiltoun of Orbistoun went to Court, and sent with him a letter to the Marques. Item, one to Erl Roxbrugh. Item, one to Erl Stirling, with the signators of Dean of Chapell anent exemptioun from taxatioun. Item, the Biibhop of Edinburgh his letters to Lord Panmuir. Item, Thomas Maxwell's to Erl Annandaill, with my own to Lord Panmuir and him, and one to my sone. 13 Fehruar 1635, Fryday.

This day the Earl of Dumfries, and a fervand of the Erl of Traquhair's, went to Court, and sent with the Erl of Traquhair his servand letters to my fone, quhairin to himself, to Erl Stirling, to Lord Panmuir, to Hary Alexander, to Mr. Walter Nesche.

Memorandum. The Erl of Traquhair his man went not at this tyme, and this pacquet remaynit in the Erl of Traquhair's hands vntil the 27 day.

Item, on 25 Februar gevin to Mr. John Lawfoun, to be put in my Lord's pacquet, letters to Lord Panmuir, quhairin to him with the Bilhop of Brichen his letter to me. Item, letters from Mr. Patrik Lyndsay.
27 Februar 1635.

Delyuerit to John Murray letters to the Lord Panmuir, and within it a letter from Mr. Patrik Lyndsay, and one from me to my fone, and within it one to the Lord Lorn.

Item, sent to James Levingstoun a letter anent Lord Banff, anent Arthor Nesmyth his agreement for L.lb sterling, anent the Lady Samuelltoun her drauchts of Poffill.

All thir delyuerit to the Erl Traquair his fervand, quho went on Fryday 27 Februar 1635.
2 Merche 1635.

Reffauit ane pacquet from the Erl of Stirling of 17 Februar, and within it letters to John Pilmour, quhilk I delyuerit to James Murray. Item, letters to Mr. James Gordoun, quhilk I also delyuerit to Mr. James Gordoun.

7 Merche 1635, Setterday. Pacquet sent be me to Erl Stirling, quhairin the contract betwix his Majestie and the Erll anent copper coyne. Item, my licence for wynning of mineralls in the baronies of Craighall and Kynninmonth. Item, letters to Lord Panmuir, to Alexander Narn, to Sir Alexander Home of Manderstoun, and last to my sone. 12 Merche, Thursday, 1635. Sent with Mr. Alexander Belsches letters to Erl Stirling, Lord Panmuir, and Lord Lorn, and to my sone. 16 Merche, Mononday, 1635.

Sent with Coronell Hepburne ane pacquet to Lord Panmuir, quhairin one 21 Merche.—The to him anent the Bishop Canterbury, the Erl Airth, Jon Maul, and the Vmermach precentory of Masondew. Item, within his a letter to the Archbischop of Canterbury, and ane other to my sone.

Item, within this pacquet one from the Erll of Lauderdaill to Lord Panmuir. 21 Merche, Setterday, 1635. Memorandum. The former pacquet went not with Coronell Hepburne. But it with ane other to Lord Panmuir, with ane to the Countess of Roxbrugh from the Lady Fleming, and one to the Erl of Ancrum. Item, one to Erl Stirling, and one to my sone, all tyet in ane pacquet, sent by pacquet from James Prymrois on 21 Merche 1635. 26 Merche 1635.

Delyuerit ane pacquet to the Lord Alexander, quhairin to Lord Panmui", defyring him to acquaint his Maiestie with the way to mak all cheiffis ansuerabill for thair clanes, and fpecially Marques of Huntly, and defyring to haif his Majesties mind to the Counsell for that effect. Item, to acquaint his Maiestie with the decreit of mariage agains Erl Burgleish, and reduction of the heritabill office of Ischeary; and if he haif occalioun, to pray at his Maiestie for my signator with the mineralls of my hail lands. Item, to the Erl Stirling anent the samyn. Item, to James Levingstoun anent the samyn. Item, to Hary Alexander anent the samyn, and to my sone Mr. Alexander anent the samyn. Item, wret to the Erl of Annandaill anent his offices. Item, within this pacquet to the Lord Panmuir, ane nott of the last proceidings aganis the Lord Balmerinach on 20 and 21 Merche.

My signator of Craighall, with mineralls.
28 Merche 1635.

Item, this day sent with the Lord Alexander ane other pacquet to Erl Stirling, Lord Panmuir, and my son, quhairin is my signator of Craighall with the mineralls, sent to Erl Stirling, with the forme of the dockett, and the doubil of the forme of the docket sent to Lord Panmuir and my sone.

Last Merche, Twysday, 1635.

This day the Erl Traquair and Lord Alexander went to court, and sent with them ane letter to his Maiestie, with ane accompt of my proceidings in his Majestie's feruice. Item, ane letter to Lord Panmuir anent Patrik Maull, quhilk wes judgit this day in counsell. Item, a letter to the Erl Stirling anent the nonentry of Dawik. Item, a letter to Erll Annandaill, and last a letter to my sone, with the doubill of my precept of 2000lb sterling.

Item, delyuerit to the Lord Traquhair ane doubil of my accompt to his Maiestie, with the doubil of my docket of my signator of Craighall, with the draucht of my precept of 2000R. surth of the annuity.

Admiralitic.
Panmuir.
2 AprylL Thursday, 1635.

This day Sir James Lockhart went to court, and als Mr. W. Quhytfurd; and I wret one to Erl Stirling for Sir James Lockart, anent his signator of the fisching for surnisching of the countery, and vther two with Mr. Walter to the Erl Stirling and Lord Panmuir, to suit for him to get aither of the places of Galloway or Abirdein, quhilk ar both vacand, and als I ansuerit the Lord of Panmuir his letter anent Admirality yesterday, and recommendit to him to affist Mr. Walter Quhytsurd.

Item, at this tyme Babethan went to court, with quhom sent a letter to his brother Doctor Chalmer.

3 Apryll 1635, Fryday. Item, sent with the Lord Justice Clerk letters to Erl Stirling, Lord Panmuir, and my sone, with the toun of Carraill their signator.

This day my deir neice Margaret departit.

6 Apryll 1635, Mononday. Sent with the President of Seflioun (quho, with Bilhop Ross and Clerk of Register, went to court) a letter to the Lord Panmuir, and within it one to the Erl of Stirling, quhairin I acquaint them with the questioun anent the patronages of Roffe.

Item, thairefter sent in a pacquet to my sone a letter to Lord Panmuir, This sent with with a nott of the patronage of Ross thairin, ane other to the Erll Traquhair bell. CamP with the lyk nott, a letter to the Lord Marquess, and a letter to the Erl Roxbrugh, reserring him to my commentarie of the Erl of Traquhair anent violent followers of publik, and the Morn In the particulers of it flat contrair.

7 Apryll, Twysday, 1635.

Delyuerit to Archibald Campbell my pacquet to the Erl Stirling, quhairin Mem.—Archibald the twa renunciatiouns of Kintyr. Item, letters to the Lord Alexander and qufJjj,"01 Hary Alexander. Item, letters to the Lord Lorn. io Apryll.

Item, an vther pacquet to my fone within this, quhilk conteinis all that is Lome, mentionat above in that to him, quhilk fould haif gone with the President, but he wes gone.

Item, an vther pacquet to my fone, quhairin L. Quhythill his signator, with letters to Erl Traquhair, Erl Stirling, and Lord Alexander.

11 Apryll, Setterday, 1635. This day pacquet sent be James Prymrois, quhairin the Commiffioun of the Borders, with my letter to the Erl Traquhair to gett one vnder the feill of Ingland, and to fie this quhilk is sent seillit with Ingland's seill at the left. Item, letters to Erl Stirling from Archbischop of Glasgow, in quhilk, presentation to Mr. G. Bennet of Libertoun, with my ernest recommendatioun. Item, sent to the Erl Stirling the signatour of Masons and Wrychtis renuncit be Sir Anthonie Alexander. Item, letters to Lord Panmuir, Sir James Carmichael, L. Ley, Erl Traquhair, acquainting him with the Commifsioun of Borders. Item, letters to my fone, and within the letters from John, Thomas, James, and als a letter from me to Hary Hope, and to him one from Alexander Lowrie. 13 Apryll 1635, Mononday. This day left with my fbne at my going to Craighall, to the suneralls of my good Lord Melvil, ane pacquet to be dispatcht, quhairin to Erl Stirling, Erl Traquhair, Erl Panmuir, only to acquaint them with my going to Fyff. But the cheif erand is a letter to the Erl Buchan, with a presentatioun to Mr. George Bennet of the Kirks of Liberton and Quodquhon, vacand he the deceifs of Mr. John Cheislie, quhilk ar incloffit in a letter to my fone Mr. Alexander. 24 Apryll 1635.

Mr. Alexander my Sent by Erl Mar to my fone Mr. Alexander jcxx doubill angels,!""K--quhairof for jewellis to Mary lxxxxfi). sterling, the remanent extending to 301b. st. to himself.

3 Junij 1635, Weddinsday. Sent with Charles Mowat, servitor to Erl of Buchan, ane pacquett to Lord Panmuir, quhairin the new deputatioun of Admirality, with the nott how to mend it, and reffons thairoff. Item, the forme of the letter to me from his Majestie anent my signatour, quhilk is past. Item, one to him from my fone Sir John, with thanks for promiffing to interpone anent kneiling. Mr. Alex. Hope. Item, within his letters to Mr. Alexander from Sir Thomas, but none from me, saif on the bak chyding him for the paying Mr. Vdward 50flE) sterling. Item, letter of thanks to Lord Duik for Kynninmonth, quhilk wes oppugnit be Bischop Ross. Item, thanks to Erl Buchan for Mr. George Bennet's presentatioun to Libertoun and Quodquhoun.

Item, letter to Erl Stirling from Mr. James Gordoun, and one to him from my self.

Item, an pacquet from Orbistoun to my Lord Marques his Maister Houshold.

Item, letters to Mr. Alexander from his mother and Sir John, and within it my lynes, appointing him to returne at Michaelmas nixt. Item, letter from Erl Traquhair to Erl Mortoun.

Item, becaus of Charles Mowat seiknes I direct ane pacquet to the Erl Stirling on Setterday, at 8 hours of nycht, 6 Junij.

8 Junij 1635.

This day being Mononday, I producit his Majestie's letter in Exchekker for paffing of my signatour,quhilk wes regiftrat, and therefter my signatour past.

11 Junij 1635.

Gevin to hir to gif Alexander Lowis fFor Malvesie and Cor Alexander Lowis to be sent forth to the Low Countryes, 6 Rosnobles, 2 x merk pieces off thair awin stamp, and 1 doubill pistollet.

Item, gevin to my wyff iiijc merkis,

in sull satiffactioun off all the money Thomas Bennet and annuell thairof, quhilk scho tuk of the money pertening to Thomas Ben-payit of alL net, fone to George, and that by and attour iijcfi) affignit to him to be payit be Thomas Forman.

13 Junij 1635, Setterday. This day letters delyuerit to Mr. James Gordoun, to be sent to the Erl Stirling, quhairin to the Erll and Lord Alexander. Item, to Lord Panmuir, quhairin from me and Sandsurd. Item, to Mr. Alexander, quhairin a letter to the Lord Duik from the Countess of Mar, and from me to Erl Ancrum. Item, one to James Levingstoun, with letters to him from Sandsurd. Item, one from Sir John to with the affignatioun from George Hope to Capringtoun's band of 5000 merkis. Item, one from Sir Thomas to him, to caus delyuer my Lord Duik's letter by another than himself. Item, a letter to Sir James Carmichaell. 17 Junij 1635.

Sent with Sir James Leslie letters to Lord Panmuir, and within them the Copie of the Renunciatioun, to be subscryvit be the Lord Marques of Hamiltoun, in savors of Lord Panmuir of the teind bolls affignit out of Moniky to Garvok and Panbryd. The principal delyuerit to Orbistoun, to

D be fent be him-with my letter to Lord Panmuir, quhilk went with Sir James Leslie as said is.

19 Junij 1635.

Memorandum.—Theis went not with Sir James Leslie, becaus I gaif them to Orbistoun, quho slipit him.

Item, sent ane pacquet with Mr. Andro Lermonth, quhairin twa to the Lord Panmuir, one to Erl of Annandaih, with one from Richard Maxwell, one to Henry Alexander, one to Erll of Ancrum, with one from his fone.

Item, one from John and Thomas to Mr. Alexander.

20 Junij 1635.

Sent with Mr. Thomas Murray ane pacquet to Lord Panmuir, quhairin Orbistoun's pacquett to Sir James Hamiltoun, within quhilk ar all theis that sould haif gone with Sir James Leslie. Item, to Hary Alexander anent the Lord Melvill.

24 Junij 1635.

Mr. Alexander This r. Nathaniel Vdward his fervand presentit to me a tikket to

Hope, my sone, 131b sterling, him from Mr. Alexander, testifying that he had borrowit of him only xiij ft sterling, quhilk I did instantlie pay and retene the tikket.

29 Junij 1635.

Letters sent to Erl Stirling with his servand, quho come from him in his way hither at Standsurd, and defyrit him to direct a pacquet to his fone Hary, quhairin ar letters to Lord Panmuir. Item, letters from Bischop of Dunblane to Hary, with Mr. Wuliam Bellenden his presentatioun. Item, letter to Lord Panmuir from Patrik Maule.

4 Julij 1635, Setterday. This day the Erll of Stirling cam from Court, and in his chamber in Mr. John Layng his house, the Erl Traquhair promisit in the Erll of Stirling his presence, to advance to me my pension for a 3eir, if I prevaillit in the matter of Bancreiff aganis Sir P. Murray.

11 Julij 1635, Setterday. This day a packet sent be Mr. James Gordoun, and sent in it a letter25 September 1635. to Henry Alexander, and within it a signatour of Sir Alexander Homes of RoterTBrouncT Threipdailly. Item, a letter to Lord Panmuir to be appendit to the packetJohn Glass'that my deir nephew, in case to meit him be the way, and if not to be sent bak to me be Hary James Hope, deAlexander. ff f,?chen in July 1635.

15 Jusij, Weddinsday, 1635. This day the Master of Daell subscryvit the presentatioun off the Kirk of Libertoun and Quodquhoun in savors of Mr. George Bennet. 29 Julij 1635.

Gevin to my fone Sir John jc merkis for bigging of the He in Crawmond Yle of Crawmond Kirk, quhilk with jc merkis gevin of before to Mr. William Colvill, Minister, 28 December 1635 makis ijc merkis. — To the wrycht,

Item, the Minister wes superexpendit in his accompt vi ft) xvj tf, quhilk wes payit to Thomas Jamesoun, 23 November 1635.

5 August 1635.

This day payit to my fone Sir John ane vther jc merks for the He of Crawmond Kirk, quhilk makis 300 merkis.

9 August 1635.

Item, gevin to him to gif Mr. William Colvill to pay the masons and wrychts jc merks, quhilk makes 400 merks.

22 September 1635.

Sent letters with Mr. Eleazer Borthuik to my fone Mr. Alexander, quhairin This day theCouna letter to him from Sir Thomas in my name. Item, letters from me tothtSeptemBischop Brichen, Mr. Dalzell, James Levingstoun, and Sir James Lockart. ber *2i* September 1635.

Sent letters in the pacquet direct be the Erll of Stirling. Item, to James Levingstoun from Justice Clerk in savors of my fone Sir Thomas. Item, from Sir Thomas to Mr. Alexander. Item, from me to Sir James Lockart, testiseing the Lords Resolutioun anent the matter of the fifehing.

Item, this samyn day delyuerit a letter to L. Ernok, quho went journey direct from me to James Levingstoun anent the communty of Dunbar.

25 September 1635.

Payit be myself to James Aytoun, meafoun, ix dollars.

26 September 1635.

Item, letters sent with the goodman of Orbistoun his pacquet delyuerit to 30ung Brounley, viz., one to Mr. Levingstoun from Justice Clerk, anent my fone Sir Thomas, and one from Sir Thomas to Mr. Alexander his brother.

28 September, 1635. Item, letter from me to James Levingstoun, in ansuer of his anent Sir Thomas, and als letters from the Justice Clerk to that samyn effect, quhairin a nott sent vp that the Wardie lands fould be first offerit to James Levingstoun, and this sent be John Inglis, younger fone to John Inglis, skynner, burgess of Edinburgh.

Last September 1635. Delyuerit to the Lord Justice Clerk a letter to James Levingstoun anent my Lord Cranstounridell. Item, ane other to Mr. William Elphinstoun anent the Justice Court, and Reformatioun therof.

2 October 1635.

Sent a pacquet with Alexander Pirrie, and thairin writtin to Mr. Alexander by myself. Item, to Mr. Dalzell, Sir James Lockart, with the copie of the Counsell's letter to his Majestie, anent the fifehing, to the Erll of Ancrum, and to Vicount Belheavin.

7 October 1635, Weddinsday. Delyuerit to the Erl of Traquhair at his going to Court, the two Commiffiouns of the Borders; one vnder the Gret Seil of Scotland, and the vther vnder the Gret Seil of Ingland, with ane new Commiflioun dockettit be me. Item, the signatour of the Erl of Queiniberie'S als dockettit be me on the fycht of on dockettit be the Erll of Stirling, and signed be his Majestie, quhilk conteins a taxt of the ward and manage of the lordship of Torthoruid, quhilk was nevir taxt of befoir. Item, delyverit to the said Erll ane pacquet to my sone Mr. Alexander, quhairin to his sacred Majestie, with 22 articles of accompt of his Majesties service. Item, to Erl Stirling, Hary Alexander, Justice Clerk, Mr. Dalzell. Item, to Sir James Lockhart. Item, two pacquets to James Levingstoun, and within one of them my ansuer to his Majestie anent James his rycht to the Commonty of Dumbar, and with a new signator to James, dockettit be me, and ane letter from John Sempill to James Levingstoun. 15 October 1635.

Gevin to James Prymrois his pacquet letters to Erl Stirling, quhairin to my son, and within his to Erl Traquhair and Justice Clerk, and also one to Serjant Young, from Mr. John Lyndsay, nepho to the Dean of Winchester. 19 October 1635.

Sent letters with Richard Foulertoun, and givin to Orbistoun to be gevin to him, viz., to my son Mr. Alexander, quhairin to Erl Traquhair and Erl Stirling generall letters allanerly, except from suiche off the factioun in Aberdein, anent the cheising of thair Magistrates.

Item, this same day, at nicht, delyverit letters to the Lord Panmuir, viz., 20 October, Lord one to himself, and within it the form of the warrand for his and my TMmr went *10* annuity, and price to be dischargit. Item, to Erl Stirling, Erl Traquhair, my sone, and Hary Alexander.

22 October 1635.
Mr. James Law and Kavertoun australe promisit 100 dollars. Item, Mr. Alexander Hepburne voluit, &c.
24 October, Setterday, 1635. Sent ane pacquet to Erl Stirling, quhairin letters to himself, with one to him from Mr. John Paterfoun's wyfF, for Mr. Alexander Hepburne. Item, letters to William Murray from hir, with myne to him, and within it the signatour of bastardie of Mr. Andro Mickle to Mr. Alexander Hepburne. Item, letters to the Lord Panmuir, and within it one to the Erl Traquhair, quhairin for Mr. Andro Mickle his gift. Item, letters to my fone Mr. Alexander, and within it letters to the Dean of Winchester, from myself and Tilliquhilly, directit to Serjant Young. Item, letter to Sir John Gordon, from John Peter, in savours of Mr. Alexander Hepburne. Item, a letter to one Mr. Nicolsoun, from Mr. Thomas Henrysoun. Item, in the letters to the Lord Panmuir, sent the toun of Brichen thair petitioun, with two presentatiouns blank, one of the preceptory of Mafondew, the other of St. Salvators. 27 October 1635, Thursday. Delyverit to Mr. John Raa, sone to James Raa, a letter to Mr. John Lothian, in his savores. Item, a pacquet to my son Mr. Alexander, quhairin a letter to the Erl Annandaill, and within it from Thomas Maxwell. 28 October 1635.

Gevin to the Lord Panmuir his litill boy, quho went be sea, an letter to the Lord, and within it one to Mr. Alexander, compleining of his obscure wryting, and commanding him to wryt particularlie of his estait and attendance.

Last October, Setterday, 1635. Letter sent to Lord Panmuir, and within it one from Mr. Henry Sinclair, advertiseing him of the deces of Mr. Andro Drummond, minister at Panbryd. Item, a letter to Erl Stirling, and another to Erl Traquhair, sent in a pacquet dire6t to the Lord Alexander by James Prymrois, quhilk pacquet went on Sounday, the first day of November 1635.
2 November 1635, Mononday. Gevin be me to James Aytoun, measoun, in sull satiffactioun of the bigging of the He of Crawmond, 14 dollars, and to his men 1 dollor.

Deir Mr. John Rig deceiffit. The Lord prepare me, for I am now the Mr. John Rig. only and last of that stok of mankynd.

Item, this days report cam off the Erl of Marfchell his deceiss, at his Erl Marscheil. awin hous in Fettereffo, of 8 dayis seiknes, about the 29 or 30 of October.

5 November 1635, Thursday. This day an pacquet sent to Erl Stirling be me, quhairin letters to the Erl from Mr. James Gordoun, and from me, anent the signet. Item, to Lord Panmuir, with Mr. Patrik Lyndsay his letter. Item, ane accompt of his effairs, viz., that Mr. Montgomerie's tak is acceptit. Item, commiffion past in Counsell anent the slaers of blak fysche and fmoltis for a 3eir, quhilk wes opponit be Sir John Hay, becaus of the thesaurer's absence. Item, I wret to him anent the toun of Queinsferie, thair signatour. Item, letters to the Erl of Mortoun, with the signatour; and letters from Erl Wyntoun and Erll of Dunsermling. Item, letters to James Maxwell from Erl of Wyntoun to that effect. Item, my letters to Erl Traquhair, to Erl Stirling, to Hary Alexander, to that effect. Item, letters to my fone, quhairin letters to Erll of Annandaill, with Mr. M'Brair his accompt. Item, a letter from John to Mr. Alexander. Item, a letter from Lord Dalkeith to the Erl of Mortoun, his sather. 13 November 1635. To the sklaitter x dollors. Item, mair to him, 13 dollars. 16 November 1635, Mononday. This day gevin to John Dalzell letter to the Master his brother, anent Pensoun, and thanks for the advertisement anent the exceptioun takin anent the signatour of Meyneris, presentit be Mr. Charles Geddice. Item, letters to Lord Panmuir, anent the calling of his caus; and to 20 December, and anent the Master of Donypace; and within Lord Panmuir his letter one to my fone, anent his money to be surnishit to him. 19 November 1635.

This day the Erl of Traquhair returnit from Court, and delyverit to me Erl Traquhair. his Maiesties letter, anent the signatour of my haill lands, with the blensche taxt ward and few holding;

with a copie of his Maiesties warrand to him for discharging the pryce of annuity.

Item, on 20 November, in Counselhous, I enterit in fpeeche with him anent the afsise of error, and he promisit to me a precept of 2000 lb scotts if I fould obteine it, quhilk I acceptit.

21 November 1635.

My sone Mr. Alex-This day delyverit to Alexander Narn of Sandsurd, to the vse of my fone "sandsiird068 Alexander, to be gevin him quhen he comes to Court, fiftie tuelf-pund pieces of gold.

Item, sent with Sandsurd a letter to Mr. Levingstoun, and ane other to the Justice Clerk.

Item, a pacquet to my fone, quhairin to himself, to Lord Panmuir, Erl Annandaill, Mr. Dalzell, James Maxwell, and Mr. Ebenezer Borthwick.

27 November 1635. Sent letters with young Gicht to the Lord Panmuir, quhairin to my fone, with letters to John Nicolfoun from his sather. Item, letters to Lord Panmuir from Dumbarro. 4 December 1635, Fryday. This day letters sent to the Erl Stirling, quhairin to himself, with his pensioun of Tillicultry dockettit be me. Item, to Lord Panmuir, ansuer of his last, with the signatour; and contract with the Lyoun, and my opinioun thairanent. Item, to James Levingstoun, ansuer anent his lignatour, and within his to Justice Clerk, anent the Commiffioun of Justiciary. Item, to my fone Mr. Alexander, to Sandsurd, to Sir Robert Gordoun, and to the E. Annandaill. Erl of Annandaill, anent his effaires, and his promise of 1c wedders on the Lowmonds.

Item, sent to my sone Mr. Alexander a letter, and within it the letter from Mr. Bankis to Horff, anent the Grenland schip. Item, a letter to Lord Panmuir anent Ylaw, and the Erl Traquhair his oy to it; and within it one from Mr. Patrik Lyndsay: and all thir inclosit on the bak to the Lord Panmuir.

Memorandum.—This day the Lady Roffe reffavit from me hir signatour Lady Rosse. of Craig and Balgone, to be advysit with be the Erll of Traquhair; and hir Ladyship promisit to me, at the returne of the signatour vnder his Maiesties hand, fiftie pieces.

11 December 1635.

Gevin to the Erl of Traquhair my letter to his Majestie, anent the Lady This went not Ross, for Balgone, with my report inclosit thairin, togither with the signatour TMw 9 De" of Balgone, dockettit be me. Item, writtin to the Lord Panmuir, and sent to him L. Morphie's letter, reffavit 8 December. Item, the copie of the decreit arbitrall; and, last, intreatit him to affist the delyvery of my letter to his Majestie anent Balgone, with the paffing of the signatour; and als writtin to the Master of Dalzell, anent the success of his caus with Mr. Dauid Perfoun.

12 December 1635. Memorandum.— Nothing gevin to the Erl Traquhair bot his Majesties letter, and report within it, with the signatour dockettit be me; and all vthers my letters inclosit in an pacquet, and direct; to the Erl Stirling, and delyverit to Mr. James Gordoun, quho sent the samyne to the Erl Stirling, with the Erl Traquhair his fervand; and I addit to the former letters a letter to the Erl Stirling himself, a letter to Justice Clerk, with Alexander Nesmyth his letters to him and James Levingstoun. Item, a letter to Bishop Brichen. Item, a new letter to Lord Panmuir, anent the L. Cadder his seu duty, cravit be the Erl Traquhair. Item, a letter to my sone Mr. Alexander. Item, a letter to Erl Annandaill, with the renunciatioun of his pensioun in his Majesties hands. 21 December 1635.

This day being Monondday, my fone Mr. Alexander returnit from Court My sone Mr. Alexto Edinburgh, and partit from Londoun on Setterday, 5 December; and sofVotTcourTMl wes in journeying 16 dayes.

24 December 1635.

Gevin to John Hamiltoun of Orbistoun ane letter to the Marques of Hamiltoun, quhairin ane ansuer of that quhilk he wrett to me anent Mr. George Winram. Item, ane accompt of the contract of Arbroith; and, last, thanks to his Lordihip for my fone Mr. Alexander.

25 December 1635.

Mem.—He went The Erll of Traquhair sent a servand to Court, and with him sent a ber!rt one'esterTM Packet to Lord Panmuir, quhairin two to him, with the College of Abirdein noon, being Twys-jjij. letter to me, anent the teinds of Haltoun. Item, a letter to the Bishop day.......

of Brechin, and within it tho signatour of the Monastrie of Arbroith, and defyring him to agrie to a contract betuix Lord Panmuir and him and the toun of Brichen, anent the nominatioun of the baillie. Item, a letter from John Pilmuir. Item, another pacquet gevin to Mr. James Gordoun, direct to the Erl of Stirling, with one to himself and one to Hary, anent Queinfberrie. Item, within it a pacquet to the Justice Clerk, quhairin to himself from me. Item, a pacquet to him from my sone Mr. Alexander. Item, to Alexander Narn from me, and als from Sir Thomas. Item, one to Mr. Dalzell, one to James Levingstoun, one to the Erll of Annandaill, and one to the Erll of Ancrum and Sir Robert Gordoun; quhilk all I haif defyrit L. Sandsurd to delyver.

With this servand the Erl Traquhair sent a letter subscryvit be him and Arbroith. me to his Majestie, anent Arbroith, with the twa contractis, dockettit be

Lady Rosse: me; and als sent with him my letter to his Majestie, with the signatour of Balgone. Balgone, quhilk I recommendit to Lord Panmuir, and defyrit that it mycht be returnit to me.

Last December 1635, Thursday. Sent letters with Alexander Alexander, servitor to the Erl of Stirling, viz. To Erl Stirling, acquainting him, that albeit his fone and I wer of the Committee of the North, 3 et we wer not on the Cabinet Counsell, for a letter wes writtin to his Majestie thairanent, to quhilk nather his sone's hand wes nor myne. Item, a letter to the Lord Panmuir, defyring him to misknaw that quhilk I wret to him anent Ylaw and the L. Caddell, and in his nixt to gif thanks to the Erl Traquhair for his savors to me. Item, a letter to Erl Annandaill, and within it the nott of the teinds sauld be Lord Stormonth; and als within it a letter from Erll of Rothes to Lady Griffell Seytoun. Item, letters from Thomas Maxwell to the Erl of Annandaill; and last, letters from my fone

Mr. Alexander to Hary Alexander: all inclosit in ane gret pacquet to Erl Stirhng.

Item, sent thairefter, on 1 Januar, with the said Alexander Alexander, This went not ane letter to the Erl of Stirling, and within it the signatour of kills and 1'™"' owenis, and making of malt, dockettit be me. Item, a letter to Hary Alexander his fone, and als ane letter to Sir Robert Gordoun, quhilk wes left out of the former packet. Item, in this letter I wret to the Erl Stirling anent the L. Quhythil, for a letter to the Exchekker anent his buflines of Dingwall. Item, a letter to James Levingstoun, and within it a presentatioun to the kirk of Stentoun, blank, vacand be Mr. Patrik Cook his deceis; and I told him of Mr. William Mortoun, for quhom Lady Borthwik and Lord £eti,er, and Mr. John Lauder, for quhom the Lord Dury.

2 Januar 1636, Setterday, at 5 houris at nycht. Sent with Wallace of Auchans, letters to Alexander Narn of Sandsurd, from my self and Sir Thomas, anent Mr. Andro Stevinsoun for the kirk of Stentoun, vacand be the deceise of Mr. Patrik Cook. 5 Januar 1636.

Sent with a Frensche gentilman, quho come to sie the country, and returnit post, a pacquet to Lord Panmuir, quhairin one to him, to wrytt to Erl Traquhair, for renewing of his renunciatioun off the annuity. Item, a pacquet to Erl Roxburgh, with letters in it to the Erl of Lauderdaill, anent Mr. Andro Stevinsoun; but none from my self, but from Mr. Robert Burnett, Mr. James Adamsoun, principal!. Item, letters from me and my fone Sir John to James Levingstoun, Justice Clerk, Alexander Narn, for it. Item, ane pacquet from my fone Mr. Alexander to the Master of Dalzell.

8 Januar 1636, Fryday. This day letters cam from Court to Sir Alexander Home, bering that the Quean's Majestie wes delyverit of ane maid child, in St. James, betuix 7 and 10 in the morning, 29 December 1635, being Twysday. 15 Januar 1636.

L. Binning. Sent with the Lord Bynning letters to Lord Panmuir, and within it from John Pilmuir. Item, letters to Erl Annandaill, and within it the gift of 1c wedderis. Item, letters to Erl Stirling, Bishop Brichen, and to James Levingstoun, with a form of warrand from his Majestie to the Bilhop of Edinburgh, anent Stentoun kirk. Item, letters to Justice Clerk and L. Sandsurd, quhairin I wrytt of the signatour of Justiciary, but send it not, becaus John Bellenden wes not ready.

16 Januar 1636.

This signatour of Justiciary dockettit be me, 15 Januar 1636, with a letter to the Justice Clerk, and another to Mr. William Elphinstoun, inclofit in a pacquet direct to the Justice Clerk.

Item, a letter to the Lord Panmuir, and within it my fone Sir Thomas his 2 signatouris, one vpon L. Chester Cheslie? his dimiffioun of place and pensioun; the vther a simpill ratisicatioun of AdvocatDeput; and a letter to theErl off Stirling: to dockett aither of them, as the Lord findis his Majestie inclynit.

Thir sent inclosit in a packet direct to the Erl of Stirling, quhilk I delyuerit to Mr. James Gordoun, 16 Januar 1636.

23 Januar 1636, Setterday. Sent a pacquet to the Erll of Stirling, with a brother of Mr. Robert Burnettis, quho wes going to the young Erl of Merschel, quhairin twa pacquets to Lord Panmuir, with the contract of the bailliery of Brichen. Item, the Erl of Mar his letter to him and Erl of Stirling. Item, my letter to the Erl Stirling. Item, my letter to the Erl of Annandaill, with a tikket thairin anent, and Thomas Maxwell's letters. Item, a letter to James Maxwell from Sir John Scott.

Quean-s Majestie delyverit of a dauchter, 29 December 1635.

25 Januar 1636, Mononday. Sent with the Erl Kynnoul a letter to Lord Panmuir, defyring him to afls from the Erl Merfchell his servand, that pacquet quhilk cam from John Pilmuir, quhilk wes not inclosit in myne, becaus I had delyuerit myne befoir it cam; remitting to his consideratioun a matche betuix the Erl and his dauchter; and als in this sent a letter to Erl Ancrum, to caus prent Franciscanis Vllisemus Florentius Volusenus?, or to send him heir to me to be prentit, becaus Mr. Robert Balcanquell wes importuning me to haif him restorit, as ane auld monument of Scottis antiquity. 30 Januar 1636, Setterday. Packquet delyverit to Mr. James Gordoun, direct to Erl Stirling, quhairin to him self. Item, a pacquet to Lord Panmuir, quhairin two to him self, with the copy of Abirdein thair letter; and the vther anent the Mem.—This went Bilhop of Aberdein and Mr. William Gordoun, thair defyr of a sarther 4 Fe" duty, ratiseing the auld tak, and geving of new for that sarther space, and for the rector's lystyme, and 5 yeiris efter. Item, a letter to Justice Clerk. Item, to L. Sandsurd, with a letter to the Countess of Home, anent Erls Murray and Lauderdaill. 6 Februar 1636.

The young L. Mynto Steuart went post, and sent with him a letter to the Lord Panmuir, anent my conserence with the Bilhop of Brichen efter his return, anent Maffondew, and the bailliery. Item, anent my reffait of the writtis of Innerpeffer, from Sir Andro Fleschor, to be transumit; and, last, anent L. Morphie, if I sal perfew him on the decreit arbitrall, becaus he hes gevin me no ansuer of my letter anent the setting and choising.

11 Februar 1636.

Sent with young L. Barnis Cunyngham a pacquet, quhairin to Erl This Thursday, Stirling, anent the signat our for xvico merkis yeirly, and the superplus to CTj0,, doun the come to the Secretary. Item, to Lord Panmuir, anent admiffioun of M.dollors t0 lvi » quhilk wes in

Robert Norie be the Bischop of Brichen and cheptor. Item, to caus him stantlie proclamit. wrytt to the baillies for the sundatioun, quhilk, as the Erl of Southesk sayis, Ib in thair hands. Item, letters to James Maxwell anent the licht of May, and a letter to the Master of Dalzell. Item, a packet from my fone Mr. Alexander to the Lord of Panmuir.

12 Februar 1636.

Delyverit to Alexander Bruce a pacquett to the Lord Panmuir, quhairin to him, advertising him of the letters from E. Southesk and Orbistoun to the Lord Marquis of Hamiltoun, with his bak band, quhilk I defyr him to ask bak from the Marquis. Item, defyring him to send bak the contract anent the bailliery of Brichen. Item, a letter to James Levingstoun, and within it one from John Sempill.

18 Februar 1636.

Item, delyverit to Alexander Bruce ane vther letter to the Lord Panmuir, and within it the presentatioun to the vicarage of Panbryde to Mr. Arthour Granger, scholemaster of Arbroith, but his name blank, becaus it is blank in the prefentatioun to the perfonage signed be the Kingis Majestie.

19 Februar 1636, Fryday. Sent with Sir James Lockart a pacquet to Erll of Stirling, quhairin a pacquet to the Lord Panmuir, and in his a letter to his sacred Majestie, with the paper of my accompt of his Majestie's effaires. Item, a nott of the form of his Majestie's letter to me, quhilk beris the approbatioun of Ylau.

24 Februar 1636, Weddinsday. Mr. Alexander and This day my two fones Mr. Alexander and Mr. James tuik journey, the journey this day. one to Court, and the other to France; and gevin to Mr. Alexander xxxvij doubill angels, quhilk, with the 13 quhilk he had, makes 50 doubill angels; lton,gevmto and jjg gevm him j 0f rydals of gold for his journey. Item, gevin to 51 Ps. in letters Mr. James 50 doubill angels, with a Portugal ducat of gold. Item, to him 1 merkis of gold for his journey, with sum 30P sterling of xijl? pieces.

Item, thair mother gaif to ilk of them 2 rosnobles. Item, I gaif ather of direct to them selfis.

them the buik of Imitatioun of Chryst, of Thomas Kempis, with command, ilk day, in morning and evening, to reid ane cheptor thairof; and, last, I gaif them my bliffing. God send me a happie fycht of them both.

Item, efter they went als sar as the Patterraw, they sent for x dollors, quhilk I gave, and vther ten dollors wes borrowit be Mr. James from Hary Hope, quhilk I payit.

26 Februar 1636, Fryday. Sent with David Seytoun, servitour to the Lord Frendraucht, ane pacquet to Lord Panmuir, and within it one to Mr. Alexander, and another to my fone Mr. James. Item, a pacquet to Erl Annandaill, and within it Thomas Maxwell his letter. Item, ane letter to James Levingstoun, advertising him to pay to Dauid Muirheid 50Ib sterling for Arthor Nesmyth, becaus Arthor had subscryvit and delyverit the discharge, and gevin band to warrand him of the teinds. 1 Merche 1636, Twysday. Sent with Captain Leslie a pacquet to Lord Panmuir, quhairin anent the Erl of Murray. Item, one to my fone Mr. Alexander, quhairin also anent the Erl of Murray. Item, a letter ta the Countess of Home, and within it one to the Erl Lauderdaill, anent the Erl Murray. 4 Merche 1636, Fryday. This day William Butter went to Court, and sent with him a pacquet to the Lord Panmuir, quhairin to him self, with the L. Dwn his letter anent Luchur, to be continewit vntil Junij. Item, anent Mr. James Raa, minister at Marykirk. Item, a letter to Erl Traquhair. Item, one to Erl Stirling. Item, a pacquet to Justice Clerk, and within it to Sandsurd, and within it my fones letter to Robert Hope. Item, a letter to Erl Annandaill. Item, a letter to Sir Robert Gordoun. 9 Merche 1636,

Sent with Mr, John Dik a letter anent the Greneland fisching to the Lord Panmuir, and within it one to my sone Mr. Alexander, and within his one to Mr. James. Item, ane vther from me and Mr. Hary Futhy to Lord Panmuir, anent St. Salvator's chaplanrie.

Hary Hope and he H Merche 1636, Fryday.

returnit to Brunt iland on 19 Octo-This day my nephew Hary Hope tuik schip at Leyth for Londoun, and ber 1636, and abaidfrom thence to d advancit to jcfo qulf my sone Sir John in the schip till)' J thai gat libertie gaif hand for him. on 3 NovemDeTto Item, gevin to him from me, at his parting, v douhill angellis. come furth, in respect of the feir off the plaig. 14 Merche 1636.

This Mononday Mr. Eleazer Bortlmik went post to Court, and sent with him an pacquet to the Lord Panmuir, with Pittarlie's letter anent guildrie. Item, ane pacquet to my sone Mr. Alexander, quhairin to himself, and his brother Mr. James. Item, to Erl Mortoun, in ansuer of his to me anent Kirkcaldie, with a defyr to thank the Erl of Traquhair for his savor in the way to pay my precept. Item, ane to the Erl Traquhair, anent Cragyvar his taking of 8 men of Gilliroy. Item, to Erl Ancrum, anent his sone's sone, borne 9 Merche 1636.

Item, letters sent to Erl Stirling, Lord Justice Clerk, and to all the remanent, with Mr. James Robertfoun his pacquet and signatour for his seall of Justice Deput, quhilk I dockettit.

17 Merche 1636.

James Murray, 3ounger, went to Court, and sent with him a pacquet to the Lord Panmuir, quhairin to himself, with a letter to Bromhil, to put the Marquise in mynd of the bakband. Item, a letter to the Erl Roxburgh, in ansuer off his reffavit laitlie. Item, to Justice Clerk. Item, to Erl Traquhair. Item, to my sone Mr. Alexander, anent the bakband to be socht from the Marquise.

21 Merche 1636.

Packet sent to the Erl Stirling, quhairin letters to himself anent the signett. Item, ane pacquet to the Lord Panmuir, with letters about his effaires. Item, letters to my sone Mr. Alexander, and within them to Mr. Levingstoun, with a presentatioun to Mr. John Moir of Stentoun, and the Bishop of Edinburgh his letter to that effect. Item, a letter to the Lord Panmuir from John Pilmuir.

28 Merche 1636, Mononday. This day Sir William Hamiltoun, brother to the Erl Abircorne, went to Court, and with him sent a packet to the Lord Panmuir, quhairin a new presentatioun of St. Salvator's. Item, a letter to the Erl Stirling, anent the new offer of the signet for the xiijIb of the and jcxxviij merkes of money. Item, a letter to my fone Mr. Alexander. Item, in the Lord Panmuir his letter, the nott of my behavior in the matter betuix Erls Murray and Lauderdaill. 5 Apryll 1636, Twysday.

This day the Justice Court held vpon Patrik Glass and Neill MeFathrik, with 6 otheris of Gilleroyis followeris, takin be L. Cragyvar.

Item, Mr. James Gordoun went to Court, and sent with him letters to Erl Stirling. Item, a pacquet to Lord Panmuir, and with it one from John Pilmuir; and als letters to him from L. Cragwar his lady and mother. Item, a pacquet to my fone Mr. Alexander, quhairin from myself, and my sones to him and his brother Mr. James. Item, from me to George Hope. Item, to Erl Traquhair, to Lord Justice Clerk, to Sir James Lockart, to Erl Annandaill, with the doubil of the licence gottin from Denmyln. Item, to Hary Alexander.

6 Apryll, Weddinsday, 1636. The toun of Edinburgh thair Commiffioner went, and sent ane pacquet to Lord Panmuir, quhairin to himself, schawing the docketting be me of the signatour of albeit I thocht the nullity absolut,

To Erl Stirling. Item, to Erl Traquhair, and anent Erl Queinsbery. Item, to my sone Mr. Alexander, and within it to the Countess of Home.

T 14 Apryll 1636.

Grantoun. Delyuerit letters at Grantoun to Sir Alexander Home, quho went to Court on 18 Apryl thairefter, viz. ane pacquet to my sone Mr. Alexander, quhairin to Erl Stirling, to Lord Panmuir, acquainting him with the contrary letters from his Majestie anent John Steuart and L. Wedderburn, and defyring him to bring my letter. Item, a letter of thanks to Sir Robert Dael. Item, one to Justice Clerk, defyring him to haisten Mr. Levingstoun his ansuer anent Stentoun. Item, one to the Erl Traquhair, acquainting him with James Grant his Item, one to Erl

Annandaill, in ansuer of that reffavit 12 Apryll. My sone Mr. Memorandum. —This 14 Apryll, at Grantoun, reffavit a letter from my James Hope. fone daitit at Diep, 14 Aprill 1636, anent his saiff arryvel thair.

22 April 1636.

This day direct a pacquet from Edinburgh to Erl Stirling, quhairin to himself; and a packet to Lord Panmuir, and within it letters to my fone Mr. Alexander; quhairin to James Levingstoun, Mr. Narn, and Justice-Clerk, anent Stentoun. Item, from John Sempill thairanent, with the instrument of resusall of Mr. Andro Stevinsoun and Bistiop of Edinburgh. Item, a new presentatioun to be subscryvit be Mr. Levingstoun and returnit. Item, a letter to Mr. Levingstoun from the Bistiop of Edinburgh.

Item, I inclosit within Sandsurdis a letter to me from the Bishop of Edinburgh, quhilk I defyrit him to conceil. Item, letters from Mr. Alexander Burnet to Thomas Maxwell. Item, a letter from me to Erl Traquhair, anent the Erl Annandaill his offer to acquaint the way how to reduce, quhilk I defyrit the Erl of Traquhair to signisie to his Maiestie, and to get his Maiesties plesur thairin. Item, a letter to the Erl Annandastl from myself. Item, a letter from my sone Sir John to his brother Mr. Alexander.

23 April 1636.

Mr. Alexander, Payit be me to Patrick Wod, according to the letters of exchange drawin 2600 merkis. e my fone r. Alexander, ccvj0 merkis, quhairof xjc merkis for himself, and the rest for gownis to Mary.

5 Maij 1636.

This day packet sent be James Prymrois, and fend in to a pacquet to Erl Stirling; quhairin to himself, to Erl Annandaill, with the letter from his agent in Ireland. Item, to Thomas Maxwell. Item, to Lord Panmuir, with Melgoun and John Pilmuir's letters. Item, to my sone Mr Alexander, and within his to Erl of Traquhair, with a nott of the depositis made be James Grant, his bastard fone; quhairof also a doubill sent to Lord Panmuir. Item, a letter from Sir Thomas to his brother.

23 Maij 1636.

The Erl Traquhair returnit from Court; and on 24 May the Counsell Eril Traquhair held, quhairin he wes sworn High Thesaurer. saurer!"11 3 Junij 1636.

Packet sent with the Lord Thesaurer's servand; quhairin the new signatour of Exchekker dockettit be me, the Commiffioun of the Borderis, the Commiffioun for revising the book of Raites, and the signatour of Mr. of Mynthous, blank to be fillit vp be the Counsell, at the return. Item, I sent ane pacquet to Lord Panmuir; quhairin letters of 21 May, and 25 May, and last of 3 Junij; and within it to the Lord Panmuir himself, defyring to send letters to his freinds of Commiffioun for advancing of Mr Laurence Skynner, minister of Navar, his defyr anent adjoining sum

of the lands of Lethnot and Menmuir parochis to Navar. Item, his wil l anent the gentilmen of Luthriemuir, anent Constabil of Dundie, and anent Mr Alexander Norie for Masondew. Item, a nott to him anent my sone Sir John, to caus him wryt to the Thesaurer for adjoining him to the Exchekker. Item, letters to Erl Stirling. Item, to James Levingstoun, with Sandsurd's and John Sempill's, anent Stentoun. Item, to the Justice Clerk. Item, I defyr to know of Lord Panmuir and Erl Stirling, if a thing wes movit laitlie anent Colleg to me, and quhat wes his Majesty's ansuer, and quhat is thair counsell.

Item, sent at this tyme to the Lord Panmuir the contract of Brichen, subseryvit be them with the old contract.

Item, as this pacquet wes going, word cam that Gilleroy wes takin be my Lord Lorn, as he wes paffing from the Lennox throuch Glenco to the north, fra quhilk he wes chasit be L. Cragyvar.

Memorandum.—This pacquet went not till 6 Junij, and I sent in it a letter to Lord Panmuir, with a form of ane letter from his Maiestie to the Commiffioun of Teinds, anent the kirk of Navar.

14 Junij 1636.

I sent letters to Erll of Annandaill and to his lady, in ansuer of theis reffavit from Thomas Maxwell.

15 Junij 1636.

Item, delyverit letters from me and Sir Thomas to my fone Mr James by Mr. Andro Marjoribanks, with a letter of thankis from Sir Thomas to Doctor Davidfoun, for his kyndnes to Mr. James. Item, letters from my fone John to him and to Doctor Davidfoun.

17 Junij 1636.

Sent to the Erl Stirling a letter, and within it the Commiffioun anent the Signet of Seffioun. Item, to the Lord Panmuir, with a letter from John Pilmuir. Item, a letter to the Erl of Ancrum, in ansuer of his to me. Item, a letter from me to Mr. Alexander, and within it one from my fone John to him, complening of his ryotous fpending.

25 Junij 1636.

Pacquet sent be the Lord Alexander, quhairin a pacquet from me to Erll Stirling, and within it to the Lord Justice

Clerk, and to my fone from myself, Sir John and Sir Thomas.

Item, ane uther pacquet to Lord Panmuir, or, in his absence, to Mr. Alexander, quhairin one from myself, one from Melgum, and one from John Pilmuir.

Item, one to my fone Mr. Alexander from and from the samyn man to Mr. Eleazer Borthuik.

3 Junij 1636, Gilleroy takin. 9 July 1636.

Letters sent with Michell, brother to William Michel, or with the Erl Traquhair's servand, if he gois; quhairin is a pacquet from me to Erl Stirling, anent xxiiij00 merkis off the signet. Item, letters to Erl Ancrum, from the Erl of Lothian his fone. Item, from me to him, signifying that I will leive Sir Thomas and Alexander to his savor next to my Maister's, and defyrs to know his acceptance thairoff. Item, letters to the Lord Justice Clerk. Item, letters to my fone Mr. Alexander, and within them letters to my fone James, and letters from the Bishop of Brechin to his fone Mr. John, to be sent to France.

17 Julij 1636.

A packet gevin to Mr. James Gordoun, quhairin to the Secretar, anent the Signet, and new Commiffioun thairanent. Item, to James Levingstoun anent Stentoun, with Mr. Robert Davidsoun his letter. Item, to Lord Justice Clerk, and to my fone Mr. Alexander.

30 Julij 1636.

This day the Lord Alexander went to Court, and send with him letters to the Erl Stirling his sather, to Erl Ancrum, to Justice Clerk, and to Mr. Alexander, from myself, my two sones, and Lord Cragyvar. Item, within myne one to my fone Mr. James, to be sent with the first occasion.

1 August 1636, Mononday. This day the Marques of Hamiltoun cam to Edinburgh, to quhom I gaif thankis for my fone Mr. Alexander.

Item, this nycht, about 8 hours at evin, I mett with my Lord Traquhair, Lord Traquhair

Tliestii i nor

Thesaurer, (at defyr of the Lord Panmuir;) quhair, efter mony kynd expressiounis, my Lord proseffit he had an abfolut defyr to be in a inteir refpect with me, both becaus of the neirnes of the places quhilk his Lordship bruikit, and myne, quhilk he affirmit had ane more fpeciall relatioun to utheris than ather Register or uther offices, and becaus of the particular frindschip hes bene betuix us; and proseffit, that if he wer affurit of me, he wald trust more to me nor the Thesaurer Deput, and communicat all that concernit his Majestie's services.

And I, on the uther part, relatit how sar I wes bund to his Lordship for my pensioun, for my precept, for my inseftment of Kynninmonth, and for my sone's admiffioun of Exchekker, and how grevously I tuik his Lordship's offense on Fryday the 22 July; for Lord Cranstoun and John Steuart, and last for my sone's signatour of confirmatioun of the deputatioun; and wes readie to gif to his Lordship all the testimonies of thanksulnes, in obeying quhat he commands, in pressing to knaw how he is affectit, and in difposing myself, in Counsell, Seffioun, and Exchekker, to follow his intentioun, so sar as I could with an honest mynd.

And quhil we wes in conserence, the Earl Southesk superveynit, quhom I defyrit to be good for me, quhilk he acceptit.

2 August 1636, Twysday. Thesaurer. This day about 9 we mett in the Counsell hall, in presence of Lord Panmuir, quhair all the preceiding fpeeches wes repeitit, and hands schokin with acceptatioun. The Lord mak me thanksull to my good God, quho hes turnit the wrath of man to his prayse.

This day letters sent to Mr. James by James Murray, to John Clerk his sactor, for surnishing of him.

Item, this day Prestoungrange told me, that Mr. James wes at Orleans, befoir his coming from Paris.

11 August 1636, Thursday. This day the Bishop of Ross went to Court, and fend with him a letter to his Majestie anent the patronages of Ross with L. Innes, quhilk I dockettit be directioun of his Majestie's Thesaurer, and, according to my humill promiss, sould be ready to follow the ordour, for reducing of patronages to the Croun; and I trustit his sacred Majestie wald be myndsull of my painsull labors and gret lossis sustenit be me since my entrie to his Majesties service.

Item, a letter to the Archbishop of Canterbury, acqainting the Bishop of Ross of my fidelitie in performing of my promiss, and making him my fponsor.

Item, a letter to the Erl Stirling, and within it one to him from the Lord Kilcreuch?

7 September 1636, Weddinsday. Tlns day the Counsell held on particular affairs two dayis, and on Friday the 9 September the Thesaurer's compts wer made, quhairin the charge Thesanrer's cam to vcntl pund, or thairabout, and he found super-expendit in vijlb, orComPtlsthairabout.

Memorandum.—In this is allowance takin of ijcft) sterling to me for my pensioun and annuity of Whitsunday 1636, quhairupon I gaif discharge, but hes nott gottin payment.

10 September 1636. This day the maist part of the Counsell being away, the Counsell held anent the coyne; and eftir long debait afoir none, it wes voittit to douncry the dollors to lv tf, and eftirhone it wes of new movit to cry doun to liiij fl, quhilk wes continewit till Mononday. 12 September 1636, Mononday. The dollors cryit doun to liiijfl. Dolloris cryit doun.

Memorandum.—The Erl of Traquhair tuik journey to Court on Setterday, 17 September 1636.

23 September 1636.

Memorandum.—This day, at Windsor, my sone sworne ordiner carver to Mr. Alexander his sacred Majestie, in place of Mr. John Cokburn. ordiner carver.

3 October 1636.

This day being Mononday, I sent ane pacquet at the defyr of the Lord Panmuir, quho wes presentlie come from Angus, and thairin a letter from him to the Erl Stirling. Item, letters to Mr. James Gordoun from George Hadden. Item, letters from me to my sone Mr. Alexander, quhairin letters to his Majestie for humbill thanks. Item, to the Marquis of Hamiltoun. Item, to Erl Ancrum. Item, to Erl Stirling. Item, to Lord Thesaurer. Item, to James Levingstoun, with one from Mr. Robert Dauidsoun. Item, to Justice Clerk. Item, to Sir Alexander Home. Item, a pacquet from me, and my wyff, and sons to James Hope my sone, being at Orleans. This pacquet delyverit to the Postmaster at 10 hours of nycht.

5 October 1636.

The Lord Panmuir went to Court, and sent with him letters to Erl Traquhair, Thesaurer; Erl Stirling, Secretar; my sone Mr. Alexander.

Item, letters to my sone Mr. James.

Item, gevin him a letter with all my instructions.

Sent to Mr. Alex-Item, gevin to him 50 tuelf-pund pieces, to Mr. Alexander. pun" pieces" Item, 50 doubill angels, to be sent to my sone Mr. James. And the item, to Mr. James Lady's sones quho goes to France, hes for thair pedagog Mr. Robert 50 doubill angels. T-r,

Bennet, brother to Mr. James Bennet. 24 October 1636, Mononday. This day Janet Gourlay deceiffit in the Pannis, and wes brocht to Edinburgh, and buryit 26 October, Weddinsday. 25 October 1636.

Sir Robert Gordoun and William Freir went to Court, and sent with them letters to my sone Mr. Alexander, quhairin to himself, to Justice Clerk, and Mr. William Elphinstoun, thanks for concerting with him to agrie with Taverner to putt off the Chancellar his Maister from Mungo Murray, in the suit of the place of carver, for quhilk Mr. Alexander is to pay to Taverner 150 lb sterling.

Last October 1636.

This day Gawin Burnet returnit from Court, and reportit that Sir James. Carmichael wes made Thesaurer Deput, and John Hamiltoun of Orbistoun Justice Clerk.

3 November 1636.

Pacquet gevin to Mr. James Gordoun to be sent to the Erl Stirling,
quhairin to himself. Item, a letter to Erl Annandaill, quhairin one from Alexander Aghan, his agent in Ireland. Item, a pacquet to my sone Mr. Alexander, quhairin to himself, from me and his 2 brethir. Item, to Erl Ancrum. Item, to Sir James Carmichael. Item, to Lord Panmuir. Item, to James Levingftoun, anent Stentoun.

4 November 1636, Fryday.

This day the Erl Traquhair, Thesaurer, returnit to Edinburgh from Court, and ane warrand to me to delay the litting off the Commiffioun of Teindis till his Majestie wer plesit to gif ordour for sitting thairoff.

7 November 1636, Mononday.

Pacquet to Lord Panmuir, quhairin letters to him from John Pilmuir.

Item, advertisement of the doubtis made be the toun of Brichen, with my ansuers.

Item, advertisement of Henry Fyiffis inseftment and surrander.

Item, sent ane procuratory to be subscryvit be the lard, for accepting of the surrander from Henrie Fyiff, oy to David Fyisf, of the auld rent of 12 ft. victueu, surth of the 3 part of the Newtoun of Carmyllie.

12 November.

Sent letters to my sone and Lord Panmuir, with the L. of Ernok.

19 November 1636. This day Henry Alexander returnit to Court, and sent with him, in a purfe, to my sone Mr. Alexander, ane hundreth threttie fyve doubill angels, Mr. Alexander, quhilk ar all doubill, except 36 singell, ansuering to 18 doubill, quhilk gold150 1b-8teriin &my sone is to give to Mr. Taverner for his surtherance to his place of carver; and moving the Erll of Pembrok, Chancellar, maister to Taverner, to pass from his suit for Mungo Murray.

G 21 November 1636.

Hary Alexander went not befoir this day, and sent with him letteris to Lord Panmuir, and within them the letter to be schawin to his Majestie anent Scone, and my imployment of my sone Sir Thomas thairin; and that to incourage me in the work, his Majestie wald be plesit not to extinguish my hope befoir I die, and to let hope live efter my death in the perfoun of my sone. Item, letters sent to the Lord Panmuir, certiseing him of the Commiffioun past anent the Kirk of Navarr, to be reportit 9 Januar.

Item, letters to my Lord Erl Stirling.

Item, letters to my sone Mr. Alexander, with an A, B, C, quhairof I haif the doubill.

Item, letter to Erl Annandaill.

Item, at this tyme one Peter Loch, a footman, wes sent up to serve my sone Mr Alexander, to quhom wes gevin fyve dollars.

3 December 1636. This day Hary Hope, my nephew, went be sea to Diep. The Lord watche over him; and I gave him 4 doubill pistolls and 5 sex pund pieces. 7 December 1636.

Packet sent to my sone Mr. Alexander with George Stirling, brother to the good man of Ardoch, quho went up with the Earl of Tullibardin his son; and in this pacquet sent letteris to my sone Mr. Alexander from my self and my 2 sones; letters to the Lord Panmuir from me from Melgum and John Ersldn. Item, from my Lord Cranstounriddell anent Sir James Murray. Item, letters to Earl Stirling from me and L. Cranstounriddell. Item, letter to Erl Annandaill. Item, letter to Robert Nicolsoun from his sather. Item, letters to Dean of Winchester from me, and Mr. Henry Scrymgeour, minister at Forgund. Item, letters from me to Mr. William Elphinstoun, with thanks for his savor to my sone.

This day L. Sandsurd told me of a gentilwoman callit Elizabeth Nevill dauchter to Sir Hary Nevill, quho hes 200 Bb sterling of portioun, with quhom my sone Mr. Alexander may haif matche.

11 December 1636. 12 November 1637,

This day Agnes Nicolsoun maryit on Sir Patrik Murray, in the Qycbtut«pt Freir Kirk, be Mr. Andro Ramsay, about 4 efternone. Thomas.

J 16 November 1637,

Scho departit this 12 December 1636. Gevin be me a pacquet to the Erl Stirling, to be sent to him be his sone my Lord Alexander, quhilk he did send with the Lord Thesaurer's servand George Peacok; and in this pacquet thair wes letters to Lord Panmuir. Item, to James Levingstoun, with letters from Thesaurer-deput and Sandsurd anent his consent to the tapestar. Item, letters to my sone Mr. Alexander to Erl Annandaill.

13 December 1636. This day George

Pacok went to court, and with him sent theis quhilk ar above, and gevin to the Lord Alexander; and by theis also a pacquet gevin to the Erl Traquhair, direct to the Lord Panmuir, quhairin to him self and Erl Stirling anent John Roy, takin be the Erl Angus. Item, to Mr. Alexander, and within his to Erl Roxburgh, in ansuer os his letter anent the kirks of Kelso. Item, to James Levingstoun, and within it a letter from Thesaurerdeput and Sandsurd, with a nott to be subscryvit be James Levingstoun, for taxing the expenffes of the merches anent the tapester to ic merkis. 20 December 1636. This day the Lord Traquhair produeit in Counsell his Majestie's letter for the Service-book. 27 December 1636. Letters sent to the Lord Panmuir, quhairin a packet from my sone to Mr. Alexander anent Cragyvar's escheit. Item, letters from me to the Lord, Mem. —This pacwith a letter to the Marquis, and ane other to the Erl of Roxburgh, for -jAie'x1tdte0rn'y ing the treuth of the rumor anent the motion made to his Majestie be Erl 27 December 1636. Traquhair, for a second or succeffor to me; with a nott to my Lord Marques anent the proceding in my sone Sir Thomas his deputatioun, and the injury done to me thairin. Item, letters to the Erl and Countess of Annandaill. Item, letters to Mr. Alexander, quhairin I defyr him to get the Lord Marquise his ansuer; and als defyrs him to send me the band made be the toun of Queinfferrie to Hary Alexander of vic merkis. 29 December 1636.

Mr. James 500 30ung James Murray schew to me twa letteris of exchange, subscryvit be This payit to James my one r. James, one m Juty 1636, quhairby he reffavit from John Clerk, Murray, viclb. at servitor to the said James Murray, iic franks, and an vther in November, 24s. the frank,..... « payit 9 Januar quhairby he grantis the reffait of iije franks, to be repayit at demand.
1637.

Januar 1637.

First Januar 1637, being Sounday, John Vetche, 30unger of Dawik, went suddenly to Court be direction of my Lord Thesaurer; and I sent with him a litill packet to my sone, quhairin to himself, to the Erl Stirling, and to the Lord Panmuir, of no busines, but to declar that I wald not omitt the occasioun; and dois rest on thair ansuer to my former letters, and of new defyring my sone to send to me the band of the toun of Queinfferrie.
7 Januar 1637.

My Lord Alexander told me that he wes to send a pacquet, and I sent a letter to my Lord his sather, in ansuer of that quhilk I reffavit, 5 Januar, from George Pacok, servitor to my Lord Thesaurer, at his returne; togither with a letter inclosit thairin to the Lord Panmuir, in ansuer of his quhilk I reffavit at the samyn tyme; and within it one to Mr. Alexander, regraiting his negligence in not wryting.
9 Januar 1637.

Mr. James Hope This day payit to James Murray, younger, for my sone Mr. James Hope, vc franks, takin from John Clerk, sactor to the said James, at Paril5, at 24 P. the frank, inde vilb.

Item, sent a packet to Mr. James from me and my two fones, with a letter 500 frankis.
from me to Mr. Nicoll Brown, quhilk pacquet wes gevin to James Murray to be sent to John Clerk. 14 Januar 1637.

Delyverit to the Lord Alexander ane pacquet to my Lord Stirling, quhairin to himself and to his sone Hary. Item, to Lord Panmuir, quhairin to himself one, with another bering the articles quhilk I intend to send to his Majestie, having his approbatioun. Item, in his a pacquet to my sone Mr. Alexander, quhairin to himself from me and my two sons, and from Mary. Item, letters to be sent to Mr. James from me and his two brethren and Mary. Item, a letter to Prince Palatine, in ansuer of that quhilk his highnes Prince Palatine, sent to me in savors of Coronel Monro. Item, a letter to the Erl Annandaill. Item, one to Sir Robert Gordoun, in ansuer of thairis writtin to me.

Item, thairefter sent in this samyn packet of my Lord Alexander a packet to my sone Mr. Alexander, quhairin to himself, to the Lord MarquiO of Hamiltoun, with a nott of my ansuers aganis the motioun of a counsellor. Item, a letter to the Lord Panmuir thairanent. Item, a letter to James Levingstoun.

Item, 17 Januar 1637, addit a letter to this samyn packet to the Lord Panmuir, anent the taking of the money of Haw fra me, and advertisement made to me thairanent be Archibald Campbell aganis promiss5 and othes.
19 Januar 1637.

This day at Counsel the contest betuix the Lord Thesaurer and me, anent Lord Thesaurer the reffaving of interrogators in the actioun persewit be John Ed3er of Wed-anent Wedderle-Vderlie with my concurfe, for ravisching of Elizabeth Ed3ar, his dauchter, be Richart Ed3ar of Newtoun, and George his sone, and Thomas Ker of Mersingtoun.
31 Januar 1637.

Pacquet sent be my Lord Alexander, quhairin I sent letters to the Erl Stirling, to Erl Roxburgh, to Erl Annandaill. Item, a letter to his Majestie to licentiat me to fie his Majestie. Item, a letter to the Marquil? of Hamiltoun anent 19 Januar. Item, to the Lord Panmuir with the contract of Brichen, with Mr. Laurence Skynner his letter to the Lord anent Navar. Item, a pacquet from Bishop Brichen to the Lord Panmuir. Item, a pacquet from Sir Alexander Home to the Erl Stirling, quhairin he insert the trew estait of the contest of 19 Januar. Item, a letter to Sir Robert Gordoun anent the pasting of his confirmatioun of the teindis. Item, letters to my sone Mr. Alexander, and inclosit within them a trew insormatioun of all the buffines betuix the Thesaurer and me. Item, letters to him from Sir John and Sir Thomas, his brethir.

Item, efter all thir, a letter to the Lord Panmuir, and within it one to Mr. Alexander, acquainting them with the mitigatioun of the contest betuix the Lord Thesaurer and me; but defyring the lord to haist to me a letter to divert the Thesaurer from brangling my affignatioun of Ylaw.
31 Januar 1637.

Item, this samyn day gevin to Thomas Liddes, quho wes going by schip to Londoun, a letter to my sone Mr. James, to be sent to him at Orleans, quhairby I ordour him not to leive his studies for a tour to be made till I sould gif him ordour.

2 Februar 1637.

Mr. Elea3er Borthuik went to Court, and sent with him a pacquet to Mr. Alexander, quhairin one to Lord Panmuir, schewing him of the incresce of his sple. and praying him to haist his letter. Item, another to my fone Mr. Alexander to the samyn effect. Item, letters from Thomas to his brother; with a letter to the Erl of Roxburgh anent Humbie. Item, a letter to my sone James, to be sent to him with diligence, to stay his tour, and to command him to attend his studies.

11 Februar 1637.

Pacquet gevin to my Lord Alexander, quhairin to Erl Stirling. Item, to Lord Panmuir, with the copy of his band. Item, a letter to my sone Mr. Alexander anent 13 Februar 1637.

Item, in this samyn pacquet of my Lord Alexander, sent a letter to the Lord Panmuir anent Ylaw, and within it one to Mr. Alexander; and another from Sir Thomas anent his pretendit vow, qnhilk I haif revokit.

17 Februar 1637.

Delyverit to William Butter, quho went post, the signatour of Bruntiland for Halhill, with 2 letters to Erl Stirling and James Maxwell from me; and in James Maxwell's I touch generally the stormes and woundis heir, and am loth to let them blow so far as Court till I can do no better. But if I haif neid I must mak vse of his favor.

Item, Sir John Scott sent letters to him anent his goodfather the Lard of Halhill.

Item, I delyverit to William Butter a litill pacquet to the Lord Panmuir, Contract with the quhairin a letter to himself, with the subscryvit contract of the College of jeege of Abir" Abirdein to be subscryvit be him, with a doubill to be writtin thair, and subscryvit also and returnit. Item, a letter to my sone Mr. Alexander.

21 Februar 1637.

The L. Auldbar went to Court, and sent with him a letter to Lord Panmuir, schewing him of the subscryving of the decreit of the Merches of Brichen Muir, and of the new commiffioun subscryvit be the haul heretors for devyding of the samyn.

23 Februar 1637. Coronell Dowglas returned to Court, and sent with him letters to my sone Mr. Alexander, and within it one to the Erll of Stirling, and one to Lord Panmuir anent the Laird of Creichis offer of jc pieces, and if thai wald offer L Creich. ii00 merkis, that I wald accept it, havand his warrand.

25 Februar 1637.

Packet sent be George Hadden, in absence of my Lord Alexander at the court of Jedburgh, to the Lord Stirling, with a letter to the Lord Panmuir, in ansuer of his resavit this day, and with it a letter from his servand Mr. Patrik Lyndsay; and als a letter from me to Mr. Alexander, complaining of his not wryting with this pacquet.

Last Februar 1637. Laurence Kinneir, merchand, went post to Court, and Mr James Gordoun sent with him certain letters; and I sent to Mr. James Gordoun a litill packet to Erl Stirling, quhairin one to himself. Item, one to Lord Panmuir, and within it one to Mr Alexander, and with it the 2 contractis of excamL. Morphie. bioun with the L. Morphie of Haltoun, Balmaver, and Balmeno, and the band of *vm* merkis.

9 Merche 1637.

This day delyverit to the Lord Alexander a pacquet to the Erl Stirling, Mem.—I desyrit his fathir, quhairin one to the Erl of Stirling himself, one to the Lord Panprepare me a ludg-muir, regrating the licknes of his lady, with a letter from David Souter. ing in Apzaird in Item, one to Mr. Alexander, and with it a second letter to his Majestie, of Kingistreet.

dait 13 Merch, for licensing me to come to Court. Item, a letter to James Maxwell, in ansuer of his to me. Item, sum letters from my sone to his brother Mr. Alexander, and to George Hope. 11 Merche 1637.

Delyuerit to Sir John Seytoun of Barnis letters to my fone Mr. Alexander, and within it to Lord Panmuir, advertising him of the former, quhilk wer sent be pacquet with his Majestie's letter thairanent.

13 Merche 1637, Mononday. Lord Lome anent This day the Lord Lorn went to Court, and at his parting gaif strait Ylaw-command to the Laird of Caddell, under the payne of his difplesur, to pay the vjflb of Ylaw to my Lord Thesaurer, quhilk wes to my gret prejudice.

Ps. bookis.

14 Merche 1637.

This day in Counsell his Majestie's letter red, prohibiting the prenting of the auld psahnes, and geving command to sing the new of the Erl Stirling.

15 Merche 1637.

Delyverit to James Boyd, sone to the last Bischop of Ergyll, ane pacquet to my Lord Lorn, and within it a pacquet to the Lord Panmuir; and within it to the Lord Panmuir, anent the Lord Thesaurer his proposing of the signatour to Sir Lues Steuart for counsellor at law, quhllk he fpak oppinly in pre-For Sir Lues sence of the Lords on 14 Merche, but on the morn went from it. Item, to Steuartmy fone Mr. Alexander. Item, to the Erll of Stirling.

1-7 Merche 1637.

Dauid Seytoun, servitour to L. Frendrauch, went to Court, and sent with him a pacquet to Sir Robert Gordoun, quhairin one to him, and another to my fone Mr. Alexander, for affisting of the paffing of the L. Frendrauch's signatour.

This day the Queanis Majestic delyverit of a maid child at St James, 17 Queanls Majestie Martij 1637, being Fryday, betuix thrie and 4 in the morning, quhairof theeritofamai' report cam hither on Weddinsday the 22 Merche, and the ordinance schott out of the castell.

25 Merche 1637.

Pacquet sent by directioun of the Lord Alexander, quhairin a pacquet from me to my Lord Stirling, in quhilk one to himself, one to the Lord Panmuir, and within it one from the Bischop of Brichen, and als to my fone, with letters to the Lord Duik from the Countess of Mar in my favors, and my awin letter to the Lord Marques of Hamiltoun.

28 Marche 1637.

Sent a pacquet to my fone by William Patoun, servitour to James Nesmyth, quhilk wes delyuerit to Alexander Lewis, quhairin to my fone. Item, a letter to Lord Panmuir, and one within it from John Pilmuir. Item, one from Mr David Dalglesche to Sir Wisiiam Balfour.

2 April 1637, Sounday. Communicat in Pencaitland.

H 3 Aprilis 1637, Mononday. This day mett with the Lord Thesaurer in his awin hous, in presens of the Erl Southelk, the Thesaurer-deput, and with me my two sones Sir John and Sir Thomas, quhair, efter long conserence, the matter resolvit in this, that he sould gif way to Sir Thomas his signatour of deputatioun, and affist the paffing of the pensioun of vjc merkis, and fould never incroche upon my place, nor daill for ather councill or colleg thairin; but fould affist me for my son Sir Thomas, and I to haif present payment of the vjIb of this 3eir in recompenle of Ylaw.

4 Apryl l 1637. This day the Clerk of Register went to Court. 5 Apryl l 1637, being Weddinsday. This day my Lord Alexander went to Court, and sent with him a pacquet to the Erl of Stirling, his sather, quhairin one to my Lord Annandaill. Item, a pacquet to the Lord Panmuir, with L. Morphie his letter, then instantlie reffavit be me, togither with letters from L. Melgum and Jolm PUmuir. Item, a pacquet to my fone, signifying the staying of my journey, and that I wold send vp my 2 sones to deil l for me in his matche with the gentUwoman. Item, letters to the Archbishop of Canterbery from the Bishop Ross, with one from me to excuse that I did not delyuer the samyn myself as I did expect and wes resoluit; but that the occurrent neceffitie of sum of his Majeftie's affairs did insorce my stay til l the Lord Thesaurer his returne. Item, letteris to the Marquii? of Hamiltoun from Sir John of Reidhous. Item, letteris from Mr. John Ker to Mr. Maxwell, anent Mr. John Mcgie. Item, letters from John Sempil l to James Levingstoun, anent Patrick Quhytlaw his Inhibitioun. Item, letters from the Erl of Hadingtoun to his son Sir James. Item, letteris from Peter Algeo to Sir William Anstruther. 7 Apryl l 1637, Fryday. My sones to Court. This day my sones Sir John and Sir Thomas went to Court, and gevin to Sir John lx doubil l angells, and to Sir Thomas xxv doubil l angells.

Item, sent with Sir Thomas Dunfyr ane signatour of Arbroith for the Prince, with letters to Archbilhop Canterburye, &c.

This day word cam of the battel of Dresdan, quhair Banier alledgit to be Dresdan. killit, and %it the Suedens caryit the victorie; thair being 150 0 of the Imperial fyd left on the grund, and Banier saiff.

8 Apryll 1637.

This day I sent a pacquet to the Lord Panmuir, quhairin one to himself, advertiling him of the President his upcoming, and of my letter to his Majeftie to recommend to the President the actioun of the conversiouns of the property and the reductioun of Scone, quhilk writs I sent not, but delyuerit to the President himself, being of dait 11 Apryll 1637, as being consorme to the tyme of his being at Court. Item, a letter to the Lord Thesaurer, acquainting him also thairwith, and a letter to the Justice Clerk.

10 April 1637.

Memorandum.—Gevin to my Lord President at his going to Court letters Lord President, to my sons Sir John, Sir Thomas, and Alexander, with one to Lord Panmuir, to caus him speik his Majeftie to inquyre the Lord President anent myself and Sir Thomas.

Item, this day Dauid Mecall subscryvit me an affignatioun to iiijnt) viijc David Mccall. xxxiij merkis money, difponit to him be Mr. John Oliphant in satisfactioun of ij00 merkis and xij 3eiris byruns, and of vc merkis more payit surth be Dauid to him for his sull rycht of the saids soms; Reservand Jonet Allane hir lysrent, the relict of vmquhile Dauid Alexander, quhilk Dauid Mccall; and for this I am bund to pay to him the annuels off his somes, beginning at Whitsunday 1637, quhilks somes comes to iij00 vijc merkis, and the annuel thairof is 3eirly ijc lxxxxvi merks, quhilk is ic xlviij merks at the terme.

Memorandum.—If Jonet Allan leive long, this blok may prove not much advantageous to me; but I remit this to Dauid his awin consideratioun.

13 April 1637.

Mr. John Dik went post to Court, and sent with him a singell letter to my

Lord Thesaurer, advertising him of the examinatioun of Donald Steuart, and confirming of him with the Mc Jockies.

Item, a pacquet to my fones, and writtin to them all thrie to try iff the Kingis Majestic hes gottin knauledge of the compromise, and if sua be, to mak his Majestie knaw the treuth.

Item, sent a letter from my dauchter Margaret to hir husband, anent the barn Elisabeth hir stay, upon occasion of William Barbor in Kirkcaldy his promise to lern hir.

Item, letter to Sir Thomas, schewing him of my reffait of the tapistrie, and that I intend to join the samyn, that the pryce may come to the behove of the Lord and Lady BafP, quhairupon I wret a letter to James Levingstoun to haif his consent to the comptis to be done be fycht of my Lord Thesaurerdeput, and I to retene so muche as efferis to the foumes contenit in Isaak Jonstoun his decreit, and the pryce of the rest to come to thair mayntenance, and to no vther use.

22 April 1637.

Lady Fanmuir Reffavit letteris from the Lord Panmuir, schewing of the departur of decis8it. his lady.

1 May 1637.

Reffavit letters from Court from my fones.

7 May 1637.

Communicat in Crawmond.

8 May 1637.

Reffavit letters from my fones from Court, and als letters from my Lord Thesaurer.

My barne Elisabeth.

Tapestrie.

13 May 1637. Reffavit letters from my fones and from the

Lord Thesaurer.

15 May 1637.

Ressavit letters from the Archbischop

of Canterburie, complaining of my going to Pencaitland.
23 May 1637.
This day being Sounday, the Service-book urgit but resistit.
27 May 1637, Setterday. The Lord Thesaurer returnit from Court. 29 May 1637, Mononday. This day, about 3 efternoone, Thomas Erl of Hadingtoun, Lord Privie Lord Hadingtoun Seill, deceiffit. God prepare me. deceissit. 30 May 1637, Tuysday. My sons Sir John and Sir Thomas returnit from Court in saifty, blifftt be the Lord.

Reportit be them that thai had gevin band to Sir David Cuningham for Mr. Alexander Mr. Alexander, thair brother, of 312 Ib. sterling, to be payit at Martimes312 ft sterlmg1637; but that the money must be prepared heir agane Lambmes, that it may be sent up in gold, quhilk I know is not poffibill.

Junij 1637, Thursday. 1 Junij 1637, Word cam that the Lord Stirlingis twa men departit of the plaig.
7 Junij 1637.

Letters sent by Mr. James Gordoun's pacquet, viz. one to the Lord Stirling apart. Item, ane pacquet to Lord Panmuir, quhairin to himself. Item, within it to my sone Mr. Alexander, quhairin to himself, with the alfignatioun of 320 Ib. sterling of my pensioun and annuelrents of the tennis of Martimas 1636 and Whitsunday 1637. Item, the nott of the contest to be schawin to the Archbischop of Canterbury. Item, ane letter to the Archbischop, in anfuer to his Grace. Item, letter to Erl Annandaill. Item, one to Erl Ancrum. Item, one to Sir Alexander Home, and one to Dean off Winchester.
14 Junij 1637.

Gevin to Patrick Wod to the within pacquet a letter to Lord Panmuir, quhairin one to him self, with a letter from the L. of Creich to him, offering iijft) merkis, with an affignatioun to the gift of his ward to an blank perform, to be subscryvit be the Lord. Item, a letter from my wyff to Mr. Alexander, forbidding him to send the watche, and chyding him for his fpending.
21 Junij 1637.

Letters to the Lord Panmuir with John Pilmuir his letter. Item, within it letters to Mr. Alexander, and within it one to him from my son Sir John; and als an packet from me to Andro Pitcarn, Mr. salconer, with forther his discharge, and letter to his uncle, with a declarator to be subscryvit be the said Andro in savors of his said nephew.

Last Junij 1637.
Delyverit to Mr. James Gordoun to go in pacquet, ane litill pacquet to Erl Stirling, and within it one to himself, one to Lord Panmuir, and one to Mr. Alexander.

1 Julij 1637, Setterday. Item, gevin ane uther letter to Mr. James Gordoun to be put in his pacquet, viz. a letter to the Lord Panmuir, to knaw if he will continow Navar to November. 5 Julij 1637. Gevin to Lord Crichtoun letters to the Erl of Annandaill, anent the offices of his brother Sir Richard, laitlie deceiffit. Item, with them a letter to my Mr. James my sone Mr. Alexander, and within it one to be sent to his brother Mr. James, "ono. to Bourges in France, quhairin I haif directit him to return about Michael mes next; and if I do not send provisioun to him befoir tent of August, to tak from John Clerk in PariP so muche as he neids at 24 f l the franc, providing he exceid not v franks.
8 Julij 1637.

Sent my letters to the Erl Stirling, quhairin to my fone Mr. Alexander, and within it to Mr. James for his returne, ut Jupra. 11 Julij 1637.

Sent a pacquet to Erl Stirling, quhairin anfuer to his, quhilk I reffavit on 9 July, signifying the surcease of the Commiffioun till his Majestie declare his surther plesur. Item, in it a letter to the Erl Annandaill, and one from Thomas Maxwell, anent the Dean, his brother, laitlie deceiffit. Item, in my Lord Annandaill his letter, one to Mr. Alexander, my fone, defyring him to haist to Mr. James his letter. Item, to advertise me if he had schawin my nott to the Archbishop of Canterbury, becaus I had reffavit on ij July an anfuer of his letter; and last, defyring him to haist his new letter for his mony to the Lord Thesaurer, with advertisement to my fone to tak notice of document gevin to him in restoring his access to Court, be occasioun of his speiking with Mungo Murray, quho wes schut vp for the plaig. The Lord preserve him.
19 July 1637.

Delyverit to the Lord Alexander a letter to the Erl of Stirling, and within it one to my fone Mr. Alexander, defyring him to acquaint me if Sir David Cuningham will tak his mony heir, and to schaw me the best way how to haif it conveyit to him.

Item, a letter gevin be me to James Arnott, to be sent to Mr. James, my fone, to reffave from Francis Kinloch, factor to James Arnott, 40 tuelf Mr. James pund pieces of gold, at 12 frankis the piece. But on the bak defyrit him tosranksreffave 500 frankis, for quhilk I payit to James Arnott, 19 July, 41 tuelf pund pieces of gold, and 8 Ib of other gold, to mak out 500 franks, at 12 frankis for the 12 h piece.
21 July 1637.

This day Lord Panmuir and Mr. Maxwell cam to Edinburgh.
23 July 1637, Sounday. Senke-book. This day the Service-book begoud to be read within the Kirks of Edin burgh, and wes interruptit be the women, &c. 26 July 1637.

Anent the vprore Pacquets went from the Counsell to his Majestie, advertising his Majestie tmikh23 July6 of tumm vproir in all the kirks of Edinburgh, anent the reiding of lfi37 the Service-book vpon Sounday the xxiij of July.

Item, sent be me in the Lord Alexander his pacquet, quhilk went with the Lord Thesaurer his servand, ane letter to the Erl Stirling, and within it one to the Erl Mar, in anfuer of all his former.
27 July 1637.

This day John Murray sent with the Lord Thesaurer's pacquet, and I sent with him letters to my sone Mr. Alexander, quhairin is ingroffit the nott of the proceidingis in Counsell betuix the Lord Chancellor and me about the Dean of Edinburgh his speiche; quhairin efter 2 dayis debait the matter turned to this, that the Lord Chancellor granted his fault and error.

Item, act of Counsell declaring all calumniators of Counsellors to be lyabill to that samyn payment, to the quhilk the counsellor wald be subiect if he wer guilty, if he do not prove the insormatioun.

28 July 1637, Fryday. This day, and not foner, John Murray, sone to Sir John Murray, went with the pacquet.

[Item, this day reffavit letters from Mr. Alexander to pay to Patrik Wod Mr. Alexander for 70 lb sterling, quhilk he had borrowit from Mr. Smyth, his factor; to the 7on) sterling. quhuk I wret ane very angrie letter, and his mother another, quhilk wer sent with John Murray, directit to him in his mother's name.]

Item, befoir this I had beine grevit aneugh for the soume of 312 Bb sterling, item, 312 ft borrowit from Sir David Cuningham, for quhilk my sones Sir John and Sir Sterlins Thomas ar cautioners. But this superveining so immediatlie *rupit patientiam*.

August 1637, Twysday.

5 August 1637, Setterday. Hary, my nephew, went by sea to Calif, and Hary Hope, gevin him fyve tuelff pund pieces off gold; and at his return he promisit to serve sum merchand in Amsterdam.

Item, this day pacquet sent be the Lord Alexander, and in it I sent letters to Erl Stirling, and within it letters to him, the Lord Panmuir, and als letters to Mr. Pitcairn, with the declaratioun in savors of his nephew.

12 August 1637, Setterday. This day I went to Craighall, and left with my Lord Alexander to send to Court, ane letter to his father, and within it one from Sir Thomas to Mr. Alexander, becaus I wald not wrytt myself; albeit 3esterday I reffavit his letter of excuse anent 70 lb sterling. Item, I causit Sir Thomas tell him that Mr. Alexander, I haif payit 312 lb sterling to Patrik Wod, and that Wod hes gevin band to?0'ft.t2Lg. pay it to Sir David Cuningham. 23 August 1637, Counsel day. This day a letter from James Murray from my fone Mr. James, schewing My [sone Mr] that he had reffavit from John Clerk, factor to James Murray, iijc franks, jj' fr 3 and James Murray wes content to reffaue thairof iijc xv lb Scottis, quhilk ansueris to 26 August 1637.

Gevin to Mr. James Gordoun a letter to the Erl Stirling, and within it one from the Lord Panmuir, quhilk Mr. James wes to send in pacquet with the Erl of Traquhair his servand, quho gois with the Counsell's letter to his Majestie anent the Service-book.

Item, gevin to the Lord Alexander ane vther letter to my L., his father, to go with his L. quhen he takis journey to Court, quhilk is to be on Mononday, 28 August 1637.

27 September 1637. Pacquet to the Erl Stirling, quhairin to him and the Lord Alexander, and within it to Mr. Alexander, quhairin one from my self, 2 from his elder, and 2 from his second brother Sir Thomas; one to the Erl of Roxburgh, with a nott of the proceidings in Counsell; one to Erl Mar; one to Sir Alexander Home; one to Erl Annandaill; one to the Countef l of Annandaill; and one from the Erl of Lothian, or Lord Balmerinach to the Erl of Ancrum.

Counsell and
Sessioun at
Linlithgow.
17 October 1637.

His Majestie's letter cam to the Counsell, ordering the Counsell and Seslioun to sit at Linlythgow till 3um, thaireftir at Dundie.

Item, this day a greter tumult of the pepill of Edinburgh for the Service-book.

28 October 1637. The L. of Panmuir returnit to Court. 30 October 1637. I returnit from Craighall to Edinburgh. Mr. James, 323 ft. Item, payit to James Murray for thrie hundreth franks surnischit be John Clerk, his servand, to my sone Mr. James, 323 lb. 1 November 1637, Weddinsday. Mr. James cam This nycht my sone Mr. James cam to Edinburgh from France, and he Item moreoo me tnat ne a(taken up from James Arnottis sactor, not only the vc franks, and 23 lb franks, but also iijc franks more, and als 23 lb sterling in Londoun from James Steuart. sterling.]

Linlythgow
Exchekker.
2 November 1637. The Exchekker held at Linlythgow. But thair wes not a number of Counsell.

3 November 1637. Gevin to Mr. James Gordoun letters for the pacquet to Erl Roxburgh, Erl Stirling, Lord Panmuir, and my sone Mr. Alexander. 12 November 1637. Pacquet sent to the Erl Stirling, gevin to Mr. James Gordoun, quhairin to himself, to Lord Panmuir, to my sone, styllling him Wester Grantoun. Item, to him from Sir John and Sir Thomas, &c. 14 November 1637. I sent ane pacquet my self to the Erl Stirling for John Sempill, quhairin to the ErlL to the Lord Alexander, his sone, to James Levingstoun, to my sone Mr. Alexander, and to the L. of Panmuir. 17 November 1637. Letteris sent to Erl Stirling, quhairin to him self, to Lord Alexander, to Lord Panmuir, and to my sone, anent the Counsell dyet of Linlythgow. 23 November 1637. This day the Lord Wauchtoun went to Court, and sent with him letteris to my sone, and within them to the Lord Panmuir; and I wret to my sone that I intend in the place of Joseph To 6 December 1637, Weddinsday. My dauchter D. Heleine Raa delyverit of a man chyld, quho thaireftir on Twysday 12 December wes baptiut Alexander be Mr. Hary Rollok, in the gret kirk of Edinburgh. 7 December 1637.

The Counsell held at Linlythgow.
Linlythgow.
12 December 1637. The Counsell held at Dalkeyth.

[My dauchter D. M' Murray delyverit of a maid chyld, quho thaireftir baptisit on Setterday, 23 December 1637, Heleine. The Lord gif his blliffing to both.]

15 December 1637.

Letteris sent in his Majestie's pacquet direct be the Lord Thesaurer, quhairin to the Lord Panmuir from me two, and other two from L. Melgum and John Pihnuir. Item, to the Erl Mortoun, Erl Stirling, Erl Annandaill, James Levingstoun, Sir Robert Gordoun. Item, from my self and Sir Thomas to my fone Mr. Alexander, and thairwith sent to him a signatour of my pensioun of 200 lb sterling to me in lysrent, and eftir to him. Item, one to Lord Sandsuird.

Item, he cravit 250 lb sterling per annum, and I wret bak that I wald gif him

2 3eris of my pensioun, reserving 3eirly thairof to my self 50 Ib sterling; and sarther wald gif 700 fl) sterling to by him a pensioun at Court; and I wret to Lord Panmuir that I wald gif of that and 1000 Ib sterling, quhilk, with 100 ijcIb sterling alreadie bestowit on him, wes a sair portioun for my 3 fone.

Item, if the signatour be signed be his Majestie, I wret it fould be keipit quyet till I fould gett the Lord Thesaurer his approbatioun thairof.

Memorandum.—Payit for Mr. James to James Steuart 23 Ib sterling. Item, payit to James Arnot for him (by the vc franks) iijc franks, for quhilk I gaif James Arnot xxv tuelf pund pieces, as my nott beris, made in November and December 1637; and als thaireftir, viz. at Martimes 1638, payit to James Steuart ijc xxvij merkis, for taking of a suit of clothes to Mr. James at his coming to Scotland, 1 Novembris 1637.

19 December 1637. Gevin ane pacquet to my Lord President direct to Lord Painnuir, and within it ane from my fone John to him, for L. Cragyvar his warrand. Item, one from me and my fones Sir John and Mr. James to Mr. Alexander, quhairin I tell him of the offer made be me to the Thesaurer-deput of xr0

Mr. James,
23 Ib sterling,
25 tb sterling.
merkis for his penfioun of 1501) sterling. Item, one from his mother to Mr. Alexander, him, with the nott of the aittis, peifl, cheitf, lalmond, and hering sent to ® JJJS "alfboll him. peiss, 12 chesis,

The President wes stayit till Setterday, 23 December 1637, and then JdTaodabalf went tymouslie. barrells hering.

6 Januar 1638, Mononday. Delyverit a pacquet to my Lord Thesaurer, to be sent to the Lord off Panmuir with ane servand of my Lord Duickes, quhairin wes a number of letters from Angus to the Lord. Item, one from my self to him, and within it the copie of the petitioun quhilk he cravit to be sent to him. Item, one to Mr. Alexander, and within it one to the Erl Hadingtoun, anent the matche

betuix my sone Mr. James and Anna Foules, dauchter to Mr. Robert Foules. 11 Januar 1638, Thursday. This day the Contract of Mariage betuix my fone Mr. James and Anna Mr. James his Foules wes subscryvit, and thaireftir celebrat in the Grey Freir Kirk be Mr. TMgg ith Andro Ramsay on 14 Januar, being Sounday immediatlie eftir the preiching. Anna Foules. 15 Januar 1638.

Delyverit to my Lord Justice Clerk ane pacquet to my fone Mr. Alexander, quhairin to him from me with ane Retroceffioun of my penfioun, to be subscryvit be him.

Item, to him from his brethir Sir John, Sir Thomas, and Mr. James. Item, from me to the Lord Panmuir, and within it the nott of the actis of Parliament aganis the Service-book. Item, to Erl Stirling, Lord Alexander, Sir Hary Alexander. Item, to Erl of Mar. Item, to Erl of Mortoun. Item, to Erl Annandaill, and within his the first article anent Scone.
17 January 1638.

Delyverit to my Lord Thesaurer quhen he went to Court a pacquet to Murw went t0

Court.

Lord Panmuir, quhairin a letter to his Majestie, with my articles and the last anent the Service-book. Item, a letter to the Lord of Panmuir. Item, a pacquet to *my* sone, quhairin one to him, schawing the proceidingis of his brother's mariage, and the exceptioun takin aganis it be my Lord Thesaurer deput. Item, a letter to the President of Selsioun. Item, a letter to Mr. James Gordoun, remembring him of John Sempill anent the clerkschip of Hadingtoun.

24 January 1638, Weddinsday. Gevin to Patrik Wod for the commoun pacquet, ane pacquet to the Lord Thesaurer, and within it one to the Lord Panmuir; with letters from the L. Thorntoun and L. Dwn, anent his dauchter's mariage.

Last Januarij 1638, Weddinsday. Sent with John Arnot, servand to the Erl of Mar, ane letter to the Erl his maister. Item, ane litil pacquet to my fone Mr. Alexander, quhairin one to the Lord Thesaurer, one to Lord Panmuir, and one to the Justice Clerk; and within the Lord Panmuir's one from John Pilmuir

to him, but he went not till Fryday the 2 Februar.

6 February 1638, Stirling. The Seffioun mett at Stirling, and continowit till 29 Merche, quhilk wes the Thursday befoir Good Fryday, and then rose and sat not doun agane. But in all this tyme not a caus difputit, nor ether subiectis or advocattis to plead. 14 Februar 1638.

The Lord Thesaurer returnit from Court, being Weddinsday, and I mett him at Dalkeyth, and saw his Majestie's warrand for the proclamatioun.
19 Februar 1638, Stirling. The Lord Thesaurer, quho com from Court, 14 Februar, went to Stirling on 19 Februar, and then wes the proclamatioun past aganis Convocatiounis under the payne of treafoun. 1 Marche 1638.

The Counsell mett and resoluit on the causis of the publict commotiounes Counseii. for the Service-book, the book of Canones, and high Commiffioun, with thair opinioun for the remedies, and directit the samyn to his Majestic by one of thair number, viz. Sir John Hamiltoun of Orbistoun, Lord Justice Clerk.
5 Merche 1638.

I writ with the Justice Clerk to the Erl Stirling, Lord Alexander, and Lord Panmuir; and sent to Lord Panmuir the nott of the proceidingis at Counsell, with my awin opinioun.
7 Merche 1638. Justice Clerk went to Court. 21 Merche 1638.

Gevin to James Murray, 30unger, a letter to be inclosit in his awin, to be directit to the Lord Panmuir with the merchant pacquet, quhairin I acquent the Lord that my pacquet is coming with James Arnott.

This day Sir John Hamiltoun of Orbistoun, Justice Clerk, returnit from 21 Merche 1638, Court, quha wes sent from the Counsel at Stirling, 5 Merche, and he brocht reTuraH from warrand to call vp the Lord Thesaurer, the Lord Privie Seill, and the Lord Court, of Lorn, quhilk wes concludit at Stirling. Counsell at
Stirling.
22 Merche 1638.

I retenit my pacquet from James Arnott, and sent it with more letters to the Lord Panmuir, in ane pacquet direct from Dalkeyth, be my Lord Thesaurer.

Item, I wret letters apart to Mr. Alexander, and within it one to Patrik Wod, to end with Sir Dauid Cuningham. 28 Merche 1638, Weddinsday. This day Mr. William Burnet (having returned from Court on 23 Merche, to quhilk he went with letters from the Lord Thesaurer to his Majestie,

Pacquet to the
Lord Panmuir.
29 Merche 1638, the Lord Thesaurer went to Court.

quhairin wes insert my ansuer to the questiounes movit be his Majestie anent the nobility and gentry) wes sent again to Court to prepare my Lord Thesaurer his lodging, with quhom I sent letters to Erl Roxburgh, Stirling, Lord Alexander, Lord Panmuir, and my sone. 29 Merche 1638, Thursday. The Lord Thesaurer went to Court, and I gaif him the signatour os the new Commiffioun of the Borderis. Item, the erectioun of the Lordschip of Dalkeyth and Muffelburgh in ane Justiciarie and Steuartry. Item, a gift of the place of Justice and Steuart to Erl Traquhair during lystyme. 13 May 1638, Lord Thesaurer returnit from Court. 15 May 1638, Twysday. The Lord Thesaurer cam to Dalkeyth from Court, and I ressavit a letter from his Majestie to draw vp ane Commiffioun to the Lord Marquis of Hamiltoun, for quyetting of the disorders; according to quhilk I drew vp tua commiffiouns, and dockettit the samyn, quhairof I haif the copies. 17 May 1638, Thursday. Mr. William Burnet went to Court, and with him writtin to my sone, and within it ansuer to Coronell Lyndsay. Item, ansuer to Erl Stirling. Item, ansuer to the Lord Panmuir, and within his one from James Murray, 30unger.

Memorandum.—I went to Craighall on 24 Maij, and returnit 26 May 1638.

Lord Alexander 26 May 1638, Setterday. As I wes coming from Craighall, ressavit letters from Court (of the death of the good Lord Alexander) sent to me be Sir Thomas, my sone, from Edinburgh.

Marquis of
Hamiltoun
Commissioner for his Sacred Majestie.
5 Junij 1638, Twysday.

This day the Marques of Hamiltoun, as his Majestde's Commiffioner for sattling of the disorders of the Kirk, cam to Dalkeyth.

Item, my sone Mr. Alexander cam this nycht to Edinburgh, being in companie with the Lord Marques.
7 Junij 1638.
[I spak with my sone Mr. Alexander, and aikit him of his debt auchtand My sone Mr. Alex.
tmdcr Hope to Patrik Wode, quho grantit 153 S) sterling, payit to Sir David Cuningham, and 3211 lb Scottis, quhairof he had gevin band.

And he grantit that this being payit, that I haif furnischit to him above two thousand four hundreth pund sterling, quhilk, with my pensioun of ijc lb sterling, wes a sufficient portioun, and he wald expect for no more, seing I had his 2 fisteris to provyd, and als to fulfil Mr. James his promises according to his contract of Mariage; and I delyverit him the gift of pensioun of 200ft) sterling, past on my demiffioun under the privie seill. Jr farmily meaces

And albeit I haif takin affignatioun from Patrik Wod to him of the bandes My discharge to maid to the said Patrik be my sone Mr. Alexander, 3it I intend to mak nohu'soumes'- vse of them except in the cace of neceffitie; and thairfoir, if I do not suit theis somes in my awin tyme, nor affign them to sum of my barnis, or gif order to suit them efter my deceitf, it is my will that the samyn be nowayis exactit from my sone Mr. Alexander be my airs or exequitors efter my decese, and that thir presents sal serve to him for ane discharge, except in the caces forfaids, writtin and subscryvit with my hand, 25 Junij 1638, Sir Thomas Hope. 26 Junij 1638.

This day the pacquet went by Mr. James Gordoun, and I delyuerit to him 26 Junij.—This a letter to the Erl of Stirling, acquenting him with the Commiffioun cravit Kynnoal admittit be the Marques of Huntly for a surther tryel of Frendrauch, quhairin I amon Counsell. omittit, and Sir L. Steuart and Mr. J. Gilmuir appointit to supply my place in the criminal perfuitis quhilk I did stay on 21 Junij last. Item, a letter to James Levingstoun, anent the Lady Samuelstoun hir dauchter, quho allegis him to be lyabill to a penalty of vc lb sterling, if he do not satiffie hir for hir rycht of Poppill.
29 Junij 1638.

[Payit to Hary Hope, quhen he went to Amsterdam, his compt of 285 lb Hary Hope. 16s) 8d.
K
Sessioun in Edinburgh.
Lord Dalzell.
[Item, gevin to him for tokins, 1 quadryit pistoll, 1 doubill ducat, and an hatt peice of gold, God bleffe him, and prepare a way of savor to him in his journey.]
30 Junij 1638, Setterday. This day the Counsel mett at Halyruidhous, quhair, be warrand of his Majestie, the Counsell, Seffioun, and vther Judicatures, ar appointit to hold at Edinburgh, and the Seffioun appointit to begin on Twysday, the 3 Julij. This day the Lord Daell admittit on Counsell. 3 Julij 1638, Twysday. The Seffioun satt, and my Lord Commiffioner the Marques of Hamiltoun cam to it about xi hours, convoyit with sex coches, quhairof I wes, with 6 horfes; and being in seffioun, recommendit to them the accelerating of justice, to supplie the tyme quhilk wes spent of befoir; and having stayit about half hour, he returnit to the Abbay, accompanit with a number of the Counsell.

Eftirnone.

Eftirnone, the Counsell mett at Halyruidhous, quhair the Erll of Kynnoull and the Lord Almond wer reffavit Counsellors.

Proclamatioun anent the discharge of the Service-book.
4 Julij 1638, Weddinsday.

This day the Counsell mett at 9 hours, quhair the Marques exhibit his Majestie's declaratioun, and told the Counsell that he had warrand of his Majestie's princelie

The declaratioun being red, it wes approvit be all.

And I, being askit, movit to haif all

maid according to his Majestie's directioun thairin contenit; to haif the service book and actis maid for introducing thairof, or of the book of canones to be annullit; nixt, to haif his Majestie's pardoun of all bygane escapes of the peopDl; quhilk, I said, wes in effect contenit in his Majestie's declaratioun.

The first wes grantit, and act; past annulling the act in December 1636, and the uther in Junij 1637, anent the Service-book; and declaring the subjects frie thairof, and of all penalties thairin contenit, and of the vther Mem.—The nobiacts, warrands, and proclamatiouns made thairanent from the beginninglIty PTOte8tit to , ,,. hmrd to supplicat thairof, and in all tyme coming; and as to the Canones, thay thocht thair anent the remanent nedit no act, seing it had no act of secreit Counsell for the warrand thairof. aiTpetitiotins

But as to the second, my Lord Commiffioner said, that he wald declair itand tuikinstru to be his Majestie's intentioun to pardoun all; but knew it wes not the tMrcc'e' nobilmen's defyr, becaus they had not tranfgreffit, albeit the vulgar had.of Edinburgh

And so that wes left till the morrow.
5 Julij 1638.

The pacquet went, and I sent a letter to the Erl Stirling, in the Lord Panmuir his pacquet.
9 Julij 1638, Mononday.

This day, at 5 in the morning, the Lord Marques returnit to Court; Lord Marques reand sent with the Lord Panmuir (quho returnit with him) ane lettertumit t0 Courtto the Erl Stirling, and within it one to James Levingstoun, anent the Commiffion of Frendrauch; to acquaint his Majestie with the wrong done to me; and offering to trye the if his Majestie sal be plesit to committ the tryell of it to the Justice Generall, Justice Clerk, and myself.

Item, my sone Mr. Alexander convoyit the Marques on his journey, and I gaif him a letter to the Lord Panmuir, contening the reffones of the injustice of the Commiffioun of Frendrauch, and the lyk offer as that quhilk is in my letter to James Levingstoun.

Item, this day dockettit the Commiffioun for hering the Lord Thesaurer his accomptes, and a letter sent with it to the Lord Stirling, in the quhilk I wrytt alfe much to his Lordship anent Frendrauch, as I did in the vther to the Lord Panmuir and James Levingstoun.

Item, this day good Mr. John Aird deceiffit, and I went to his suneralls Mr. John Am. at Newbottill, vpon the Thursday thairefter, 12 Julij.

20 Julij 1638, Fryday. This day William Jamesoun, painter, (at the ernest desyr of my sone Mr. Alexander,) wes sufferit to draw my pictur. 27 Julij 1638. Item, a second draucht be William Jamesoun.

Last Julij 1638, Twysday. Mr. Alexander The Seffioun rose, and a packet sent to Court for the place of Thesaurer rierk" Clerk, vacand be Mr. William Chalmers his deceitf, in savors of Mr. Alexander

Burnett, quhilk I secondit; with a pacquet to the Lord of Panmuir, quhairin to himself, to the Erl Stirling, and to James Levingstoun, thanking him for moving his Majestie anent the Marques of Huntley his commiffioun aganis the Lord Frendrauch, quhairin he patt Sir Lues Steuart and Mr. John Gilmor to supply my place.

7 August 1638.

Hary Hope. This day Hary Hope returnit from Amsterdam.

Lord Cragivar. Item, this day the Lord Cragivar and Mr. Andro Skene of Haerds mett anent my sone's buffines of Rewing, and brak vp; and my fone thairefter, on 24 August, subscryvit ane consent to him to sell, sore aganis my will.

9 August 1638.

Lord Marques. This nycht the Marques of Hamiltoun returnit from Court, and with him the Lord Panmuir. God giff a bliffit succetf in the publict buslines of Godis trewth!

13 August 1638.

This day the Erll of Murray deceiffit at Dernway.

23 August 1638, Thursday.

Jesuit. This day the Jesuit Abirnethy reffavit in the Greysreir kirk.

24 August 1638, Fryday. This day the difput betuix the Lord Daell and his tenants, befoir the Counsell, anent thair band os Combinatioun aganis thair maister, quhilk wes sund Null, and thai fynit in *ujm* merkis. 25 August 1638, Setterday. Marques returnit This day the MarqueB tuik journey to Court, and promisit to return with to Court. ansuer 20 September. 27 August 1638, Mononday.

My sone Mr. Alexander took his leve of me for Court, and I gave to him My sone Mr. the King of Sueden his gret piece of gold, weighing ane vnce and mair,Alexanderquhilk I gatt from the Vicount of Airdes.

Item, he defyrit os me to advance to him, within a 3eir, X00 merks to by ane pensioun or a pack, and he wald crave no more of me; quhilk I did not grant, but said, if I wer frie of debts, and iff the Lord bliffit me with so muche by, (the rest of my children being provydit,) I wald think upon it.

Memorandum.—This day he subscryvit to me ane abfolut discharge of his portioun natural, and ot all former bands and provisiouns, and specially of the band of xx0 0 Ib, daitit in Apryll 1635; quhilk discharge I delyverit to my sone Sir John.

Item, gevin to Mr. Alexander, to mak his expends in his journey, x doubill angells.

To his man Andro Lyne, 3 dollors.

To his cocheman John, 3 dollors.

29 August, Weddinsday, 1638.. This day I went to the Kerf, and from thence to Craighall, quhair I cam on Setterday, 1 September. 18 September 1638.

I returnit from Craighall, be letter from the Lord Thesaurer, advertising Marques returnit me of my Lord Marques his returne, quho returnit on Setterday, 15 Sep=P,1=x38³=tember 1638. 19 September 1638.

This day I mett with my Lord Marques at Halyruidhous.

Item, reffavit from my sone Mr. Alexander my rod, with the King's Majestie's portrait on the head of it, of porcupine penne, or of the schell poddokis.

26 September 1638. I returnit to Craighall, quhair I abaid till 20 October. 20 October 1638, Setterday.

This day I came from the Queanis

Ferrie to Edinburgh, about 7 hours in the morning; and mett with my Lord Marques at Halyruidhous.

Item, Hary Alexander went to Court, and sent with him letters to my Lord his father, to Sir Alexander Home, and to my sone Mr. Alexander.

Item, I had conference with my Lord Marques on 25 and 27 October, and then I reffavit from him his Majestie's letters, with certan questiounes to be ansuerit.

28 October 1638, Sounday. This day the Communioun wes celebrat at Edinburgh; and efter sermon wes red the sumondis againes the Bischopes, to compeir in the Generall Affemblie at Glasgow, 21 November nixt. 29 October 1638.

This day I mett with the Lord Marques, and gaiff him the nott of the act of Generall Affemblie in July 1580, red in the kirk on the last Sounday; and in respect thairof, counsellit him to acquent his Majestie or he sould proceid sarther in urging of the subscriptioun of the Conseffion of Fayth, except his Grace be sully myndit to bind the subiectis be the oth to exclud episcopacie; for I declarit in respect of it, that I am bund be othe to abjure it, and that now I cannot be frie to ansuer the questions.

Last October 1638, Weddinsday. The Lord Marques sent for me, and cravit ane ansuer of the questiounes, quhairof I thocht myself exonerit, be reffoun his Grace had said on Mononday, that I nedit not be haistie in ansuering of them, till his Grace sould advertise me.

Item, in conference with his Grace, I sand him to mak many sliiftis anent the oth of the Conseffioun 1580, that it did not intend disciplin, and albeit it did, that disciplin wes changeabill; quhilk wondersully affectit my mynd, for now I sand that he wes purposit to putt a gloffe vpon the othe, quhilk I said wes impoffibill.

Immediatlie efter my returne from him, I humblit myself on my kneis to Last October 1638, my Lord, and in prayer vowit to adhere to my oth, with ha3ard of allVow t0 my Lord perrellis, and thairto cravit the Lord's help and affistance; and if the nobilmen had absteynit from than: protestatioun, and subscryvit the Conseffioun 1580, according to thair awin explicatioun thairoff, quhilk is according to Godis treuth, and the trew meaning of the Conseffioun 1580, thai had putt the bane foundlie in.the sutt of thair adverfaris. But in respect of thair resusall, thay haif put a wapon in the Kingis handis, at leist the pretense of one, that in thair disobedience to his command, quhilk is of a thing commandit be God, thay haif another end nor the matter of religioun; but God is the gret difposer of menis myndis and thochtis.

1 November 1638, Thursday. This day the Lord Commiffioner cam to Seffioun, and urgit the Lords to Confeffioun of subscryve the Conseffioun 1580; quho all did it except the L. InnerteiL the *Fath* in. S0"" Lord Dury, my sone the L. Craighall, and my Lord Scottistarbett. 2 November 1638.

Delyverit my pacquet to my Lord Juftice Clerk, to be sent in the Lord Packquett. Marques his pacquet to my sone; and within the samyn one to the Erl of Stirling for John Sempill, ane other for him to Mr. James Gordoun, anent the Sheriff-clerkschip of Hadingtoun. Item, ansuer to Sir Alexander Home his letter anent his signatour. Item, in my letter to my sone Mr. Alexander insert a nott of my proceiding in Counsell on last of October, quhairin I opposit episcopacie as contrair to my oth.

About this tyme Hary Hope, my nephew, tuik schip from Dundie to Hary Hope. Diep. The Lord preserve him from the tempest of sea.

8 Novembris 1638.

Ane pacquet sent with George Halden his packet, and in it to the Lord Pacquet to the Panmuir, with the twa blensche signatours off the baronie of Balmakelly, to his blenthe the Lord Panmuir and his sone Hary; and of the barony of Cragis, 2 part signature, and 3 part; the lands of Lour, and lands of Leyis, to David Carnegy, appeirand of and to Jeane Maul, his spous, in warrandice of hir lysrent, and conjunct fie, lands, and teinds. Item, a letter to the Erl of Stirling, testifeing that the ward's lands ar not the tenth part of his eftait, and Athie's ward lands not a sext part of his eflait, according to the rentalls gevin vp be them to the Lord Thesaurer, according to his Majestie's reserence. Item, a letter to the L. from James Murray, 30unger. Item, a pacquet to my fone Mr. Alexander, quhairin from me and his thrie hrethir.

14 November 1638.

My sone Mi. Letters from Mr. Alexander to Sir Thomas, in quhilk he wryttis of

A. lex u nil It.

Mres. Muire, relict of Sir Patrik Achesoun, and only dauchter to Sir John Muir, Knycht, Keiper of his Majestie's Signet.

16 November 1638, Fryday. Marques of Uamil-This day the Marques and the Counsell went to Glasgow, to attend the toun to Glasgow. Qenerajj Affemblie, quhilk beginnes thair on Weddinsday, 21 November. My sone Mr Alex-Item, this day sent letters to Lord Panmuir, and with them one to Mr.

ADlit *V* X ML TTlOrlc

'Alexander, quhairin I defyr him to borow the x0 0 merks (quhilk cravit be his letter of 5 November, ressavit 15,) thair, and draw vp an band, be himself as principall, myself and his 3 brethring as cautionars, to be payit within thrie 3eiris, and annuel in the mean tyme.

Item, in the letter to the Lord Panmuir, I acquaintit him with the Lord Marques his going to Glasgow, and that he had gevm me warrand to stay at home.

22 November 1638, Thursday. Letters ressavit from Mr. James Gordoun, quhairin from the Erll of Stirling, Lord Panmuir, and my sone, on 21 November; and ansuer returnit this day, by pacquet sent by Mr. James Gordoun.

Pacquet.

26 November 1638, Mononday. Packet sent with Mr. James Gordoun, his packet to Erl Stirling, quhairin to the Lord Panmuir, with the tikket in it anent the penall affeffor. Item to Mr. Alexander, and within his to James Levingstoun, quho went away to Court on Fryday the 16 November. . . '. ". 5 December 1638.

A letter sent to the Lord Panmuir, and within it one to my sone, schaw-Lord panmuir. ing the Lord Panmuir of the reffait of his, and off Athie's blensche signatours, and that the Thesaurer hes promisit to pass them in Exchekker on Setterday nixt. Item, schawing him that the Marques dischargit the Affem-Assemblie. blie on Weddinsday, 28 November; but that thai continow thair sitting.

Item, the letter to my sone Mr. Alexander, anent his pensioun of ijc ft sterling, for the Mertimes Terme 1638; to defyr him to wryt, and to caus Lord Panmuir wryt to the Thesaurer thairanent.
8 December 1638.

Sir Mark Ker proponit to me the purpose of dealling with the Lord Sir Mark Kerr. Thesaurer, and defyrit me to name quhat I would haif for my concurrance, quhilk I resuflt; and he said he wald gif me the tenth part of that quhilk sould be gevin to him be my Lord Thesaurer, quhich I said wes to muche; and he ansuerit, " Thair is my hand 3e sal haif it. " 9 December 1638, Sounday. This day, about 8 at nycht, thair wes a gret thunder; quhilk wes thocht Thunder, prodigious, being in wynter.
10 December 1638.

The Marques, High Commiffioner, cam from Hamiltoun to Halyruid-Marques, hous, to hold Counsell to-morrow, being Twisday, xj December 1638.
11 December 1638.

The Counsell held not; but the Marques delyverit to me a pacquet from My sone Mr. my sone, and within it ane band of 550& sterling, according to the Inglische Alexanderforme, quhilk I keip befyd me. And I sent letters in ansuer of his, on Lord Panmuir. 12 December, by the Lord Dal3ell, inclofit within the pacquet to the Lord Panniuir; and in the Lord Panmuir his pacquet is sent the procuratory of resignatioun of the barony of Balmakelly, to be subscryvit and returnit; but this went not till 17 December, at quhilk tyme I gat the pacquet from Lord Dal3ell, and gaif it to my Lord Thesaurer.
13 December 1638.

Hischopes excom-This day thir Bischopes following wer excommunicat, be ordinance of the municat.

Generall Affemblie, in the Kirk of Glasgow, be Mr. Alexander Henderfoun,
Moderator; viT,.., Sanct Androis; Glasgow; Mr. John Maxwell, Ross; Mr. Thomas Sydserf, Galloway; Mr. David Lyndsay, Edinburgh; Mr. Walter Quhytsurd, Brichen; Mr. Adam Bellenden, Bischope of Aberdein; and Mr. James Wedderburne, of Dumblane.

Item, depryvit Mr. John Guthrie, of Murray; Mr. George Grahame, of Orkney; Mr. James Finlay, of Eng3ie; and Mr. Neil Campbell, of Yles; and ordanit to be excommunicat, if they do not obey the sentence of the Affemblie.

Item, sufpendit Mr. Alexander Lyndsay, of Dunkeld, and Mr. John Abirnethy, of Caithnes; and in cace of obedience to the Affemblie's ordinance, appointit to be admittit to seuerall kirks; vi3., Mr. Alexander Lyndsay to St Madoze, and Mr. John Abernethy at;and in cace of disobedience, to be excommunicat, 16 December 1638.

Item, thir sentences of the Affemblie red and publischit in the kirks of Edinburgh, on Sounday, 16 December 1638. 17 December 1638. This day I went to the Abbay, and mett with my Lord Commiffioner; and wes to tak my leve of his Grace, but he tauld me that he wes not to go away suddenly, and that he wald fend for me befoir he went. Mr. Walter Quhyt Item, heir the Bischope of Brichen, Mr. Walter Quhytsurd, (as I wes haviour. standing in the gallery, with my Lord Lauderdaill, and my Lord Maitland, his fone,) cam surth from the Marques, and I, being unwilling to salut him, turned my bak, and as fone as he wes past by, I went into the chamber at the end of the gallery, and I wes not long thair but Mr. Walter Quhytsurd cam and callit for me; and I told him, that thair hes benc inteir acquaintance betuix him and me of befoir, but now I must sufpend it. And he askit, quhairfor? And I said, because of the intimatioun of his excommunicatioun gesterday, quhilk I hard red. He ansuerit, that I wes bund be promil? to his Majestie to assist Episcopacie. I ansuerit, that my promifl wes in civill privileges, but not in thes quhilk concernit spiritual and ec-

clesiasticall power. He replyit, that I had solicitat bischopes to admitt ministers. I ansuerit how I did it, in refpect they had then both the keyis in thair hands, but now they wantit one of them, quhilk wes the chese part, vi3., Affemblie. And then he sell out in thir disdainsul words: "3e 31 our Pert, that dar haif refpect to any actis of that rebellious Affemblie, seing his Majestie dischargit them to sitt vnder the payne of treasoun." And with this he flew away. 18 December 1638, Twysday. This day, about 2 hours efternone, Patrik Wod deceiffit. Patrik Wxl. 21 December 1638, Fryday. This day his Majestie's letter exhibit in Seffioun, prohibiting to grant any His Majesties letletters or vther exequutioun upon the actis of the late Generall Affemblie, AssemTM &c.; quhilk being red, the Lords tuik to be advysit thairwith till the morow.blie 22 December 1638, Setterday. This day the Lord Thesaurer declarit, in presence of the Lords, that my Lord Commiffioner, being humblie intretit be the nobilmen and gentry, wes willing to suppres the letter anent the Affemblie, rather nor to gif occasioun to mistak ather to the Lords or to his Majestie's subjects. (Bliffit be God.) 24 December 1638, Mononday. This day William Murray, gret uncle, deceffit suddanlie. The Lord William Murray, prepare us. 27 December 1638.

Item, the Marques of Hamiltoun tuik journey from Dalkeyth to Court MuesofHami1this day. The Lord direct his Grace in his report to his Majestie, that the Kirk of God may be in peax. Pæquet. Item, this day sent letters in Mr. James Gordoun's pacquet to the Erl Stirling, and within it to Lord Panmuir and my lone.
29 December 1638.

Lord Panmuir and This day sent letters to the Lord Panmuir, and within it to my fone, niy soii6 from myself and his mother, anent the x0 0 merks quhilk he cravit, and that I delyverit to my Lord Thesaurer his pacquett.

Item, this day the Counsell convenit, for a warrand to my Lord Gray to levye j00 men for the Frensche King's service.
31 December 1638.

Lord Panmuir. Letteris sent in Mr. James Gordoun his pacquet to the Lord Panmuir, and within it a letter as from Henrie Maul, being a trew narratioun of the extent of Episcopacie in anno 1580. 1 Januar 1639, Twysday.

Erl Roxburgh and Letters fent with the Erl Roxburgh to the Lord Panmuir, and within it Lord Panmuir. the copy off the ansuers to the questiounes anent Episcopacie, movit to me be the Erl Roxburgh.

» 10 Januar, Thursday. Mary contractit. My dauchter Mary contractit with Charles Erfkin. 25 Januar 1639.

Anent his Majestie Reffavit letters anent his Majestie's purpose to come to York on 1 Aprill; coming to York. ansuerit the samyn day, in letters writtin to Lord Panmuir, Erll of

Annandaill, and Erl of Stirling.

29 Januar 1639, Twysday. His Majestie's let-This day, in Counsell, his Majestie's letter wes red, declaring his Majestie's iu tihiira.iLiit. pUrp0se to come to York about Easter nixt, to accommodat all affares in a fair way, quhilk wes ever his Majestie's purpose, and to that effect made his Majestie's approche the nerar; and defyris the Counsell to advertise his Majestie, if in the meantyme any thing occur concerning his Majestie's service, and that his Majestie will rely muche on thair judgement; lyk as his Majestie declars, that his Majestie will acquent them with his Majestie's surther procedingis betuix and that tyme.

Last Januar 1639, Thursday. This day sent a packett with one Mr. Graham, Inglischeman, quho had Mr. Alexander his the procels aganis John Dyn and John Park, to my sone Mr. Alexander; cuningham of quhairin is a band, be him as principall, and be myself and my two sones556 ft sterling, as cautioners, of the some of 556 Ib sterling, to Sir Dauid Cuningham of This payitNovemAuchinhervie, Thesaurer of the Principality of Walles, to be payit at theber 1641. termes Whitsonday 1640, 1641, and 1642, and anuel in the meantyme, with 15 S) sterling of penaltie for ilk terme's sau3ie, and with power to charge without requisitioun, daittit penult Januar 1639, Item, letters from Sir John and Sir Thomas to him; and a letter to my Lord Panmuir, and within it one from John Pilmuir.

5 February 1639, Twysday. This day my dauchter Marie and Charles Erskein maryit, be Mr. Andro Mary maryit. Ramsay, in the Gray Freir Kirk, about 4 efternone; quhair wer present, the Countess of Mar; the Lord Auchterhous; Alexander, John, and Mr. William Erskinis; myself, and my thrie sones, John, Thomas, and James; John Carstairs, Mr. John Rollok, &c.

» 9 February 1639.

Taken from Anna Foules the jowel 1 quhilk scho had of Marie at her Anna Fowlls, for 1 fair jowcll mariage; and I gaif hir a tikkit to gif it bak, or als good, betuix and Whitsonday nixt.

Item, this day pacquet went with John Murray, and sent letters to the Pacquet with John JVlllITftV

Lord Panmuir, anent Cunnaquhy his reductioun of the horning and decreit, and to know if I sall attend his coming in Marche, as he promisit. Item, writtin to Erl Stirling anent his gudson Sir William. Item, a letter to Mr. Alexander, to chaip ane jowell, and to send me word of the number and bignes of the diamondis, with the pryce.

10 February 1639.

Lord Angus on The Lord Angus reffavit on Seffioun Extraordinar Lord, in place off the Lord Alexander.

Sessioun.

13 February 1639, Weddinsday. William Seytonn, William Seytoun, of Marry, defyrit me not to be aganis him in the of Many. reductioun of Meldrum's horning; and promisit, if he wan the caus, fiftie doubill pieces of gold. 23 February 1639.

LetterU to the Letters sent in the Lord Thesaurer his pacquet to the Lord Panmuir and Lord Panmmr. sone, in ansuer of theis reffavit from John Murray, 21 February 1639.

1 Merche 1639, Fryday. Counsell-s letter to This day the Counsell satt, and a letter drawin vp, to be fent to his his Majestie. Majestie, with the nobilmen's supplicatioun, complening and craving justice of Stirling, for wryting of ane letter to Berwick to Mr. Thomas Sydserff, affirming that the nobihnen wes levying money and men to invad Ingland.

L. Thesaurer to Court.

Letters to Lord Panmuir.

2 Merche 1639, Setterday. This day the Erl of Traquhair went to Court, and sent with him a pacquet to the Lord of Panmuir, quhairin to himself anent Cunnaquhy, and to my fone, and to the Erl of Annandaill, with Thomas Maxwell his letter to his L.

7 Merche 1639.

Letters from Lord Reffavit from the Lord Panmuir letters, with the proclamatioun maid be Proclamatioun at his Majestie at Quhythall, February 1639, aganis the procedingis of the Quhythall.

Scottis nobility, &c.; and a pacquet, sent in ansuer of the said letter, that samyn day, quhilk I delyverit to Mr. James Gordoun, and quhilk he promisit to dispatche the morow befoir tuelf hours.

9 Martij 1639.

Doctor James Chalmers, phisician to his Majestie, and to the Prince, Doctor Chalmers.

(efter the closing of his actioun with the L. Meldrum and L) went to Court; and gevin to him a pacquet to my sone Mr. Alexander, and within it one from the Countess of Mar to my Lord Duk's Grace; and within it one to the Erl of Traquhair, Lord Thesaurer, anent the haill of hir and hir twa sons' pensioun of iiijc h sterling. 16 Martij 1639, Setterday. This day Sir John Hay tuik journey to Ingland; and 3esterday the Countess Home's Countess of Home went also. "requisition to
Ingland.

21 Merche 1639, Thursday. This day the Lord Thesaurer returnit from Court. Lord Thesaurer returnit from

Item, this nycht, betuix 4 and sex at nycht, the Castel of Edinburgh Court, braschit be pittardis, and takin In be the nobilitie.,Ca8tfU 0f.'" r burgh takin.

22 Merche 1639.

This day, being Fryday, the Seffioun

satt; quhair Sir Robert Spottiswod, President as toun. President, the Justice Clerk, and Thesaurer Deput, wer present; but att nycht, the President went as toun.

23 Merche 1639.

This day, being Setterday, the President went as toun; and ane number of the Seffioun mett, and wer requyrit be the nobilitie to subscryve the Covenant.

Item, this day ane number of the Covenanteris went to tak in Dalkeyth, Daikeyth takin in and tuik it in.

24 Merche: 1639, Sounday. Lord Thesaurer. This day I gat a letter from the Lord Thesaurer, (daitit at Cranstoun, to quhilk he retirit efter he left Dalkeyth, in the place pertening to the Scheriff of) defyring me to insorme his Lordlhip of the forme of prorogatioun of the Parliamenf from July, quhilk I ansuerit; and thairwith delyverit a letter to Sir John Vache, to be sent to Lord Panmuir, and within it on to my fone, if the Lord Thesaurer sould go presentlie to Court. 25 Merche 1639, Mononday. Lord Thesaurer. Mett with my L. Thesaurer this day, about 6 at nycht, in the Borrowmuire, quhair he defyrit to be clerit in the points of my letter; and he told me that thai had insormit his Majestie, that the prorogatioun behovit to be vpon 40 dayis preceiding the dyet; quhilk, I said, is trew in ane new indictioun off a Parliament, but not in the continuatioun, quhilk behouit to be *eodem die* that the Parliament is senGt; but his Majestie may notisie his plesur to haif it prorogat quhensoever his Majestie pleffis.

I rememberit his Lordlhip of my letter to Lord Panmuir, quhilk he promisit to delyver to him, and als to reid my marginall nott to his Majestie, quhairby I cleir myself of all the calumnies and hard insormatiounes made of me, except the point of judgement and conscience, as I did expres it in Counsell.

26 Merche 1639, Twysday.

Waponschawing. This day the waponschawing of Edinburgh, quhairin thair wes of musketiers j00 vc, and of pikmen j00, by commanders. Item, of the College of Justice, of musketiers ijc lxx, and of pikkis jc lxrj, by commanders; and theis quho wes with the 4 Lords quho went befoir, vi£, Durie, InnerteiL Craighal, and Scottistarbet, and ane number of the auld advocattis and wryters; sua that all the College of Justice wes about vc.

Dumbarton Item, this nycht sure word cam that Dumbartan wes takin in, on Soun day, 24 Marche, be a stratageme.

Hary Hope. Item, this nycht Hary Hope, my nephew, cam from France.

27 Merche 1639, Weddinsday. This day the Lords of Seffioun sent the Lord Justice Clerk to his The Sessioun sends Majestie, to acquaint his Majestie with the trew estait of the countrey; and t0 his Majesty, to deprecat his Majesties wraith of the sam. 30 Merche 1639, Setterday.

This nycht his Majestie cam to York. His Majestie at

York.

1 April 1639, Mononday. 2 April 1639, Twysday.

This day, being Twysday, about 6 at nycht, the Lord Naper, Lord The-Aneiltthe melting saurer Deput, and Lord InnerpefFer, cam to me and told me that thai had and Sessioun. mett with my Lord Durie, and that thai hard the Kingis Majestie wes come to Newcastell, and wes to be at Bervick on the morow; and that it wes fitt that the Counsell, with the Seffioun, fould meitt togither and resolve, all to go toward his Majestie, and present themselfis befoir his Majestie, and deprecat his wraith from his peopill. And accordinglie letters wes writtin to the Counsell, and to suche of the Lords of Seffioun as wer absent.

Item, as I awaked on Weddinsday in the morning, I sell in ane ernest Words spokin and incalling of the Lord, that his Majestie wald pittie his peopill, and vindicat jg03tnpril them from the power and rage of thair adverfaries, and wald establische the morning, glorie of his bliffit trewth in the land. And quhills I wes praying, thir wordis wer fpokin, but quhither be me or some other I dar not say, but the wordis wer, " I will preserve and saiff my peopill." Quhairupon I awakit out of my drufines; for I wes not sleiping, but as it wer oppreffit with greiff and teires, till theis words wer fpokin and certanlie hard be me. Bliffit be the Lord, quho hes a cair of his awin. And askit my wyff if scho hard any fpeiking, quho hard not; and I told her quhat I hard.

6 April 1639, Setterday. This day 7 of the Counsell and 9 of the Seffioun mett in the Seffioun-Meiting of Counhous, to advyse for sending of some of thair number to his Majestie, tosellan esS,ounLord Thesawer deprecat his wraith aganis the countrey; and in the meiting hard from the confinit to his hous... in York. Erl Wigtoun, that the Lord Thesaurer wes commandit to keip his hous in

York, and prohibit his Majestie's presence. Eri Lauderdaiii. Item, I mett thair with the Erl Lauderdaill, quho said that he rememberit his promise, and wald do it; and I ansuerit, that I wes in no doubt of it, but I wald haif had his Lordlhip's tikkit, to schaw it to the Erl Murray; and he said, " I sall tell him myself that I haif done it." Lord Wodhall Item, this nycht, about 12 hours in the nycht, the Lord Wodhall, Sir lcceissit.

Adam Cuningham, deceiffit.

10 April 1639, Weddinsday.

Meiting of Secreit This day the Counscll and Seffioun mett to advyse anent the deprecating

Counsell and Ses-...,,. ,,..., ,,, sioun. of his Majestie's wraith of the country, and resoluit all to go and cast them selfis at his Majestie's royall feit; and prevailit the Thesaurer Deput to try his Majestie's acceptance.

Item, my sone Sir Thomas his barnis went to the Kerf.

11 Apryll 1639, Thursday.

This day the Act made and subscryvit be Erl Mar, Erl Perth, Erl Wigtoun, Erl Galloway, Erl Lauderdaill, Erl Southcsk, Lord Elphingstoun, Lord Nepar, Advocat, and Thesaurer Deput, of the Counsell; and be Lord Dury, Lord Innerteil, Lord Innerpeffer, Lord Balcomie, Lord Fotherance, Lord Cranstoun, Craighall, Lord Scottistarvett, Lord Eistbank, of the Selfioun.

12 April 1639, Fryday. Lent to my sone Mr. James my sword and twa pistolles.

This day the Erll of Southesk and young Athy took journey to Court. Meiting in my Item, this day, about 6 at nycht, mett in my Lord Durie's, Erl Ergill, une-Erl Mar, Erl Perth, Erl Wigtoun, Lord Nepar, Advocat, and Thesaurer Deputt of Counsell; and Lord Durie, Lord Innerpeffer, Lord Fotherance, Lord Cranstounriddell, Lord Craighall, Lord Eistbank, off SesBoun. And to them cam Erl Rothef5, Lord Lyndsay, Lord Lowdoun, Lord Capringtoun, George Bruce, John Smyth, and Mr. William Cunningham; quhair the Lofdis acquaintit the nobilitie, that thai had directit the Erl Wigtoun and Lord Nepar, of the Counsell, and my Lord Durie and Craighall for the Selsioun, to notisie them thair resolutioun; and that thai had promisit to come and declair thair opiniounes of it.

And then the Erl of Rothefl first, and thairefter the Lord Lowdoun, schew that thai had considerit of it, and thocht it nawayis expedient, except thay wer resoluit and satiffeit off some doubtis; and proponit, first, that thai must be sure that thay quho went vp fould be all of one mynd, quhilk thai haif reffon to doubt, since both Counsell and Seffioun had gevin forth thair contrair determinatiounis, in subscryving the Covenant according to his Majestie's declaratioun, and in resusing to gif horning upon excommunicat perfones.

I ansuerit, that the difference of judgement wes not the point now; but, seing vpon it hes rysen the apparent and instant perrell of kirk and kingdome be two armies coming to the feildis, how any happie middis may be sund to preveyne the samyn, and extremities wald not be joynit *fine medio*. This is thocht fitt, and the reffoun thairoff urgent, that his Majestie is bund in justice to try the fault befoir he punische or exequut be a bloodie warr, quhilk will affect his Majestie's hart muche. And for thair impedimentis, thai haif no place heir, for be them all mediatioun is excludit, seing the Covenanteris will not be admittit be his Majestie to mediat, and the vther i8 refusit be them; and as to the saif conduct, it wes resolvit upon. It wes ansuerit, that all mediatiounis wer usit be supplicatioun, and nothing restit; and that thair affent to this act of the Counsell wald prejudge thair caus.

I ansuerit, that thair wes no consent cravit of them, but that the Counsell wald not omitt that refpect to them to acquaint them thairwith, lest thay sould mak stop; and thay had gottin ane ansuer gracious and fauorable to all thair preceiding supplicatiounes, and nothing now restit but the matter of the Affemblie, quhairin it wes to be supplicat from his Majestie, first to try if, be the lawis of the kingdome, his Majestie, efter indictioun, mycht discharge the Affemblie, vnder the payne of treasoun.

Thairefter the Lord Innerpeffer ansuerit, that the Seffioun had done nothing contrarie to them, for thai had suhscryvit the Covenant as it wes prentit; and as to the Lord Marques his declaratioun, the samyn wes emittit efter thair subscriptioun, and quhen his Grace fpak it, thai said it wes in thir termes, that the ordinance of Counsell did nather allow nor disallow of Episcopacie.

Item, as to the vther vniformitie, if thai went vp, that it wes resoluit that none sould speik but that quhilk, with vniforme consent, sould be aggreit vpon be all.

And as to thair particular opiniounes, if his Majestie did ask them, he declarit for himself that he wald affirme, that the only fittest way to sattill all thingis wer to hold ane Parliament.

The Lord Fotherance said the samyn, but with this scrupill, that a Parliament could not be haldin wanting the Thrid Estait, quhilk is establischit be the Act of Parliament 1597 to be Bischoppes. And as to the letteris of horning vpon excommunication, thai wer not resusit, but letters writtin to his Majestie thairanent; quhairin thai had just reflbun, becaus, albeit thair be ane Act of Parliament to gif letters of horning aganis perfones excommunicat, 3et the Act 1G12 declares that none can be excommunicat but be consent of the Bischoppes.

The Lords Cranstoun and Eistbank all said the lyke; and for my Lord Durie and my sone, thai wer not doubtit.

My Lord Fotherance cravit me to cleir to him the point of the Thrid Estait of Parliament, and the Act 1597 quhairvpon it dependit, quhilk I schunit, becaus we had no tyme; butt I said, that *quoad jurisdictionem in ecclejia*, it wes sufpensive till it wer condescendit on with the Kirk; and if all the bischopes wer deid, the Thrid Estait wold (be) in vther prelattis, as abbottis and priores.

15 April 1639, Mononday. Thesaurer Deput. This day the Thesaurer Deput tuik post to Court, and sent with him letters to Erl Stirling, Lord Panmuir, James Levingstoun, and to my sone. Marques of Hunt-Item, certane word from the Erl of Montroisi and Generall Leslie, quho ley. went to the North, that the Marques of Huntley wes come in and subscryvit the Covenant, and gaif his eldest sone as pledge for his constancie. 18 April 1639.

Delyverit to Sir Robert Gordoun ane ansuer of the letter quhilk I reffavit Lord Panmuir, from him 3esterday, from the Lord Panmuir, anent the Castell of Edin-Robert burgh; and an other to my Lord Stirling, for the samyn, but generally.

22 April 1639.

Gevin to my sone Sir Thomas my putrinell or carabin, indentit of rowat PutrinelL work; reserving the vse thairof to myself, quhen I call for it.

23 April 1639, Twysday. My dauchter Mary went bak to Craighall; and gevin with hir, to my Cognisance, barne Thomas, the cognisance of Baronet, quhilk I gatt from Lord Stirling, 19 Merche 1630; and Anne went with hir.

24 April 1639, Weddinsday.

Mett with the Lord Thesaurer in Mr. Adam Hepburne's houfi at the Lord Thesaurer, South Port, quhair he told me of Sir John Hay his trecherie, in causing accuse him to his Majestie as plotter and counsellor in all the troubles; and he wes to be judgit be the Erll of Arrundell, Merchel of Ingland, becaus the armies wer vpon the seild.

He cam from York thairefter be his Majestie's warrand, and with him the Lord Dal3ell, on Thursday of befoir, to the Borderis of Scotland, being 18 April; and sent letteris to the nobilmen to meit them at Melrotf, quhair thai mett on Mononday, 22 April; and cam to the

Potterraw on 23 April.

Item, Marques of Huntley committit to the Castell of Edinburgh. Marques of Huntley.

Last Aprill 1639, Twysday. This day reffavit his Majestie's letter, daitit at York, 27 April 1639, Letter from his commanding me to come to Court. to York 110

Item, that day hard that the Lord Sayis and Lord Broghe, Inglische Lords, wer putt in prifoun at York, as suspectit to be intelligencers to the Scottis nobilmen.

[Item, this nycht his Majestie's schippis, to the number of 30 or 40, wer discoverit als sar as Dumbar.]

1 Maij 1639, Weddinsday. This nycht a servand of Coronell Erskin's cam from Court, quho affurit that his Majestie wes in Durehame. 2 Maij 1639.

Marques of Hamil-His Majestie's schippis cam to Insche Keyth, in number 29, and fend in je«te-schippisMa"taau" commiffioun to the nobilmen, quhairof the Marques of Hamiltoun General.

Charts Erakin, my Item, this day Charls Erskin, my fone, defyrit to put within my litill irne joweiu!3 08 ne kist Cn coffer with jewellis, quhilk wes done, and I gaif him the key thairof. Item, Mr. Alexander Burnett patt thairin, besoir it wes lockit, ane litill bunsche of paperis pertening to him. Thir redelyuerit to All thir, with the meikill irne kist, and writtis being thairin, ar putt in "raltem tcMrtnc cn v0 seuar» for eschewing of fyr; and committis the rest to the Lord.

Alexander Burnet.
3 Maij 1639, Fryday.

Thesaurer Deput. This nycht the Thesaurer Deput cam from Durehame, quhair his Majestie wes, to Edinburgh, with a proclamatioun offering a general pardoun, and declaring all that did not accept it to be rebellis and traitors, and all thair landis to be forsaltit.

[4 Maij 1639.

This nycht tuo men takin, quho wes to set the toun in fyre. 2 irne kistis. Item, this nycht the tua irne kistis, with the writtis and evidents being thairin, putt in the laich seller volt.

Pacquett.
7 Maij 1639..,. i;

Letteris sent in James Prymrois his pacquet to the Lord Panmuir, with the commiffioun for sencing and prorogatioun of the Parliament. Item, letter to Erl Stirling. Item, the Countef l of Merschel hir letteris to the Lord Panmuir. Item, Coronel Erskin his letter to the Erl Stirling.

11 Maij 1639.

Gevin to John More, quhen he went from my service, v auld rof l nobles. John More.

[12 Maij 1639, being Sounday, at nicht. The pacquet in paiper cam to me from Neucastell, daitit 11 May 1639, His Majestie s with commiffioun for prorogatioun of the Parliament to 23 July nixt; with ansuera letter from his Majestie, for performing of the samyn.

15 Maij 1639, Weddinsday.

This day the Parliament fencit be his Majestic's Commiffioun vnder the Parliament fencit Quarter Seill, and continewit to 23 July nixt.,ad eontinewit.

Item, pacquet sent, quhairin to his Majestie self, and to the Lord Panmuir, and Secretar, and Erl Roxburgh; in it to my sone Mr. Alexander, to be sent to him from Neucastell to Londoun; within quhilk is a letter from Hary to his mother.

Item, within this letters from the Thesaurer Deput to Erl Stirling. Item, from Coronel Erfkin to the Erl Stirling. Item, from Sir Robert Gordoun to the Erl of Stirling.

Item, this day report of the Lord Roxburgh his committing, in the MairErl Roxburgh, of Neucastell his hous.

Item, this nycht the copies gevin to Sir Robert Gordoun aganis my Lord Raa and Lord Raa and Sir James Sinclair of Murkill; and thairefter copies of oth,L-MurkiUto 25 July, sent by Alexander Young, Ikynner in Elgin, to Drennie, Sir Robert his place, 2 July 1639.

16 Maij 1639.

Arthor Stratown went to the Erll Merschell, and sent with him letters to Tutor of Piuiigo. the Lord Phillorth, and Tutor of Pittsligo.

[17 Maij 1639.

Maister of Forbes This day report of the conflict in the North, befyd Innerrory, brocht takin or hurt. bg young Ludquharne. quhair Banff, Lord Haddo, Donald

Ferquharfoun, and vtheris of the name of Gordoun, sett vpoun the Maister off Forbes and his companies, being in hortf and flit 600 men, and Banff not above iiijc, with sum seild peices; and patt the vther to flicht, without so muche as a strik on the vther fyd; and the Maister of Forbes hurt or takin, and twa or thrie killit.

[18 Maij, Setterday, 1639. Wordis hard 18 This day, in the morning, I lying in my bed, betuix fyve and sex, and,

QhiiklVard on T011 tQe off the rePort of the disaster in the North, puring forth my 3 April. hart to the Lord in prayer, and saying, " Lord, pitie thy pure Kirk, for thair is no help in man!" I hard a voce saying to me, as I did heir it of befoir, on thrid Apryll last, " 1 will pitie it." For quhilk I bliffit the Lord; and belevis that it sal be as my Lord hes now twys fpokin to me. Long carabin. Lent to John my long carabin of rowet work all indentit, with the brace iron key and gold string, gottin from Mr. John Erles?

19 Maij.

At nycht the pacquet cam to me, with letters from Erl Stirling and Lord Panmuir, testiseing his Majestie's approbatioun of the prorogatioun of the Parliament to 23 July.

20 Maij 1639.

Litill carabin. Gevin to my sone Charles my litill rowat carabin of mother-a-perll stok, to be vfit be him quhen I haif not ado thairwith, but to be readie quhen I call for it.

Contributioun. Gevin to hir 5 rosnobles, for the contributioun to the comoun caus, made be women.

Pacquet. Item, this day direct a pacquet to the Erl Stirling, in ansuer of that quhilk I reffavit on Sounday the 19 Maij instant from Neucastell; quhairin one to the Erl of Stirling, and within it one from James Prymrois, and ane vther to the Lord Panmuir, quhairof I haif ane copie, becaus it concernis the publik affares.

21 May 1639, Twysday. This day Generall Leslie, Erl Rothetf, and Lord Lyndsay, tuik journey Generall Leslie, to the bound rod. 22 May 1639, Weddinsday. This day, about fyve hours efternone, thair wes ane eclipse of the soun. Eclipse of the soun. 23 May 1639.

Coft from Andro Anderfoun, in Couper, 2 pistolles, and gevin thairfoir 2 pistollea. 2 doubisl angells; and I gave thame with the calmes key and worme to Hew Lyndsay, to keip and dress for my vse.

This day 14 or 16 of the Kingis schippis lousit from the raid. 16 schippis.

Item, Mr. Alexander Henrysoun, with Mr. Archibald Johnstoun, raid to Mr. Alexander the bound Rod. Henrysoun. 24 May 1639, Fryday.

This day ane Inglische herald brocht a new proclamatioun from his New proclamaMajestie, daitit at Neucastell, May 1639; quhairin his Majestie declaristlounthat he cravis nothing of his subiectis but civill obedience, and that he is come to hold his Parliament; and thairfoir commands all his Majestie's fubiectis quho ar gathered in armes to remoue thamselfis 10 myl thairfra, vnder all highest payne. Item, a letter from the Erl Holland to the nobility, to that samyn end.

To this the nobility gaif ansuer by a letter to the Erl of Holland, and be Ansuer thairto. sending the L. of Blacater, with instructiounis, to the nobility of Ingland, defyring to haif conserence with some off them; and in the meantyme, quhill thai gatt ansuer, sould obey, and retire thair armies and forces ten myles from the Bordour, provyding that the Inglische did also keip thair forces bak from the Borderis.

Item, this 24 May, being Fryday, the Kingis Majestie, with his armies, His Majestie at cam to Anwik. N Anwik.

25 May 1639, Setterday. His Majestie at This day his Majestie cam from Anwik to ane place callit Gosehauk, myle Bendck. pertening to a gentilman callit Hamiltoun, quhilk is within 4 myle to Bervick.

The sehippis returnit.

Packett.

Words hard, 3.
Words hard, 4.
Words, 5.

27 May, Mononday. This day the 16 sehippis quhilk went away returnit to the raid of Leyth. 28 May 1639, Twysday. The pacquet sent to Erl Stirling, quhairin one to him, and within it to the Thesaurer Deput. Item, one from me to Lord Panmuir, quhairin from the Countefl of Merfchell 2, and from Angus 3. 29 May, Weddinsday, 1639, Edinburgh.

About midnycht, as I wes regrating to the Lord tbe calamitie off his Kirk, and humblie praying his Majestie to arrise to the help thairoff, and with teares vrging, calling vnto him, Arryse! I hard thir words, "I will arryse." And within half hour efter, the horne blew with a pacquet.

Item, I went away toward Hadingtoun, to meit with the Erll of Rothef5, but he wes gone to Dumbar; quhairvpon I wont to, quhair

I stayit till 6 Junij; and on 6 Junij, being Thursday, I went to Lammermuir, toward Bervick, be the convoy of one William Wauchop; and came, about tuelf hours of the day, till Foulden, quhair I wes most courteouslie entertainit be John Wilkie and his lady, and abaid with them till 20 Junij, at quhilk I returnit to Edinburgh.

On Fryday, 7 Junij, I kiffit his Majestie's hand; and had conserence with his Majestie on Mononday the 10, and on Twysday, Weddinsday, and Thursday; as my nott made thairvpon will testisie.

On 8 Junij, lying in my bed, betuix 1 and 2 in the morning, I wes pouring surth my hart to the Lord; and in so gret necellitie, being to speik with the King, I said, "My Lord, will not thy Majestie help and affist me?" And I hard a voice saying, " I will, doubt nott."

Item, at Foulden, on 14 Junij, quhilk wes Fryday, 1639, being anxious in fpirit for the event and succefl of God's caus, I hard this voice, " Latt me work it."

Item, on Setterday the 15 Junij the articles wes presentit, and the nobilmen gatt a kiffe of his Majestie's hand.

Item, at Foulden, 16 Junij 1639, being Sounday; I being praising the Words, 6. Lord for the good beginning, and humblie praying for the accomplisching of God's work, I hard this voice, " I haif done it."

Item, on Twysday, 18 Junij, the articles of peax wer subscryvit.

Item, this day, in the morning, I being in a deip meditatioun of God's Vow to my good savors to the publik good of his Kirk, and in it to me his poore servand; IGodvowit to my Lord, (in refpect of the gret tentatiounis offerit to me, be calumniatts and vtherwais, be some of my awin, quhom I name not;) I vowit, I say, to rellrayne my soddan paffioun, and to compone my mynd, by God's grace, to patience and equanimity, and to remit all to the Lord; quhilk I pray God I may keip.

20 Junij 1639.

On Thursday, 20 Junij, I came from Foulden about 5 in the morning, and came to Edinburgh about 4 efternone.

On Setterday, 22 Junij 1639, the Castell of Edinburgh randerit to his Castel of EdinMajeftie, and to the Marques of Hamiltoun in his Majestie's name; andf uncles!)!' General Ruthven made Captane thairoff.

On Sounday, 23 Junij 1639, I rememberit the holy vowis and promiffis Sounday, 23 Junij 1639 Vowis to my Lord, for adhering to his trewthe, and puritie thairoff. And in'

refpect of his Majestie's gracious affistance of me quhen I wes befoir the

King's Majestie, according to his sueit promiffes and affurances gevin to me,

I renewit my vowis, and promisit, be his grace, to hold sast the Covenant off his bliffit treuth, and thairwith to walk in charitie, sobrietie, and all vther

Christian vertewis; and to moderat theis affectiounis and paffiounes, of impatience, anger, and vtheris of that kynd, quhilk is one of my greitest tentatiounis in bodie and mynd; and to remit all to the grace of my Lord,

to strenthen me aganis theis infirmities, and to keip me in the moderat vfe of theis thingis quhilks vtherwais ar lawfull, but not expedient for this tyme of tryel. The Lord performe quhat he hes made me promise!

On Sounday last, Junij 1639, a holy renewing of my vowis to my Lord, Renewit.

quhilk I putt on his Majestie's grace and strenth, without quhilk I am not abill to performe the samyn.

Counsell.
Indictioun of
Assemblie to
12 August.
Sessions to sitt doun 9 July.
1 July, Mononday, 1639.

This day the Counsell mett at Halyruidhous, quhair wer present, Lord Thesaurer, Lord Privie Seill, Marques of Huntley, Erl Perth, Erl Lauderdaill, Erl Kynnoull, Erll of Hadingtoun, Justice Generall, Thesaurer Deput, and Sir James Hamiltoun; and I being difeafit of a colik, wes excusit.

Heir the AffembUe ordanit to be indictit to the xij of August next.

Item, the Seffioun ordanit to sitt doun on 9 July.

The Affemblie proclamit, and the nobilmen protestit aganis the naming of archbischops and bischoppes.

On 3 July, Weddinsday, wes the tumult of women in Edinburgh, quho invadit the Lord Thesaurer, Erl Kynoul, and Lord Oboyne, in thair coches.

4 July 1639, Thursday. This day also the Counsell satt, at quhilk wes present the Lords above expreffit, and by them the Justice Clerk; and heir nothing wes movit of the tumult, but onlie how to provyd for his Majestie's cariage, and vther neceffares for his Majestie's incoming to Dalkeyth; and I wes excusit be reffoun of my disease.

My promise anent Item, my dauchter Margaret being going to Craighall, cam to visit me; my oy Elizabeth. and I flayed hn-a tyme, and told hir that I wes sorie to find my sone and hir so sad and lowring; and told thai had no reffoun, and red to hir the nott quhilk I had from my sone in Januar last; and in end told of the impediments, be reffoun of the troubles of the tyme, quhilk hinderit me to performe my promise anent Elizabeth hir j0(1 merks at this terme; but that, with God's grace, I sal pay it, and ane vther thousand, at Witsounday 1640, if the Lord spair my dayis.

9 July 1639, Twysday. Sessioun sittis. This day the Seffioun satt, and thai wer 9 of number; and admittit the Lord Halkertoun, younger, vpoun his Majestie's letter, oppin and not signettit, in place of Sir Adam Cuninghame; but nather President nor Clerk of Register wes present; and of the ordinar Lords, (by them,) Innerpeffer and Fodderance wes not come. 13 July 1639.

The Lords sent a letter to his Majestie be the Thesaurer Deput, adver-Letter from the tising his Majestie of thair sitting, and that nane of the fubiectis repairit t0 thairto; and cravit his Majestie's plesur if thai fould sitt or ryse.

18 July 1639.

I sent letters in James Prymrois his pacquet to the Erl of Stirling, Packet of letters to quhairin to him, with the commiffioun for sensing of the Parliament, and athe Secretarpacquet to him from Sir Robert Gordoun. Item, to the Lord Panmuir, and within his to the Lord Thesaurer, defyring to haif the commistloun for the Parliament to be sent befoir Setterday next.

22 July 1639.

Sent with Robert Wallace, seruitor to the L. Frendrauch, an ansuer to Letters to Lord him of his letter; with twa letteris, one to the Tutor of Pitsligo, and ane Fhlllorthvther to the Lord Phillorth, anent the slownes of thair ansuer for the writtis.

23 July 1639, Twysday. This day the Parliament sensit, and continewit to the 26 August next. Parliament. 24 July 1639.

Theis thrie nobilmen, vi3., Erl Dumsermling, Lord Lyndsay, and Lord Nobilmen went to Lowdoun, went to his Majestie, to gif ansuer to some articles; but hisBervickMajestie defyrit vtheris to come, quhairof the Erl Rothefl, Erl Montroifl, Erl Lothian, wes thrie; quho went about the 18 July, and returnit, to fetche with them the remainder.

25 July, Thursday, 1639. This day my sone Alexander, with Mr. Roo, a gentilman quho come My sone Mr

Alexander.

with him about the end of Junij last, returnit to Bervick, to attend on his Majestie; and gevin to my sone, in takin, 5 old rofl of gold; and this day Tutor of Pitsligo. reffavit the Tutor of Pitstigois letter, with the contract of mariage.j 26 July, Fryday, 1639. His Majestie-s re-This day word come that his Majestie had refoluit suddenly to go to London. K Londoun, and to tak journey on Mononday nixt, 29 July. 27 July 1639, Setterday.

Packett. A packet sent to Erl Stirling, quhairin to himself, takand my leve of him.

Item, to Lord Panmuir, and within it to my sone Mr. Alexander. Item, one to him from the Countess of Merschell. Item, another to James Levingstoun, from me. Item, another from me to Mr. Alexander, anent

Sir Hary Milmay. James his hgnatour; and one to him, to be delyverit from me to Sir Hary Milmay, Knycht, jowellor to his Majestie.

Mr. Alexander, for Item, this samyn day, about 3 efternone, Adam Blair tauld me of the deceit f of the L. Blair, and went from me; and efter that Mr. George Norwell put me in mynd to sute the gift to my sone Mr. Alexander, quhilk I wald not do without Adam Blair his knowledge, quho come to me and said he could not do it without warrand of the freinds, and fpecially of Sir Archibald Steuart of Blakhall and the Lard of Gaitgirth, the desunct's goodbrethir; but he wes content to misken it. I promisit that it sould not pass the Seills till the freinds and I wer accordit; and he told me the estait is worth 12s10 merks be 3eir, but then thair is 3 lady lyfrenters vpon it, and the burthen of 5000 Ib of debt, with 8 bairnis; quhairvpon I drew vp the gift and sent it to my sone, with letteris to Erl Stirling and Lord Panmuir, to affist him thairin.

1 August, Thursday.

Countess of Mar. 8 August 1639, the Counsell mett, quhairin no publik buffines wes treattit, (becaus his Majestie's letters wer not come,) only the particular betuix the Countess of Mar and the L. Erikin, anent the feat of the kirk of Stirling; and vpon 9 August the matter wes submittit to Erl Ergill, Erl Southelk, and Lord Durie.

10 August 1639, Setterday.

This day his Majestie's letter cam to Counsell, appointing the Erl Tra-Eri Traquhair quhair Commilsioner for Affemblie and Parliament. one0"TM18'

Item, letters sent to my sone Mr. Alexander, quhairin to himself, anent the Letter to Mr. Lord Thesaurer his promise for signing of his precept to Alexander Steuart. Alexander

Item, a letter to Erl Stirling, acquainting him with Sir James Douglas Item, to Erl Stirhis titil, aganis quhilk Patrik L. Oliphant gaif in a bill; and als remembering jmy him of a signatour to James my sone of the mynes of Waterheid, to quhilk I must haif him and his sones joyn thair consent.

Item, a letter reffavit this day from Sir Hary Milmay, joweller to his Item, Sir Hary Majestie, quhilk I haif ansuerit with this pacquet. Milmay.

12 August 1639, Mononday. This day a solemn sast in all the kirks of Edinburgh, both befoir none General Assemblie. and eftirnone; and about half hour to four the Affemblie mett in the New Kirk of Edinburgh, quhair, efter prayer made be Mr. Alexander Henryfoun, last Moderator, the Clerk callit the Roll off the Commiffioners of Presbitries, Burghes, and Collegis, quhilk held neir twa hours; and the Affembsie ordanit to meit to-morow at 10 houres. 13 August 1639.

This day Mr. Dauid Dick chosin Moderator, and the lytes wes namit to Mr. Dauid Dick be Mr. Alexander Henrysoun, last Moderator, quho namit fyve, and to them his Majestie's Commiffioner addit Mr. Alexander himself; quhairvpon thair wes a long disputt, but in end the sex stude, and the matter went in voiting.

14 August 1639.

This day the Affemblie mett, and the Commiffioner requyrit, that befoir Parie. the debaiting of matters, for eschewing of misconstructioun, that some of the Affembsie sould meit with the Commissioner, and with him some off the Counsell, at efternone, quhilk wes grantit; quhairvpon the seffioun of this dayis Affembsie rose.

Item, this day a pacquet sent be my Lord Commiffioner, and I sent

Packet to the Erl letters inclosit In the Lord Panmuir his pacquet, quhilk he sent to the wammd for Par-Secretar, with a warrand for him and his goodsone A thy, for ratifeing of imment. thair blensche inseftmentis latlie past in Februar 1639. Item, a letter from me to the Erl Stirling, and within it a warrand to be past his Majestie, for ratisicatioun in Parliament of my blensche inseftment of Craighal and Kyninmonth, in Junij 1635. Item, a signatour to Mr. Alexander my sone of the lands and mynes of Waterheid, vpoun Mr. James his resignatioun, to be past his Majestie's hand.

Act of Assemblie abolisching Episcopacie.

Packett.

17 August 1639, Setterday.

This day the Affemblie, quhilk began at Edinburgh on Mononday the 12 August, clout the point of Episcopacie, and declarit it vnlawsull, and contrair to Godis word, to the vnfpeakabill joy of all them that feiris the Lord, and waittis for his salvatioun.

Item, this nycht sent a pacquet to the Erll of Stirling, advertising him heirof, and thairwith sending him a warrand to ratisie ane rycht of patronage of Tullibody in Parliament. Item, a warrand for ratiseing James Maxwell his inseftment of the patronage of Dirltoun, and containing a suppreffioun of the abbacies of Dryburgh and Cambuskennell, and pryorie of Inchmahomo. Item, a letter to my fone Mr. Alexander, and ane other to James Levingstoun.

Packett.

Anent the 3 estait.

19 August 1639, Mononday.

This day delyverit to the Lord Commiffioner a packett to the Erl Stirling, quhairin one to him from Lord Panmuir. Item, one from me, with the presentatioun of Monecky to Mr. Henry Fithy, vpon the deceit f of Mr. John Durham, last minister; and in the end thairof my regrait of thir 3: (1.) That I never callit to be present; (2.) That S. L. at his elbo; (3.) That his splen and outragious speeches my disgrace.

Item, this day the Lord Commiffioner asldt me concerning the 3 estait of Parliament, quhilk I ansuerit in presence of Erl Southeslt and Lord Justice Clerk.

Item, thairefter I spak with the Erll of Ajrth, &c.

21 August 1639, Weddinsday. This day Colin Campbell, Tutor of Calder, promisit to me 3eirly thrie or Colin Campbell, four mairtis to attend to the Lard's affairs and his; and to begin atTutor of CalderMertimes nixt.

Item, he promisit to gif the seu-duety of Ylaw to Mr. George, to remayneYlaw. in his hands; and he wes content that I fould tak it from Mr. George, vpon surety to repay it, if I gat him not to discharge.

25 August 1639, Sounday. This day, betuix allevin and tuelff befoir none, David Mccall decelfit. David Mcall Item, sent letters to the Erl Stirling and my sone, ansuering the Erll hispj1 letter reffavit 24 August, and complaining of my sone of not ansuering his, quhilk wer sent at one tyme. 26 August 1639, Mononday. This day the Parliament sencit be commiffiouns vnder his Majestic's Parliament. Quarter Seill, and continewit to the 30 of August instant, and this Court wes holdin in the New Parliament Houfl. 30 August 1639.

The Parliament sencit, and ordanit to ryd to--morow; and this intimate Parliament, to the estates be a measer and sound of trompet.

81 August 1639, Setterday. The Parliament raid. Erl Traquhair, Commiffioner; Erl Ergyll, croun; Erl Crausuird, sceptor; Erl Sutherland, sword.

Item, this nycht letters sent to my sone, and within to the Erl Stirling.

2 September 1639, Mononday. ter Margaret brocht to bed, and fle the Lord; and gevin to Jean 1 tuelf-pund piece. The bairne wes borne betuix 3 and 4 efternone.

This day my dauchter Margaret brocht to bed, and dely verit off ane man My dauchter Marchyld, for quhilk I bliffe the Lord; and gevin to Jean Cuningham, midwyff, fret ' o

Hary Hope.

MaUter of Berridaill.

3 September 1639, Twysday.

This day Hary Hope went to Bruntiland, to schip to Newheavin; and I gave him for a takin 2 quadrupill pistolles of gold.

Item, this day the Maister of Berridaill deceiflit at Edinburgh, being heir attending the Generall Affemblie.

9 September 1639, Mononday. The baime baptisit This day the bairne baptisit in the Auld Kirk, efter the morning preiching, be Mr. William Colace; and the bairne namit Archibald. Witneffes, Archibald, Erl of Ergyll; Patrik Lyndsay, myself, Charles, Sir Thomas, James, Mr. Archibald Johnstoun, Mr. Alexander Colvill. 14 September 1639, Setterday. Pacquet. This day a letter sent to my fone, and within it to the Erll of Stirling, to tell them of the difput anent the 3 estait, and vote in Parliament. 19 September 1639, Thursday.

Packett. This day Muschet, servitor to the Erl Airth, went to Court, and come and askit if I had my letters; and with him I sent a letter to my sone, and within it one to Mr. Levingstoun, in ansuer of his reffavit be me, about the lordschip of Wauchtoun, in the matter of Beill, on 15 September instant.

Squyro Hay. Item, 21 September, Setterday, Sir James Hay of Smeithfeild, Squyre of his Majestie's Bodie, went to Court, and sent with him a letter to my fone, to be schawin to Mr. Levingstoun and to the Squyre himself, that he may schaw his Majestic I haif lost popular applause.

Words hard.

22 September 1639, Sounday. This day, about 3 in the morning, I calling to mynd the croce proceidings in Parliament, (quhairof I haif a large journall every day since it satt doun,) and the difficult and hard estait quhairin the kirk and kingdome standis, did pour surth my heart in prayer and teiris to the Lord, and betuix the seir of judgement for fyn, and the expectatioun of pardoning mercie in refpect of the glorious work alreadie done be the Lord in his Kirk; and thairefter salling in a slumbering, I hard thir words, "My work is a perfyt work." The Lord perfyt it!

And vpon the morne, being Mononday, 23 September, betuix 4 and 5 in the morning, I being regraiting the greit difficulties of the ratisicatioun of Godis treuth be the Parliament, be reffoun of the questiounes movit be the barones anent the 3 Estait, thir words cam to me, "I will do it in my awin way." For quhilk I bleffe the Lord, and belevis that the Lord will do it in his owin glorious way.

1 October 1639, Twysday.

This day I reffavit letteris from the Erl Stirling, beiring he had acquaintit Erl Stirling, his Majestie with the buffiness of the thrid Estait.

Item, on 2 October writtin to the Erl Stirling, and als to my fone Mr. My sone Mr. Alexander, and within his one from my fone Mr. James, delyverit to Wil-Ale3tander liam Leyth, servitour to the Erl Mortoun, quho is to go post tomorow, 3 October 1639.

3 October 1639, Thursday. This day Mr. Ninian Bowse maryit on Katharine Maccall, dochter to Mr. Niniane vmquhile Dauid Mccall; and gevin ane gilt coup of 22 vnce, and ane silver, coupe of 16 vnce. 5 October 1639. Packet sent to Erl Stirling, quhairin a packet to him from the Lord Pan-Packett. muir. Item, one from me to James Levingstoun.

9 October.

This day I fpok the Erl l of Lauderdaill, in the rowme above the Articles, Erl Landerdaill. about 8 in the morning, (he being thair, with the Erl Southesic and Innerpeffer, on a Committee of the Blew Book, and I, with the Erl of Southeslc, vpon the Act of Landslords in the North;) and I defyrit to knaw if he wald pay the jm merks and intrefl: And his ansuer wes, that he wald mak the *dyk of the faill;* quhen the Erl Home payit him he wald pay me; or, if I defyr, he wald affigne me so much of the Erll of Home's band. And then he askit, quhat I had done for the Erl Murray; and that he fould not pay if the Erl of Murray pay nott. To quhilk I ansuerit, that both he and the Countef l of Home had promisit. Item, I did of befoir remember him of his promise in the lobbie of the Eist Kirk, the tyme of the Generall Affemblie, in August last; quhair he said, "*Manet irrevocabile verbum!"* 16 October, Weddinsday. Commissioner. This day, at 7 hours, I went to the Abbay at 7 hours in the morning; and thair the Commiffioner askit my opinioun anent the act of Mensall Kirkis, quhilk I told in presence of Sir Lues Steuart, and reportit to the Marques of Huntley first, and then to the Lord Privie Seill; but quhen the matter wes brocht in difput this day befoir none, and the Moderator and Commiffioners of the Kirk being present in ane very great number, the Commiffioner, without any occasioun offerit be me, brak out violentlie in thir fpeiches, ester I had reffonit the point exactlie for his Majestie: "Be God, this man cares not quhat he fpeaks; for he speakes one thing to me privatlie, and evin now in my eir, and another thing publiklie, he is so impudent." Quhairanent I made ansuer, and appellit to Sir Lues Steuart, quho hard us in the morning, and als to the Lord Privie Seill and Marques of Huntley, quho supervenit efter.

Spanish Navy defait.

17 October. 1 gaif in my petitioun to the Lord Commiffioner and Articles, defyring Sir Lues Steuart and the Lord Privie Seill and Marques to be hard to declair; quhilk petitioun wes red, but resusit to gif ansuer to it, and takin vp be him and putt in his pockett. And with this he sell out in the railling fpeeches contenit in the paper apart.

Item, this day, efternone, the newis cam of the desait of the Spanische Navy be the Hollanders, quhilk wes fochtin foirent Downes Raid, on Fryday the 11 October.

19 October 1639, Setterday. This day sent a packet, with Sir Alexander Home or Mr. Alexander Johnstoun, to the Erl Stirling and my sone, with one from me to James Levingstoun, and one from my sone James to his brother, with insormatioun of the Erl Traquhair, Commiffioner, his outrageous behaviour on 16 and 17 October, and the doubill of my petitioun. 22 October, Twysday. Mr. William Burnet cam from Court, quho, and Lord Dal3ell, went to Court on Sounday, 6 October, and returnit not till this 22. 24 October, Thursday. This day the Commiffioner declarit, in Articles, his Majestie's plesur to haif the Parliament

adjornit to ane certain day, till his Majestie wer insormit of the pointis in difference. 29 October.

Sent ane pacquet to Court to the Erl of Stirling, vnder cover of the Lord Pwkett. of Panmuir, quhilk wes delyverit to one Kinloch, sactor in Paris, quhois sather duellis in the heid of Nidrie's Wynd; and in this pacquet thair is a letter to his Majestie, with the nott of my petitioun, and the ansuer thairto. Item, one to the Erl Stirling. Item, one to my sone, with copie off my letter to his Majestie.

30 October.

Item, delyverit to the Lord Panmuir ane letter to the ErL Stirling, and ane to my sone, in ansuer of his of 19 October, reffavit 23 October from Mr. William Burnet, anent making him certane of present miserie, or of freidome from greiff, by fending moneyis and sic lyk; ane vther, schawing to him how the Lord of Panmuir had purchasit the Thesaurer his subscriptioun to a precept to Alexander Steuart, for payment to him of ijc lb sterling, subscryvit 28 October; and that I had sent Hew Lyndesay to Fyiff, to defyre Alexander Steuart to accept it.

Lord Panmuir to Memorandum.— The Lord tuik journey on thursday the last of October,

Court...

about 7 hours in the morning. 31 October, Thursday. This day a pacquet sent be me to the Erl Stirling, quhairin one to himself, with a not of the debait anent the prorogatioun of the Parliament to the 14 November nixt. Item, one to Lord Panmuir, anent Alexander Steuart his resusall of my sone's precept. Item, one to Mr. Alexander, my fone, quhairin is the precept of ijc lb sterling, subscryvit be the Lord Thesaurer at Halyruidhous, 28 October 1639, for the pensioun of the termes of Martimefl 1638 and Witfounday 1639, with Alexander Steuart his letter of resusall, and instruments thairvpon. Item, a letter to James Levingstoun, anent the prorogatioun of Parliament. Erl Kynnoul. Item, the Erll of Kynnoull sent with a letter from the Counsel to his

Majestie, anent the prorogatioun of Parliament.

1 November 1689, Fryday. Item, this day the Erll of Dumsermling and Lord Lowdoun tuik journey to Court, for the part of the nobilmen, &fc.

Turnoris.

2 November 1639, Setterday. This day the turnors, be act of Counsell, cryit doun to a pennie the peice; quhilk wes recallit be ane contrair act, made 7 November 1639. 4 November 1689, Mononday. Packet. This day John Erskin went post to overtak the Lord Panmuir, and I gaif him a letter to the Lard, quhairin is a forme of a letter from his Majestie to the Commiffioner, for staying of the Act of Cariestoun; with a letter to my fone, to gett a letter from his Majestie to the Thesaurer for iijc lb sterling of his pensioun, including Martimefl 1689; and defyrit my letter to his Majestie to be delyverit with diligence, and without delay. 8 November 1639.

Packet. This day letters sent (with one Mowbray, servitour to the Erll of Kellie,) to the Lord Panmuir, quhairby I tell him of the recalling of the act maid for decrying of the turnors, made yesterday, 7 November. Item, in his packet letters to him from the Countef l of Merschell.

10 November, Sounday. This day being ane sasting day, at the very entrie of the foirnone sermon, Fyre. the exhortatioun being begun by Mr. Alexander Henrysoun, thair wes a fray in the kirk, be occasioun of a fyre in one David Murray his houtf, on Ane vther lyke the north fyd of the gait, nixt to Mr. John Skenis chalmer, on the west ofuJumj 1543.' it; quhairvpon a gritt part of the pepill, with the Prouest and Magistrates, ischit surth; and the Minister stayit till thair return, be the space os 3 quarteris of ane hour; and then, be Godis mercie, the fyre wes quenschit. 14 November 1639.

The Parliament continewit till 2 Junij 1640, be vertue of the commiffion Parliament, vnder the Quarter Seill.

15 November 1639, Fryday. This day, being Fryday, betuix xj and tuelf befoir noone, my dauchter My dauchter Marie delyverit of a maid child; for quhiDc I bleffe the Lord, and God mak a maid cMLcLTM1 f hir parentis and me thanksull. 20 November 1639, Weddinsday. This day a part off the Castel wall, quhilk is toward the entrie on the Wall of the CasteU southe, sell in the nycht, with sik a noise, that all within took it for a myne fafiknlmburgh or surprise of the Castell of Edinburgh. 21 November, Thursday. This day a pacquet gevin to Mr. James Gordoun, to be sent to the Erl Stirling, quhairin is ane pacquet to the Lord Panmuir, and ane vther to my sone, with the twa insormations anent the prorogatioun of the Parliament, Signatour of Waand anent the act of Counsell for ratiseing thairoff; and Mr. James Gordoun J6"1 of new delyverit the pacquet to Mr. William Forbes. In this is the signatour of Watterheid. 22 November 1639, Fryday. Commissioner to This day the Commiffioner tuik journey to Court, and Mr. William Forbes delyverit to some off his men my pacquet to the Erll of Stirling.

Item, this day my sone Sir John offerit to pay his mother, for Craighall, v0 0 merks for the hous, ather termelie or monethlie; and he to pay the Minister and Mr. John Craig, and Robert Bennet his annuel, as Eister Pittscotty.

The Counted of Kinghorne deceiffit 22 November, Fryday.

23 November, Setterday.

Mr. William Mr. William Cuningham went to Court with the supplicatioun of the

Cuningham to Estates: and I sent with him a letter to the Lord Panmuir, and within it Court..'' one to my sone.

24 November, Sounday.

Erl Rothes. This day, efter sermoun, the Countess of Mar and Erl Rothefl cam to sie my dauchter; and the Erl spak thir wordis to me, that the Commiffioner had perverted me.

29 November 1639, Fryday. Pacquet with Mr. Mr. James Gordoun went to Court, and gevin to him a pacquet to the anenTawUn' of Stirling, quhairin one to himself, one to Lord Panmuir, and one to my sone; with a letter to the Duik of Lenox anent Ylaw, and the insormatioun of my rycht befoir his; with a copy of both sent to my sone, to be communi-

cat to the Erl Stirling and Lord Panmuir. Last November 1639.

Thetaurer Deput The Thesaurer Deput went to Court, and sent with him a letter to the Erl Stirling.

1 December, Sounday, 1639. 2 December 1639. Walter Sieuart. Mett with Walter Stewart, consorme to the nott.

Item, letter sent with Mr. Alexander Belsches to my sone Mr. Alexander. My sone.

Item, this day, 2 December 1639, being Monoday, the report cam ofMr. John SpottUthe death of Mr. John Spottifwod, lait Chancellor; quhilk wes reportit at the buriell of Mr. Alexander Hayi8 dauchter, in presence of Sir Thomas Nicolsoun, quho thairvpoun sell out to speik of the bischoppis and abbotis jurisdictioun in the kirk.

3 December 1639.

John, sone to my Lord Lyndsay, baptisit: he was borne on day of Lord Lyndsay.

November, and he deceiffit in August 1640.

4 December 1639.

Report cam of the deceit off the Erll of Buchan at Court, on 4 dayis Erl Buchan. seiknes of a sever.

9 December 1639, Monoday. A pacquet sent be James Prymrois, quhairin I had thrie pacquets,Pacquett. one to Erl Stirling, and within it to the Thesaurer Deput, and to the Lord Annand, from the Erll his sather. Item, one to the L. Panmuir, quhairin a number of letters from Alexander Keyth and vthers. Item, a pacquet to my sone, quhairin one to James Levingstoun, to mak my excuse of not coming to Court till the spring. Item, from Sir Thomas and James to my sone. Item, from me to Mr. Maxwell, with letters from Patrik Scott, and therin the tak of Admirality of Dirltoun and Innerweik, to him from my Lord Duik's Grace. Item, in this also a letter to Captain Walter Captain Walter Steuart of Blantyre, and in cace of his absence, to my Lord Saltoun, anentSteuartthe buffines of Cragyvar; of quhilk letter I haif ane copy befyd me. 17 December 1639.

This day sent a packet to my sone, with letters from the Countess of Countess of Mar. Mar to the Lord Duik, Sir Robert Gordon, and some vtheris, quhilk wes delyverit to Captain Walter Steuart, quho tuik post this day and no foner, Captain Waiter so that my letter to him is befoir him. Steuart.

P 18 December 1639.

Eri Traquair his This day word cam that the Erl of Traquair Commiffioner wes to be in return from Court, pjjy *us* nycht.

19 December.

This day the certainty of the Commiffioners coming to Dalkeyth wes knowin.

27 December 1639, Fryday. Packett to my sone This day a packet sent to my fone or to the L. Panmuir, quhairin L. rpaVilmrderWldletters to Erl Stirling. Item, to the L. Panmuir, from the Countef l of Merschell and John Pilmuir. Item, to him, from myself, 2 letters, in ansuer of his ressauit on 12 and 16 December. Item, to my fone Mr. Alexander. Item, to him from James his brother. Item, to James Levingstoun, with a letter in it from Mr. George Noruell, for subscryving of the warrand of quhales mellit with be Sandsurd, as havand rycht, from Sir James Levingstoun of Kynnaird. This packet sent with ane Inglischeman callit Richard Wriglisworth, at the Croce Keyis in Watling Street of Londoun. 1 Januar 1640, Weddinsday. Packett. A packet to the L. Panmuir; within it to him, from the Countess of

Merschell, twa severall lettere. Item, to my sone. Item, to the Erl Stirling; all delyverit to Alexander Keyth on 3 Januar, and thai went not befoir Twysday the 7 of Januar, in a packet direct be James Prymrois, at the defyr off George Hadden. Erl Airth. Item, 9 Januar 1640, Thursday, delyverit twa packets, to the Erl Airth, to the L. Panmuir, with a letter from the Countess of Merschell to him.

14 Januar 1640.

Erl Rothes. *This* day, being Twysday, befoir 9 in the morning, the Erl of Rothes cam to my chamber, and with him Mr. Dauid Aytoun and Mr. John Smyth, and als one Mr. George Comming, merchand at Doles, and told me that he had reffavit a letter surth of Murray in sauors of Mr. George, quho is injustlie perfewit befoir the Justice for the slauchter off one John Piggott.

And thaireftir he schew me a trinkett of paper, quhilk he said he had drawin surth of a letter from Ingland, from ane good hand, quhilk he red to this sense: "I am forie to wrytt, that thair is a slap to come vpon the Advocat, sik as come the last 3eir vpon the Erl Ergyll, to draw vp *Juper inquirendis;* and thairfor, iff 3e haif any entres in him, bid him bewarr off himself."

My ansuer wes, "My Lord, I cair for nothing, I rest vpon the Lord; onlie I wische that God direct 30W, quho ar nobilmen, sua that 3 c may seik the mayne point, quhilk is Godis trewth, to be ratisiet, and lat the rest come as the Lord plesis."

He subjoynit, " That that swinger the Thesaurer hes so calumniat the haill estates to his Majestie, that albeit his Majestic wald ratine all the actis, we will not close till we gett justice vpon that traitor; and iff we gett justice, we sall rase him out off the erth; and if it be denyit, and thair be weir, we sall sueip his memorie surth of the land, and 3c sal be sully revengit off him."

I ansuerit, " My Lord, for Godis caus, latt not revenge aganis him move 30W to neglect Godis caus; and for my revenge, I leive it to God."

He ansuerit, " We haif gottin sull intelligence that the King will never quyt bischopes, but will haif them in again."

I ansuerit, "My Lord, latt no reportis move 30W, but do 3 our dewty; putt his Majestie to it, and if it be resusit, then 3 c ar wytles. But iff on thir reportis 3c preis civill pointis, his Majestie will mak all Protestant Princes sie that 3e haif not religioun for 3 our end, but the bering doun of monarchic."

With this I convoyit him to the 3ett, and I said, "For Godis caus, my Lord, haif a cair for ratifying religioun, and latt me be putt to ane effay in that, and 3 c sall sie quhat I sall do or suffer for it."

He ansuerit, "We never doubtit of yow in that; but 3e haif been sar out of the way this tyme bygain, and we had never a thocht to do you wrong."

I ansuerit, "I am more movit be one of your hard words nor with all the prejudice can be done to me; and for civill points, luik nevir to haif me to go with yow."

Item, this day, about 6 at nycht, I ressavit his Majestie's letter for confyning in Craighall, be reflbun of the story of James Grant's remiffioun, and off ane vther remiffioun to one John Steuart; vpon the reffait quhairof, I addreffit myself to Craighall. His Majestie's letter is daitit at Quhythall, 4 Januar 1640.

I was in Bruntiland a nycht, on Thursday the 16 of Januar. I cam to Craighall on Fryday the xvij of Januar, about 12 hours. My wyse, with the twa ȝoung barnis, cam to Craighall on Fryday the 14 of Februar, and went bak on Mononday the xvij of Februar. Item, on Mononday the 23 of Februar, scho, with all the rest of my samilie, cam to Craighall.

16 Merche 1640, Mononday. Packett. This day sent letters to the L. Panmuir and my fone Mr. Alexander, anent the quytting of my place, &c.; and thir sent to Edinburgh this day, in companie of my fone Craighall, quho went to Edinburgh with his bedsellow, vpon a letter from the Lords of Seffioun.

Item, this day putt ane pie in my rycht arme, quhairof the cautere wes putt in be Doctor Balfour and William Narn, on Mononday, 2 Merche, (at Craighall,) of befoir.

Erljkirlinps Item, at this tyme sure word cam of the death of the Erl Stirling.

23 Merche 1640., Packet sent to the L. Panmuir, with a letter to the Erl of Airth, and ane other to my fone Mr. Alexander; and the Erl of Airth wes anent Haltoun, and my fone's, to send me ane accompt of Sir David Cuningham's 1000 merks, and als to fend bak to me the precept of iijc sterling, presentit to Alexander Steuart; and this pacquet wes delyverit to the Lord Lyndsay, quho promisit to send it with one Capitan Ridpeth, quho cam laitlie from Court to Generall Ruthven.

Packett to L. Panmuir.

Last of Merche 1640.
Reflavit letters from L. Panmuir, and within it from the Erl Airth, daitit 24 Merche, and ansuerit the said last of Mercke, quhairof I sent the pacquet to Edinburgh with my wyff, to be gevin to my sone Sir Thomas, and be him to be dispatcht with the first sure occalioun, and be James Murray, if he will vndertak it.

1 April 1640, Weddinsday. Sent my pacquet to L. Panmuir with my wyff, quho this day went to Packet. Edinburgh, to close vp the voultis, and to sand the vpmost houlP, for seir of grenades. 12 April, Sounday. About 6 at nycht the Lord Saltoun and Walter Steuart cam heir. 13 April, Mononday. They returnit to Edinburgh about 3 hours efternone.

Item, this day gevin to Alexander Keyth a packet to the L. Panmuir, Packet, quhairin one to the Erl of Airth and one to Mr. Alexander, with a forme of ane alfignatioun to James of the iijc lb sterling contenit in the precept; and I defyrh L. Panmuir to certisie me if he reffavit mine of 16 Merche, and red it to his Majestie, anent the quyting of my place, and quhat wes his Majestie's ansuer.

1 May, Fryday, 1640.
The Countes of Rothes deceiffit.
Countes of Rothes.

17 May, Sounday, at 2 houres efternone, good Elizabeth Nicolsoun Elizabeth Nicoldeceiffit, and left me the only levand of the stok of John Hope, my guid-80unschir, in the degrie off thrid from him. The Lord prepare me. 28 May, Thursday, at 9 of the nycht, James Philp brocht me the Kingis Letter to me from Majestie's letter, commanding me to repair to Edinburgh; and I went on reEdin? Setterday, 30 May. burgh. 1 Junij 1640, Mononday. The Parliament could not prorogat for want of Commiffioners, and Parliament not the Estates satt from 2 Junij to 11 Junij inclusive. prorogat.

Battering of the
Castell.
Packet, 2 Junij
1640.
Packet, 9 Junij 1640.

Packet, 18 Junij 1640.
Packet, 25 Junij 1640.
On 12 Junij they enterit to batter the Castell of Edinburgh, and I returnit to Craighall Fry day.

The packet to his Majestie, anent the accompt of our proceidings in the prorogatioun of the Parliament, wes direct on 2 Junij, subscryvit be me and the Justice Clerk; and then I sent my ansuer to Lord Saltoun and his vncle.

Item, on 9 Junij, Mark Home, servitour to the Erl of Dunsermling, went to Court, with quhom I sent letters to the L. Panmuir, anent the manage of his dauchter with the Erll of Kinghorn.

Item, packet from Craighall to the L. Panmuir, and within it one from the Countes of Merfchell to him. Item, one from me to Mr. Alexander, and within it one to the Lord Saltoun, expostulating for the warrand to James Abirnethy; and this packet sent with my sone Mr. James, (quho went to Edinburgh on 18 Junij, being Thursday,) to be gevin to James Murray, ȝounger, to get it sent to the L. Panmuir.

Item, reffavit letters from the L. Panmuir, daitit 15 Junij 1640, vpon Thursday, 25 Junij, and ansuerit immediatlie; and the packett sent with my sone, (Craighall,) quho went to Edinburgh on Fryday, 26 Junij, with letters to James Murray, younger, to dispatche the samyn to the L. Panmuir; and within them is the copie of the letter to the Justice Clerk, anent the filling of the blank for the Parliament; with a letter to be schawin be the Lord to his Majestie thairanent.

Lord Leslie, Weddinsday the 15 of July.
Thursday, 16 July.
20 July, my sones went with the) annie, and my promise to recommend it to God. 1 July 1640, Weddinsday.

The Lord Leslie and his pedagog, Mr. James Wilsoun, came to Craighall at 10 hours, and abaid till 3 efternone, on Weddinsday, 15 July.

Item, this nycht, about 9 hours at nycht, *ira*fo£io-fof; and I haif folemnlie vowit to my Lord to absteyne from all occasioun, and if any be offence to me, to neglect it till I powrit it befoir my

Lord in prayer. This on Thursday, 16 July.

Item, the armie wes to merche out of Edinburgh on Mononday the 20 of July, and in it my two fones and Cambuskynneth; and in respect thairoff, I promisit to the Lord a restraint of thingis vtherwayis lawsull, and to recommend the neceffitie of in helth. (This promisit on 17 and 19 July, being Fryday and Sounday.).

I August 1640, Setterday.

II August 1640, Twysday. *Novus* (Oektoj; quhairvpon I renewit my former, made 16 July. 21 August, Fryday, the armie corsit Tweid. August. 24 August 1640, Mononday. This day James Murray cam from Angus, and I gave to him a letter to the L. Panmuir, and defyrit him to fend with it other two, quhiDc I sent to my sone Craighall, being at Edinburgh, (Prelident of the Committee of Parliament,) quhairof one 16, 19 August, and the vther 22 August. 28 August 1640, Fryday. Our armie corsit Tyne, and discomfitit the Inglis troupes that did prohibit Crock Tyne. them; and this samyn day the Castell of Dumbartan randerit. 28 AugU8t' *ft* day, Dumbartan

Castle randerit.

29 August, Setterday, they tuik in Neucastell. 30 August 1640, being Sounday, at nycht, a part off the place of Dunglas Dunglas bWin wes blowin vp with powder, and thairin diet Erl Hadingtoun, Robert hisvpbrother, Cornel Alexander Erskin, Reidhous, Gogar, Inglistoun; and Sir Gideoun Baillie, and Prestoungrange, hurt. 1 September 1640, Twysday. This day I gatt a letter from my fone Sir Thomas, daitit at Rytounsurd, Le"" from *Si 3* 6 ... Thomas anent the 29 August 1640, declaring the particulars of thair happie victorie, andvietorie at Neuintaking of Neucastell. CttStelL 15 September 1640, Twysday. U f Ed The Castell of Edinburgh randerit vp be Generall Ruthven, Capitan burgn randerit. thairoff. ,,.. _ L

Melting at York,

Meiting at 3or of e Peiris of Ingland, to gif anfuer to the supplica-24 September 1640.

tioun sent to his Majestie from Neucastell, and the Scottis armie thair mett, on Thursday, 24 September.

Thairefter a treatie at Ripont, within 10 myles to Allartoun, betuix some of the Inglische and Scottis nobility, held on Thursday the first day of October.

1 October 1640, Thursday. Meiting at Ripont. Thus day wes the meiting at Ripont, betuix the Inglische and Scottis nobilitie. 8 October.

This day I gatt word of the death of my good Erll of Annandaill, at Londoun, quho wes my derest lord and freind: God prepare me. He departit 22 September 1640, being Twysday.

Erl Annandaill decebsit.

Words hard.

12 October 1640, Mononday. This day, being greivit for the report of the diuisioun in the camp, occasionat be the Erl of MontrorP, I wes humbly supplicating the Lord, (remembring the words qululk I hard 22 September 1639;) and efter falling in a slumber, I seymit to heir thir words, " Aflc still, and the end salbe glorious." And efter walking and bliffing the Lord, I sell in slumber agane, and hard thir words, " And yow sal l fie it." The Lord in mercie performe it in his awin good tyme. 24 October 1640, Setterday. Ripont. This day letters from Sir Thomas, my sone, from Neucastell, daitit 20 October, quhairin he tellis the Kingis granting to them of 2500 sterling monethly, (during the treaty;) and had past commiffion vnder the Great Seil l (of) Ingland, to theis of the nobilitie quho wes namit of befoir, to end and conclud with thair Commiffioners; and that his Majestie wes gone to Londoun to prepair for the Parliament, quhilk sitts doun thair on 3 November nixt. Blissit be the Lord, and God in mercie gif the buslines a happie closing. 28 October, Weddinsday. My dauchter and My fone m£ dauchter, with the bairnes, went from Craighall to Bruntiland.

Item, Mungo Murray cam to Craighall with a letter from the Erll of Mungo Murray. Annandaill acquainting me with the death of his deir sather, and wald not stay but went to Falkland, and he told me that his Majestie wes gone from York on Mononday last to Londoun, and that my fone Alexander was gone with his Majestie.

1 November, Sounday. On 5 November, being Thursday, I returned from Craighall to Edin-Retumit to Edin "burgh.

burgh.

On 11 November a packet sent to the L. Panmuir, and within it one Packet to L. to him from the Countes of MerfchelL and also one from me to my sone, Mr. Alexander. Alexander, and within it one from Mr. James, his brother, to him with ane accompt of the Sj" merks reffavit from Alexander Stewart for his pensioun of Mertimes 1638 and Whitsounday 1639. This packet delyuerit to James Philp, quho wes to direct it, on Thursday, 12 November, at 2 efternone. Item, in it is a letter to James, now Erll of Annandaill.

Memorandum.—Efter I had closit and delyuered this pacquet to James Mr. Alexander cam (-1 _.. to Edinburgh from

Philp, quhilk wes on Thursday, 12 November 1640, being about nyneYorki2 November houres, my fone, Mr. Alexander, cam into me about ten houres in the morning, and I retired my pacquet and tuik surth Mr. Alexander his letters, and gaif them to himself.

Mr. Alexander came on Thursday, 12 November, having in companie Returnit to Court ,..on Setterday 14 with him one Mr. Samuell Dauidsoun, second sone to Sir Alexander Dauid-November 1640.

soun off Blakstoun, quho did propone to me, in name off Sir William Fennick off Meldin, the marriage of his daughter with my fone, and thai returned home on Setterday, 14 November, and I gave to my fone xx tuelf pund pieces, and promisit, if the Lord spared me, so long as I wer abill, to relieff him of Sir David Cuningham's debt, and iff the Lord callit on me, to leive my mynd thairanent to my son Craighall; and als I told Mr. Alexander off my contracts of Saltoun, and promisit if I gatt that vi00 iiij Sb from the L.

Saltoun to gif it to him. Item, Mr. James advancit to him 50 doubill angells.

19 November 1640, Thursday. Parlia-

ment. This day the Parliament mett, and without sencing, honors, or robbis, cheisit the Lord Burley president, and continewit the Parliament till 14 of Januar 1641.

Anna Foules de lyuerit.
Lord Boyd.
21 November 1640. Anna Foules delyuerit of a man child, being Setterday, baptizit Thomas. Item, this nycht advertisement cam of the death off the good Lord Boyd, at his hous of Kilmarnok. 1 December, Twysday, 1640. 8 December 1640, Twysday, pacquet gevin to James Philp, direct to the L. of Panmuir, and in it answer to the Marques of Hamiltoun his sals challenge. Item, letters to Mr. Alexander, my sone, and within a letter to the Lord Saltoun (quhairof I haif reservit a copy) to answer to betuix 15 Januar 1641.

Item, sent with this packet annext thairto, ane pacquet to be delyuerit to my sone Sir Thomas at Neucastell, quhairin thair is the complaint quhich L. Lamingtoun recommendit from the committee heir, with ane new supplicatioun to be followit their aganis him.

Item, this day sent a letter to the Erll of Caithnes, requyring the byruns of the lu for xxvi 3eir extending to xiije lb., affuring him if he do not tak ordor with it betuix and Candlemes next, that I will be forcit to persew. Sent by David Monro to Commiffar of Caithnes. Item, a second letter sent with G. Sinclair, his base sone, 29 December 1640.

My sone Sir Thomas cam from Neucastell to Edinburgh on 14 December 1640, being Mononday, about 4 hours at evin.

Item, on Sounday befoir, being 13 December, and thairefter, being 20 December, I tuik the holy communion at Edinburgh, and on the Thursday befoir, being 10 December, I renewit my vow to the Lord, quhilk I pray God gif me grace to keep.

Pacquet sent be James Philp on 23 December, Weddinsday, quhairin I sent letters to the L. Panmuir, in answer of his of 14 December, reffavit 22 December 1640, and within it one to him from the Countes of Merschell.
31 December 1640, Thursday.

Item, sent to Robert Bennet in Craighall warrand for selling the beir of Hiltarbat and Seres, and the myll, and promisit him jc merks for his paynes.

Item, this day I sent letters to James Philp, to the L. Panmuir, and Pacquet. my sone Mr. Alexander, to be sent in his pacquet, but he excusit himself be his letter to me that he could not direct the pacquet till Setterday thairefter.
1 Januar 1641, Fryday. 1641.

This day gevin letters to James Philp to the L. Panmuir and my sone, Pacquet. quhilk he promisit to direct quicklie; but upon advertisement from the Lady Marqueffe of Hamiltoun, he defferit.
5 Januar 1641, Huis diei nocte insequente insomnium horribile, quasi reus maiestatis incusatus, et carceribus tradendus; sed persugio evafi—Deo fit omnis gloria. Fuit et aliud insomnium ante 2 Januar 1641, quasi densa caligine interceptus in hortis petrocellanis; sed cum clamore evigilavi, Deum invocans in mei auxilium. 7 January 1641, Payit to David Gourlay jc merks, quhilk he affirmit to David Gourlay. be awin to him of the pryce off his tenement sauld to my son Sir Thomas, and this gevin be him to his sone Thomas Gourlay quhen he was going surth off the country. 8 January 1641, Gevin to hir xxv dollors to gif to Mr. G. Bennet, for hir sister. Item, this day takin Mr. David Crausurd in service till Witsounday nixt, Mr. David Crau surd in presence of Mr. Patrick Crausurd, his brother, and Mr. Richard Keir, for meit and clothe.

Memorandum on 7 Januar 1841. I reffavit letters from the L. Pan-Packet, muir, advertising me that his Majestie had sent letters to me for continewing the Parliament till 13 April. But because James Philp sand them not, both he and I wret instantlie of the want of them, and this pacquet went on Thursday, 7 Januar 1641.
Packet.
Lord Panmuir.
Countes of Mar.
L. Lamingtoun.
11 Januar 1641, Mononday.

This day a pacquet to L. Panmuir, quhairin a packet to the Erl Rothes', and within it the Countes of Mar hir packet,

and my letter to the Erll conveying it, and giving him thanks for his savour (by my knauledge) in deilling with the Marques, and augmenting the Marques his injust indignatioun and outrages, but remittis them to God. Item, letters to the L. Panmuir, and within one from the Countes of Merschell. Item, in myne to him, I recommend the gift of eschiet of L. Lamingtoun. Item, letters to my fone, Mr. Alexander, from me, and within the gift of L. Lamingtoun, his escheit. Item, his brother, Mr. James, his letter to him for that caus.

This packet delyverit to James Philp on Mononday at night, but went not quhill Twysday 12 Januar 1641.
Parliament.
My oy Thomas.
13 Januar 1641.

Reffavit letters from his Majestie, daitit last December 1640, for prorogatioun of the Parliament to the 13 April nixt.

Memorandum on the night preceiding this 13 Januar I dreamit that I had in my hand ane rigne with ane pointed dyamond thairin, and that I lost my pointit diamond, quhilk putt me in ane great seir, becaus my nephoy Thomas, fone to Craighall, wes sick of the pockis. But the Lord had mercie on him, for he beguid to recover on Twysday, the 19 Januar. Bleffit be the Lord.
Prorogation of
Parliament to 13
April 1641.
14 Januar 1641, Thursday. This day the Parliament prorogat (but sencing) to the 13 April nixt.
15 Januar 1641.

Pacquet direct to the Erl Lanerk, Secretar, quhairin one to his Majestie anent the prorogation of the Parliament to 13 April 1641. Item, one to the Secretar, and within it my accompt to his Majestie, subseryvit be me, of the proceidings anent the prorogatioun of Parliament, to be schawin be the Secretar to his Majestic Item, twa letters to the L. Panmuir, quhairof the one to be schawin to his Maj estie, concerning myloffis and sufferingis, with a copie of his Majestie's letter, and a copie of myaccompt to his Majestie. Item, Anent Mr.

Alexletters to Mr. Alexander from me and Sir Thomas, and in myne to him the er my S e copie of his Majestie's letter, becaus the end of it beirs a petitionn for the supplie of Mr. Alexander. Item, a letter to James Livingstoun, defyring him to fpeik his Majestie anent my loffis and sufferingis, quhairof he is to reffaif a nott from Mr. Alexander off that quhilk I wrett to the L. Panmuir.

19 Januar 1641, Twysday. This day pacquet sent be James Philp at 3 efternone, quhairin from me Packett. to Erl of Lanerk, with the instruments of production of his Majestie's letter,19 Januar 1641and the copie of the Act of Prorogatioun. Item, to L. Panmuir, with a letter from the Countes of Merschell, and with the copies off the baihje of Brichen his petitioun to the Committee, for a localitie to the Minister of his stipend out of the teinds payit to the Bifchop, with a copie of my letter to the Erll of Lanerk, anent the calumnie, that I movit and framit the protestatioun agains Erl Traquair. Item, letter to Mr. Alexander, and within it one from Mr. James. 20 Januar 1641, Weddinsday. Reffavit 2 letters from the L. Panmuir anent my sending for to court, L. Panmuir. Packett quhilk I ansuerit instantlie, and gaif to James Philp for his pacquett. 27 Januar 1641, Weddinsday. This day reffavit letters from the Erll off Lanerk and L. Panmuir, Pacquet. quhilk I ansuerit immediatlie, and sent a pacquet be James Philp, quhilk went on Thursday, 28 Januar 1641, with a letter to Mr. Alexander, and one from Mr. James to him. 28 Januar 1641, Thursday. This nycht my oy Thomas, (efter he was convalescit of the pockis,) tuik a My o-Thomas. litill bastard sever, quhilk patt us in greit seir. But I powrit my heart befoir the Lord, and humbly prayed for him, as being the comfort of my lyff.

My sone Mr. Alexander.
29 January 1641.

Reffavit letters from my fone, Mr. Alexander, daitit 16 Januar, with the Lord Saltoun's letter, returnit to me becaus he wes going to Spayne with his uncle Walter.

1 Februar 1641, Mononday. Pacquett.

Letters writtin to Court, sent in James Philp his pacquet, viz. to L.

Panmuir, advertiling him off the treatty betuix Erl Kinghorne and the lady, sister to Erl Kintyre, and with it letters from Alexander Keyth to him. Item, a pacquet to Mr. Alexander, in ansuer of his reffavit 29 January, from me, Sir Thomas, and Mr. James. My letters ar daittit 4 Februar 1641, and sent in pacquet on Fryday, 6 Februar 1641.

Letter from the committee anent the bill offorfaltour.
Packett.
10 Feb. 1641. 9 Februar 1641.

Delyverit to me be James Philp, packet from the L. of Panmuir, daitit 4 Februar 1641, with letters to the Countes of Merschell and John Pilmuir, quhilk I delyverit to Alexander Keyth, with a letter to himself. To be directit away with surety and difpatch.

Item, this nycht about 6 hours, I had a letter from the Committee delyverit to me be George Hadden, with 2 bills to be subscryvit for sumonding the Erl Traquair, Clerk-Register, President, D. Balcanquall, Erl Nithsdaill, Sir Lues Steuart, and vthers, befoir the Parliament, to the 13 of April nixt, to heir and sie them forsalt and punishit for thair crymes and malversations; and I excusit myself that I could not do it without his Majestie's warrand, and wret a letter to that effect, quhairoff the copie is within the letter sent me be the committee.

Item, immediatlie I wret to James Philp, to direct a pacquet to quhom on 10 of February, being Weddinsday, I schew my letter to me from the committee, with my ansuer, and delyverit to him ane pacquet to L. Panmuir, within quhilk is a letter to him from the Countes of Merfchell. Item, my ansuer anent the permit of the Erl Traquair, that I wes refoluit not to do it without his Majestie's warrand.

Item, efter the wryting off my letter, quhilk I defyrit to be red to his Majestie, is the postscript anent the letter writtin to me from the committee, with my ansuer. Item, letters to Mr. Alexander, quhairin one to the Erl of Airth, excusing my not wryting. Item, letters to Mr. Alexander from Sir Thomas, and vthers

from Mr James to him.
13 February 1641.

This day being Setterday, my nephew Hary Hope saillit to Diep, and on Hary Hope Fryday befoir, quhen he tuik his leve of me, I told him that I wald pay toHeTurnedbak his mother 3eirly 101b sterling, and gaif him 5 pieces for the first termand saillit not till thairoff. The Lord bliffe him in his voyage, and send him ane happie tenlayTeli but returne. He went last on 8 Merche 1641. returnit thairefter.

Item, on this xiij of February, pacquet sent be me to the Erl of Lanerk, Pacquet from in quhilk wes a letter to himself anent the proceiding in the sumonds ofmyselftreafoun aganis Erl of Traquair and vtheris, and a pacquet to the L. Panmuir, quhairin a letter to be schawin to his Majestie anent my behaviour in the saids sumondis of treafoun, and beiring, that if the tyme wer proper, I Pacquet, i3Febwald supplicat his Majestie for reddrette ot my loftis, and my tone Mr. Alex-Sent my ander; but in respect of the tymis, will wait on better. Item, a letter to Mr. Alexander, with ane insormatioun of his brother's right off the leid mynes, and L. Lamingtoun his oppreffioun. Item, a forme of ane band to be gevin to the Erl Lanerk, quho hes stop the gift of escheit of Lamingtoun vpon his brother's horning, quhairof I haif the doubil befyd me.

17 Februar 1641, Weddinsday. Sent in James Philp his pacquet letters to the L. Panmuir, with one Pacquet, 17 Feb. from the Countes, and hire to me, quhilk beirs the calumnie anent the protestatioun. Item, letters to Mr. Alexander from me and Sir Thomas. Item, letters to the Erll of Annandaill anent his service, and to Thomas Maxwell, all daittit 16 February 1641, with letters from Mr. Alexander Burnet to my lord, and the procuratory for his service. Item, sent in this pacquet ane letter to the L. of Panmuir from James Murray, quhairin thair is one from the Erl Kinghorne to the L. of Panmuir.

Item, this 17 February, reffavit letters from L. Panmuir and my sone, daitit 11 February 1641, and ansuerit immediatlie in this samyn pacquet, quhilk wes not 3 it away quhen thir letters cam.

22 February 1641, Mononday. Packet. This day a pacquet gevin to James Philp direct to the L. Panmuir, with one to him from the Countes of Merschell. Item, ane vther from hir ladyship to him, quhilk cam this day befoir the going of the pacquet, daitit 19 February 1641, and an vther from John Pilmuir; and in myne I tell him, that I haif seine his sone's patent, but thinks it not fitt to sist William Gray, quhil first the lard prepair for himself workhouffis, leist the patent suffer. Item, writtin to him anent Robert Maul, his non entry. Item, anent my greiff be Mr. Alexander, his purpose to sell his place. Item, anent the deforcement of the leid myne. Item, letters to Mr. Alexander from Sir Thomas and Mr. James, quhairin a not of my rent, to schaw my inhability, but no letter at this tyme from me to Mr. Alexander. 24 February 1641. Relict of Mr. William Struther deceillit. 26 February 1641. David Jonkyn. David Jonkin tutor to my dauchter Anne Foulcs deceillit. 1 Merche 1641, Mononday. Ansuer of my This day reffavit letteris from the Erll of Lanerk, in ansuer of my pacquet pacquet off 18 Fe-.,,

bruary, quhilk cam lent 13 ebruar.

in 5 dayis, for it wes item, 2 letters from the Lord Panmuir, both daitit 22 Februar 1641, with delyverit at Court 18 February. a letter to Henrie Maul, quhilk I gave to Alexander Keyth, and ane vther to the Countes Merschell, quhilk I am to delyver to her awin servand.

Item, reffavit from the L. Panmuir the warrand off his ratisicatioun in Parliament, and my awin also, quhilk he reffavit from Erl Traquhair.

2 Merche 1641.

Delyuerit to James Philp my ansuer to the Erl of Lanerk, quhairin Ipacquet. excuse my sone, Mr. Alexander, for pasting escheit of L. Lamingtoun by him. Item, I promise not to affift the accusatiounes in Parliament without his Majeflie's expres warrand, and I crave returne of my pacquet to myself immediatelie, for preserving of my privilege ones or twyis in the 3eir.

Item, letters to L. Panmuir, and within it one from the Countes of Merschell, and als the draucht of a letter for the soap works.

Item, a letter to my sone Mr. Alexander, and within it one to him from Cambuskynneth; and a pacquet from the Countes of Marr to Erl Rothes, or hir sone Scottiscraig, quhilk I haif appointit my sone Mr. Alexander to delyver.

Item, twa letters to the Erl of Annandaill, and one from Mr. Alexander Burnet to him, schawing that the penult of Merche is appointit for his Lordship's service.

7 Merche 1641, Sounday. At xi hours befoir none Alisoun Rig, fpous to Mr. John Skene, deceiffit. ir j0iin Skein, his wife. 9 Merche, Twysday.

Letters writtin to the L. Panmuir, my sone, and Erll of Annandaill, Pacquet. quhilk all putt in an pacquet direct to the L. Panmuir, and delyverit to James Philp on Weddinsday, 10 Merche 1641; and within it an to the L. Panmuir from me, the Countes of Merschell, and Alexander Keyth. Item, in that to my sone is myne. Item, from his brother James, and within myne is one to Sir James Galloway, secretar, and also to the Erl of Annandaill and Thomas Maxwell. But this pacquet went not till Fryday, the 12 of Merche 1641.

Item, this day reffavit letters from my sone Mr. Alexander, with letters to his brother Mr. James, quhairin wes the twa signatours past and signed be his Majestie, one of the L. of Lamingtoun, his escheit takin to Mr. Mynes of Watter-Alexander, and in his name, and the vther of the lands and mynes of Waterheid, takin also to Mr. Alexander, his airs and affignees, vpoun Mr James and his fpous resignatioun with ane gift *de Novodamus*.

Item, 10 Merche, reffavit vtheris letteris from him, daitit 21 Februar 1641, quhilk both I haif ansuerit in this last pacquet, quhilk went not till Fryday the 12 of Merche 1641; and in this I haif acquaintit my sone with Cobburnfpeth's defyr anent the gift of Postmaister.

19 Merche 1641, Fryday. L. Panmuir. (Becaus James Philp delayit to send pacquett till he gatt ansuer of his former pacquet,) thairfoir I having befyd me 2 letteris of the Countes of Merschell to the L. Panmuir, and hering that James Patoun, sumtyme servitor to James Nasmyth, wes going post to Court, I sent to him a letter to the L. Panmuir, within quhilk wes theis 2 letteris from the Countes of MerschelL 22 Merche 1641.

Pacquet. Reffavit a number of letteris from the L. Panmuir and my sone, quhilk cam to me on Sounday at nicht 21 Merche, and sent to the Countes of Merschell, to John Pilmuir, to Dauid Souter all thir inclosit in one to Alexander Keyth quho wes at Montroifs, and writtin ansuer to the lard's letter and my sone's, and sent to him the non entry of Robert Maull, with a letter from one vnknawin to me, but quhilk William Mudie brocht me,

Mr. James Hope, and als ane letter to my sone, with one from Mr. James, quho went this day to Lanerk for the leid mynes.

23 Merche 1641. Item, on 23 Merche, being Twysday, reffavit letteris from the Countes of Merschell, quhairof one to the L. Panmuir, and ane vther to the Erll of Airth, quhilk I sent with one to aither of tham from myself, and thair letters inclosit, and thir went with this samyn pacquet on 23 Merche 1641. 27 Merche 1641, Setterday. Letteris sent to the Secretar, in ansuer of his reffavit 26 Merche, quhilk cam in the pacquet of 22 Merche, but wes inclosit in his to Mr Hary Maull, quho wes at Hamiltoun, and cam not to me till 26 Merche.

Item, letteris to L. Panmuir, and within it one from the Countes of Merschell, quhilk cam to me 26 Merche, and nothing els into it except letters from Mr James to his brother, with ane gift and dimiffioun of Mr. of Work.

Item, sent in this pacquet, quhilk went not till 29 Merche, I sent one from the Lord Oxinsurd Mr Henry Futhie.

Item, this 29 Merche, efter the going of the pacquet, I rcffavit a letter from the Countes of Merschell, and ane vther from Patrick Murray, servito r to the Erll of Kinghorne, quho delyverit a letter from the Erll to the L. L. Panmuir. Panmuir, quhilk I tuik, and pat both the letters in pacquet, and gaif them Sent with William to William Douglas, fone to James callit Nikftikks, servitor to the

Erll of Douglas of GoKarMortoun, quho went this day post, being 29 Merche, about fix hours at nycht.

Reffavit, 30 Merche 1641, letter from his Majestie, with one to the Par-Letter from his liament for continewing of it till 25 May 1641. Majestie.

Item, packet from myself to the Erll of Lanerk, certiseing off the reffait off Packett from myhis Majestie's letteris, and that I gatt not a copie off that to the Parliament, April 1641 nor any word from him thairanent, and craving to knaw his Majestie's pleffur quhat I fould do if the summondis be red in Parliament, being (in) my name, if I fould protest agains it. This sent on Fryday, 2 April, at 12 hours at none.

Item, sent letters to the L. Panmuir, quhairin to Mr. Alexander from me and Mr. James, with the Commiffioners letter to pay to the L. Panmuir 500 Ib sterling, quhilk he is to pay to Erl Stirling quhen he paffes the gift vnder the greit scill to Mr. James of the place of Mr. of Wark.

8 April 1641, Thursday. This day L. Sandsurd went journey to Neucastell, and from thence to L. Sandsord Londoun, and sent with him letters from me and my dauchter Kerf to my journey"6TM Wenl fone Sir Thomas. Item, letters to L. Panmuir, and within it one to him from the Countes of Mersehell. Item, one to James Livingstoun, and last one to my sone Mr. Alexander, defyring him to follow L. Sandsuird his counsell, both in his awin and in Mr. James his particulars. Pacquet direct to Item, this 8 of April 1641, about 10 hours at nicht, ressavit from James Erl Lanerk Sccreuncan, postmaister in the Cannogait, ane packet direct to me from the Erll of tar, daitit 4 April Lanerk, Secretar, daitit 4 April 1641, and reflavit this 8 April, Thursday, on8 ApriireSSaVIt betuix 9 and 10 of nicht, and in it a letter from the Secretar, telling me that the letter to the estates for prorogating of the Parliament was delyverit to the Commiffioners to be sent to me, and thairwith he dois fend me the copie off it, and the vther letteris wer to a number of vtheris, quhilk I delyverit to the postmaister to gif to them to quhom thai wer

directit, except theis to myself, from the L. Panmuir and from my sone Mr Alexander. 12 Aprill, Monondday, 1641. Pacquet to my self This day, about 8 in the morning, ressavit a packett to my self from the quhilkTsent 2 Erl of Lanerk, Secretar, in ansuer of that quhilk I sent on 2 Aprill 1641, APril-and in it ressavit a letter from his Majestie, daitit 6 April, commanding me not to insist nor affist the summondis of treasoun at this dyet of Parliament, 13 April 1641, quhilk holdis to-morow. 13 April 1641. Parliament proro. This day, being Twysday, the Parliament prorogat to 25 May 1641, Lord Sell0and y «wt hurley, President; and I sent ane pacquet to the Erll of Lanerk, Secretar, sent be me to the about 2 afternone, quhairin to his Majestie, with a minut of the proceidingis, Secretar3"" ' becaus I could not haif the act so sone. Item, to the Secretarie, and within his letter the minut. Item, to the L. Panmuir, and within his one from Sent be me a pac-the Countes of Mersehell. Item, one to Mr Alexander from me, and ane 1641.18 vther from Mr James. Item, a letter to the Erl of Annandaill, and ane vther to Thomas Maxwell anent my Lord's service, quhilk past on penult off Merche 1641, at Lochmaben. Item, a packet from Mr. Alexander Burnet to the Erl of Annandaill. Item, ane pacquet from Mr. James Aikinheid to John Squyre, sumtyme servitor to the Erl Stirling, and now to Erl Lanerk, quhairin is his ansuer to Sir James Galloway; and I sent at this samyn time a letter to Sir James, in ansuer of his to me, quhilk I inclosit in my letter to my sone Mr Alexander.

Item, this 13 April 1641, at 6 of nycht, a pacquet cam to James Philp, Ressavit further a daitit 8 April, quhairin I had tuo letters from L. Panmuir, ane of 3 new pacquet the r ' said 13 April 1641,

AprylL with letters to the Countes of Merfchell and to John Pilmuir, and at 6 at nycht.

the vther daitit 8 April 1641, within quhilk was inclosit one from his Majestie, to quhilk I must mak ansuer sa sone as I haif performit quhat is commanded thairin.

Item, about the samyn tyme reffavit a letter from my sone Sir Thomas, Deane ofWinfrom Neucastell, and within it one quhilk he had gottin from his brother Mr che9ter'Doctor . _ . John Young.

Alexander to me, quhilk had within it from Doctor John Young, dein of Winchester, anent Sergeant Young.

Item, in the pacquet direct be James Philp on Weddinsday, 14 Apryll, I pæquet u April sent a letter to the Erl Lanerk, and within it the act of prorogatioun, sub-dirfct James scry vit be young Durie; and als sent ansuer to Doctor Young, and within it one to my sone, within quhilk wes one to L. Panmuir, schawing that I had ressavit his of 3 and 8 April, and asking his opinioun of 2 pointis (1) if the copie can not be had, if he that my ansuer beir the impoffi bility (2) anent the supplie of the Mearnis.

17 April 1641, Setterday.

Reffavit letters from the Erl of Airth of 12 April, with one to the Countes gri Airth and of Merschel. Item, letters from the L. Panmuir, and within it one to the Lard PanmuirCountes of 9 April, quhilk sent by Alexander Keyth.

Item, letters from Doctor John Young, dean of Winchester, with serjant *ntor* John

David Young of Downachar, seriand of his Maieltie's scullarie. his band ofYoun&' Deanof 6 " Winchester.

25200 merks, payabill at Mertimess 1640, and 7000 merks of penalty to be put in register. Item, a letter to L. Coffinis and David Lyndsay of Kyn nettles, his brother-in-law. 21 April 1641, Weddinsday. This day James Philp sent away a pacquet, quhairin wes my letters to

Ansuertohis the L. Panmuir, and within them one to his Majestic in ansuer of that

Majesties letter....-,.

reliavit 13 Aprill, at b ot nycht, with ane accompt of my diligence for a Item, to L. Pan-copie, &c. Item, a letter from the Countes of Merschell to L. Panmuir. toDcanof WlnItem, a letter from me to tne Eru of Airth. Item, a letter from me to Dean Chester, and my 0ff Winchester, and one from me to my sone Mr.

Alexander. sone. 29 April 1641, Thursday. Ressavit from William Dowglas, sone to James of Gogar, letters from the ivitfromWU-paruxmir, and within them to Countes of Merschell, Erl Kinghoroe, liam Douglas. #....

L. Lour, John Pilmuir, with ane litill pacquet in hardin, quhilk all directit, viz. to Erl Kinghorne, with David Lindsay of Kinnettles, inclosit in one from myself. Item, to the Countes, delyuerit to Alexander Keyth, inclosit in one from myself, and sent to Stirling, the lady being thair. Item, to L. Lour, his gevin to Mr. George Noruell, quho past him, being at the Committee.

Pacquet.

L. Panmuir.

Last April 1641.

Sent in James Philp his pacquet letters to the L. Panmuir, and within them 2 from the Countes of Merschell, and ane from James Murray younger. Item, ane thairefter anent Keyth.

1 May 1641, Setterday. Pacquet ansuer of Th'8 7 tne pacquet from the Secretar, Erl of Lanerk, to James Philp, that quhilk went daitit 26 Apryll. at 9 of nycht, and James Duncan, the postmaister, brocht on 21 April 1641..,..,.. 2 i x,,. to me about 8 in the morning 3 letteris, viz. , one from Lrl Lanrek, bering that his Majestie was sully satiffiet with my cair and diligence in proroguing of the Parliament. Item, one from L. Panmuir of 24 April, with one from him to Hary Maul of Melgum, quhilk I inclolit in one from me to John Pilmuir, and gaif it to Alexander Keyth to be sent away. Item, one from my sone Mr Alexander, daitit 26 April, bering the ressait of myne of 19 April, quhilk went with James Philp his pacquet, on 21 April, and my sone wryt tis to me, that myne to the L. Panmuir (in quhilk wes inclosit my letter to his Majestie,) quhairoff mentioun is maid on the vther fyd in the pacquet of 21 April, but that the L. Panmuir could not gif ansuer thairoff with this pacquet.

Item, this nycht, betuix xi and xij, my dauchter, the Lady Cambuskynneth, i May 1641, my delyuerit of a man child. Bliffit be God, and the Lord bliffe him; and lyerirofson6 gevin to Jean Cuningham, midwyff, 1 doubell angell.

Item, 10 May 1641, Mononday, pacquet sent be James Philp, and in itioMay 1641. ane letter to the Erl Lanerk, with thanks for his letter, and that I expectitPackettto heir that he wes satiffiet with my fone Mr. Alexander. Item, with his pacquet to the L. Panmuir, with 2 from the Countes of Merschell. Item, to the Erl of Annandaill and Thomas Maxwell, and within his one from Mr. Alexander Burnet to the Erll of Annandaill. Item, one to my fone Mr. Alexander, from my self, and excusing Mr. James becaus he was and is at Leidmynes this 15 dayis.

Item, at 3 afternone a new pacquet of letters cam from the Countes of Merschell to the L. of Panmuir, quhilk I inclosit with a letter to him from my self, and sent by Alexander Keyth to James Philp, about 4 eftfernone, to be putt in this day's pacquet.

11 May 1641, Twysday. Marie Fleming, my proneice, spouse to Alexander Maxwell, departit at Marie Fleming de 6 in the morning. ceissitItem, this day, about 7 hours at evin, a packet cam to James Philp, daitit Packett. 7 May 1641, quhairin I had letters from the L. Panmuir, with a pacquet to the Countes os Merschell, (quhilk I chargit Alexander Keyth send the samyn nycht, inclosit in one of my awin to Seytoun, quhair the Countes wes

this nycht.) Item, one to John Pilmuir, quhilk I haif gevin to Alexander Deputie declarit

Keyth to send to him. Item, letters from the Erll of Annandaill and4"1101--

Thomas Maxwell to me anent a blank affignatioune to a debt auchtand be Robert Ellot, &c.

Item, the L. Panmuir grantis the ressait of myne of 29 April, but L. Panmuir. fpeikis nothing off that singel letter quhilk I sent anent Keyth quhilk I sent to James Philp, and he promisit to inclose in one of his awin.

17 May. . Erl Straffurd, de

Word cam of the beheiding of Thomas, Erll of Straffurd, deputie of Ire-putie of Ireland, beheidit.

Packet.

land, in the Tour-hill of London, on Weddinsday 12 May, and the King and Queen went to quhairvpon I gatt letters from the L. Panmuir and my sone, daittit 12 May, reffavit 18 May 1641.

Sent in James Philp his pacquet 17 May 1641, being Mononday, letters to the L. Panmuir, and within it the Erl of Kinghorne his ansuer. Item, lettres from the Countes of Merfchell. Item, letters to my fone, and within from James, and als letters to the Erll of Annandaill and Thomas Maxwell from my self and Mr. Alexander Burnet.

Communion.

Parliament prorogat to 15 July 1641.

23 May, Sounday.

Communicat in Cramond, quhair at tabill (being in great anxietie) I reffavit this comfort, (My grace is sufficient for ye,) for quhilk I bliffe the Lord.

This nycht, (being in Grantoun,) about 8 at nycht, I reffavit letters from the Erl of Lanerk, daitit 18 May, with a copie of his Majeflie's letter for prorogatioun of the Parliament to 15 July; but (albeit I wes defyrit to reffave the principal!) I reffavit it not.

24 May 1641, Mononday. At 10 of nycht I reffavit letters from his Majestie, daitit 20 May, acquainting me with his Majestie's resolutioun to come in his royall perfoun to hold the Parliament on 15 July, and commands me to attend the counsell quhilk wes appointit to meit, and to be resident daylie at Edinburgh for preparing suche thingis as wer neceffar for his Majestie's receptioun, and in this pacquet reffavit letters from the L. Panmuir to my self, and from him to the Countes of Merfchell, and-to Alexander Keyth, quhilk I delyuerit to him, with one from my self to the Countes. 25 May 1641, Twysday. This day, about 8 in the morning, reffavit letters from ane servand off the Lord Maitlandis, viz., one from his Majestie to my self, daitit 18 May, for prorogatioun of the Parliament, togither with one from his Majestie to the estates for that effect, and being sent for be the Committee, I went at 10 hours, quhen thai red the report of suche of thair number as wes appointit to resolve upon the fycht off the copie off his Majestie's letter, quhilk thai had, and findis in thair

report a command to me to perfew the summondis aganis the incendiaries; I opposit.

Item, thairefter the estates heing convenit in the Parliament Hous, quhair the Lord Burley wes chosin President, and I delyuerit to him his Majestie's letter, and efter reiding tuik instruments thairvpon; and quhen thai enterit to reid the act of prorogatioun (quhilk wes condiscendit to be to the 15 July 1641) I defyrit to be hard, quhen the clerk cam to theis words, commanding the Advocat to perfew, &c.; and Mr. William Scott, clerk, quho wes reiding very indiscreitlie, red on without acknowledging my defyr, till I movit the President to command him to stay; and then I said, I find thir commands so sar binding of me, that being dischargit be his Majestie, I can not sit still, but I must protest in the contrair; and rather or I did protest, I wald remove; quhairvpon I removit and returnit, and cravit the extract ot quhat wes done from Mr. William Scott and John Diksoun, and to insert thairin my removing, quho did resuse to insert, but promisit the extract; quhairvpon I tuik instruments in James Philp his hands, quho promisit to attend for that effect; and I told him and Mr. Hary Maul the caus of my removing, to be not only becaus off the command to me, but also becaus of the vther provisoes insert in the Act.

Item, about 12 hours efter coming from the Parliament, I drew vp the forme of the instrument, and send it inclosit in a letter to James Philp, being in Robert Fleming his hous.

Item, I writ all my letters, vi3. to his Majestie, and insert within it the Ansuer to his compt of my proceiding. Item, to the Erl Lanerk. Item, to the L. Report!6' Panmuire. Item, letter to the Erl of Airth, in ansuer off his to me. Item, to my sone Mr. Alexander. Item, to Erl Annandaill and Thomas Maxwell. Item, to Dean of Winchester. Quhilks 3 letters I inclosit in my fone's pacquet; and thir letters wer daitit 24 and 25 May 1641, and with them sent letters from Countes of Merfchell, Alexander Keyth, and John Pilmuir, to the L. Panmuir.
s

Letters to the
L. Panmuir.
Pacquett.
26 May 1641.
James Philp sent a letter resusing to gif in the instrument, quhairvpon I wes forcit to wrytt new letteris to the Erl of Lanerk, and to L. Panmuir; and sent in the Erl of Lanerk his letters the doubill of James Philpis 2 letteris, and of my ansuer; and the principalls to the L. Panmuir, to be returnit to me. And thir letters to the L. Panmuir wer inclosit in the pacquet sent be me to the Erl of Lanerk, Secretar, by the seuerall pacquets sent be me to the L. Panmuir apart, daitit 24 and 25 May 1641.
Counsel satt.
Pacquett, 1 Junij and 2 thairof.
1 Junij 1641, Twysday.

This day the Counsel satt, for prepareing thingis necessar for his Majestic coming to the Parliament, 15 July; quhair present, Erl Ergyll, Erl Merschel, Erl Wyntoun, Lord Angus, Lord Elphinstoun, Lord Naper, and Advocat; and Lord Elphinstoun as Eldest Preses.

This day, efter CounseU, pacquet sent be James Philp, quhairin letters from the Counsel to his Majestie, and to the Secretar. Item, from me a packet to the Secretar, quhairin one to him, with the proceidingis done in Counsell. Item, one to the Erl Stirling, anent his bill past, deputing Archibald Steuart of Hiffilheyd to be his deput. Item, letters to L. Panmuir, and within it from Erl Ergyll to Lord Lowdoun. Item, letter to my sone, defyring him to delyver the letter to Erl Stirling, and telling him the occasioun thairoff.

Item, the pacquet went not till 2 Junij, and sent in it a letter to L. Panmuir, with 2 vther from John Pilmuir and Alexander Keyth.
4 Junij 1641, Fryday.

Hary Hope. This day my nephew, Hary Hope, returnit from Diep, and cam to Edin burgh, and told that the King of France wes on the frontiers, with so i
Packett, 7 Junij 1641.
7 Junij, Mononday. The pacquet direct be James Philp, and I sent letters to the Erll of Lanerk, schawing him off the attendance of four, vi3. Erl Ergyll, Erl Wyntoun, Lord Nepar, and myself, and that we had writtin for the hail number to a dyet of 17 Junij; and in this told him that my fone had, at my command, focht his fine and wes rejeckit; and that I wald not request, not being prohibit, but trustit my silence fould work as muche. Item, letters to the L. Panmuir and Erl Airth, and within ather of thais, letters to them from the Countes of Merschell. Item, letters to my fone Mr. Alexander, complaining to him of Mr. James his submiffioun aganis my discharge; but to keip it quyet, till I sie how I can mend it.

Item, this day letters from his Majestie to the Counsell, of dait 1 Junij, Letter from his quhilk wer instantlie ansuerit; with a letter to the Secretar from the Coun-counsell of6 sell, beiring ane nott of the neceffars for his surnitor, the reparatioun of the Jwnupalice, and money thairfoir; with money for vtheris caufP. Item, the Erll of Wyntoun his remonstrance, that he wes inhabill to ludge his Majestie at Seytoun. Item, a petitioun from the houshold servands and surnischers, for want of thair preceiding fies and surnishingis, to be schawin to his Majestie. Item, letter from the Secretar. Item, reffavit letters from the L. Pan-l. Panmuir. muir, and from my fone Mr. Alexander, with letters to the Countes of Merschell, Erl Merschell, James Murray younger, Alexander Keyth, John Pilmuir, and Sir Andro Fleschor; quhilks all delyverit to Alexander Keyth, with one from me to the Countes, and hir letter inclosit thairin. Item, letters from the Erl Annandail and my fone.

Item, in this pacquet returnit ansuer to all thir, and specially of that from the Secretar challenging me, quhairof I haif a copie. Item, in myne to L. Panmuir and my fone, defyres to return the warrands for the vefl) sterling, seing his Majestie hes declarit his will, that he will not bestow the place of Mr. of Work on my fone.
9 Junij 1641, Weddinsday. Reffavit from John Lermonth, forth of the Erll of Roxburghis L. Panmuir. pacquet, letters from the L. Panmuir, daitit 28 May, with a letter to the Countes of Mer-

schell, to the Erll of Kinghorne, to James Murray, and Erl Kinghorne. Alexander Keyth; and delyuerit all to Alexander Keyth, but inclosit that to the Countes in a letter from myself to hir Ladylhip. And James Murray coming in, I told him off the letter to the Erl of Kinghorne, quho defyrit

Alexander Keyth to latt it ly ovir undelyuerit, for he wes sure that if thai did ones meit they wald aggrie, for the Erll is content to quyt the blok off the lands; as for the vther, James said he never intendit it fould be more nor 30 0 lb sterling, albeit he hard that the Countes of Merfchell fpak of 4000lb Scottis, and that surth of that quhilk the Erl cravis his 40nlb sterling; quhairvpon Alexander Keyth delyuerit bak to me the Erl of Kinghorn his letter, and James Murray promisit to wryt to the Lady thairanent. 11 Junij 1641, Fryday. Krl MontroiS. This day, about 8 of nycht, the Erll of Montroifl wes putt in the Castell be the Committie.

Pacquett. Item, James Philp directit ane pacquet, and gaif me no advertisement of the going thairoff.

14 Junij, Mononday.

A letter from his Majestie to sa mome off the Counsell as wes at EdinHis Majestie-s let-burgh, quhilk James Philp presentit to the Erl of Ergyll, quho would not be Sir James Gal-open it. Thairefter James cam to me, and I went with him to the Erl of loway. Ergyll his house; and the Erll defyrit to sie the last letter, quhairin his

Majeiste gaif ordour to sa mony off the Counsell as wes present to reffave his letteris; quhairvpon James Philp went for the letter.

Item, I tuik occafioun in the mean tyme to acquaint the Erl of Ergyll of James Philp his resusing of the instrument takin 25 May 1641.

Item, at James Philp his returne, and efter reiding of the letter, my Lord Ergyll wret to the Committie, and promisit to come to the Counsel-hous, to quhilk I went immediatlie, and the Erll went efter quarter of an hour be the bak way thruch the Banquetting-hous.

Item, efter he came his Majestie's letter wes red, quhilk in effect defyrit publicatioun to be made of his Majestie's resolution to come to Scotland, quhilk we thocht fitt to anfuer be a letter to the Erll of Lanerk, Socretar, (notwithstanding that the letter cam to James Philp, in a letter sent to him be Sir James Galloway, quho told him that it wes his Majestie's plesur to command that the anfuer thairoff be returnit to him, becaus off the Erl of Lanerkis disease,) and in the letter to the Erl of Lanerk, we told that becaus the Counsel is to meit frequentlie on Thursday nixt, 17 Junij, that thairfoir we differrit till then.

Item, efter we had writtin our letteris, the Erl of Ergyll movit me anent James Philp James Philp, and efter gret debait, James offerit to gif his othe that he remembers not, quhilk I resusit *in facto tarn recenti,* and becaus he rememberis both *ante et post,* and told that I wald perfew him befoir the Counsell on Thursday. Then thai defyrit to know the witness quhom I wald vse, quhilk I schunit, becaus I know thay will labor to divert them.

This nycht, at 8 hours at evin, James Philp send the pacquet, with the Pacquet sent foirsaid letters, to the Erl of Lanerk. Item, I sent ane pacquet to the L.14 Jun 1641Panmuir, and within it one from the Countes of Merschell and Alexander Keyth. Item, one to the Erl of Airth, and within it one from the said Countes. Item, ane other of myne to the L. Panmuir, anent James Philp his instrument, and sent thairin to be schawin to his Majestie, the nott of my cair in takand of instruments in James Philp his handis, (quhairoff I haif a doubill befyd me,) and this nott is subscryvit be me. Item, the doubill of James Philp his letter, also subscryvit be me, as a trew copie. Item, the doubill of the forme of instrument delyuerit to James Philp, bering the names of the witneffis. Item, sent to my sone a letter. Item, one to the Dean of Winchester, and within it one from Kynetlis and Nicolas his brother.

Memorandum.—On 13 Junij 1641, being Quhitfonday, I reffavit letters from the L. Panmuir, daitit 9 Junij, quhairin he schawis me that his Majestie thinks that I wes in the sault in not taking instrumentis in James Philpis handis; and the Lard sayis that I was not sairlie vflt be the Erl Lanerk in his Report, and thairfoir I dispatchit anfuer to the Lard, with the writtis within specisi-it, quhilk went be pacquet, sent be James Philp, of 14 Junij, as is withinwrittin.

Item, on Twysday, 15 Junij 1641, reffavit from William Dik 100fi) sterling, Mysone Mr. Alexbe vertew off the Committie's precept, direct to him to pay it to my fone nder s 'P01stir" r *1 r J J* ling, 15 Junij

Craighall, as for his brother Mr. Alexander, his pensioun of the terme of 1641.

Mertimes 1640, and gevin bak to William Dik the precept, with his acceptatioun thairoff with my fone Craighall his discharge on the reffait thairoff, for quhilk William Dik directit his letter of exchange to Robert Inglis, his sactor in Londoun, to be payit on 15 dayis' sicht, and I gaif to him 2 tuelf pund pieces for the exchange, quhilk is at 2 off the hundreth, and immediatlie I closit it in a letter to Mr. Alexander, with ane vther of my fone James his to him, and gaif it to the merchand pacquet this day, about 4 afternone, and thair is writt on bale 2 f l sterling to be payit for the portage. Counsell, 17 Junij Item, on 17 Junij 1641, being Thursday, the Counsell met, being onlie 164 sex, vi3 L. Awmonthe, Erl Ergyll, Erl Wyntoun, Erl Southesk, Lord

Angus, Advocat, quhair the point anent proclaiming his Majestie's coming to Scotland wes debaitit, quhither it could be done without a quorum of the Counsell, and efter debait, the buikis of Counsell ordanit to be seirchit, and continewit till the morow.

18 Junij 1641.

This day the buikis seirchit, and producit diuers actis off Counsell, quhairin the sederunt wes but sex, and I rememberit that diuers proclamationis wes past with this qualitie at the end, *Per Regem,* without, *per actum.*

Thairefter it wes accordit that the proclamatioun sould be drawin vp, and James Philp had preparit it, and it wes Cgnettit, and, being red over, mendit in some words.

Memorandum.—This day, when the Lords went to the Committie, I vrgit James Philp to gif out the instrument, quhairvpon I raifl instruments be Archibald Primrois and John Douglas.

Item, thairefter it was movit to haif the assistance off the Committie of estates thairto, to quhilk end the Lord Awmonthe, Lieutenant-generalL and the Erl off Ergyll wer sent to the Committie, quho stayed till efter tuelff. Bot the knok wes holden bak, and the croce clothit with tapestrie, quhilk the Prouest and Baillies of Edinburgh being sent for, could not find. But I causit bring als monie surth off my hous, vtherwais it wald haif bene done without couering. And word cam from the Committie to delay the covering of the croce for a schort space. And it wes ones agitat to continew till the morrow. But the croce wes coverit befoir the advertisement.

Item, quhen the Lord Awmonthe and Erl of Ergyll cam bak, they returnit ansuer, that the Committie thocht that the Counsell would not remitt the Proclamatioun, for 2 cauffl; 1. becaus not a number; 2. becaus thai sitting, and that thai aucht to do it; and vpon the Counsell's will do it be thair act, and heirupon having long debaitit, it wes thocht fitt rather to give them thair will, nor to suffer a rub in the buffines.

Item, efter proclamatioun, the Counsell mett at 4 hours at nycht, and Mungo Murray, writt a letter to his Majestie, and promisit to meet to-morrow at 8, for junyf Hmu wryting a letter to the Secretar; but the Erl of Ergyll wes excusit, betere fronl Erl of _...-.... Annandaill and refloun oi his not being weill. my sone, daitit 12 and 13 Junij.

19 Junij 1641.

This day the pacquet went, (being Setterday;) and letters sent to the Packett sent. Erl of Annandaill, vnder Mr. Alexander Burnet his cover, becaus I wald delyver none to Mr. Philp; and in this pacquet, (by that of myne to Erll of Annandaill,) sent one to my sone, and within it one to L. Panmuir, to quhom I sent a letter from the Countes of Merfchell. Item, a copy of Hary Maul of Melgum his letter to James Murray younger, anent Erl of Kinghorne. Item, the principall letter from Mr. Philp to me, daitit Philp's letter sent 26 May 1641.-Item, a letter to my sone, and within it the doubill of the jj L-Pan" letter of exchange from William Dick, direct to Robert Inglis, his factor, to pay my sone 100 8) sterling. Item, another letter to the L. Panmuir, anent James Philp his ansuer, denying that instruments wer takin be me in his hand aganis the tenor of his awin letter, quhilk he made most falslie and impudentlie; and als his schift to haif witneffis examinat, quho wil be loth to depone vpon the resusall off the Clerk of Parliament, and of quhom the maist part ar delt with not to depone aganis James, except he himself grant and subscryve the act.

22 Junij 1641, Twysday. This day sent a letter to my sone Mr. Alexander in the merchand My sone, Mr. pacquet, and within it the forme of a warrand, to be signed be his Majestie, for payment of his pensioun of 200 fc sterling of the 3eir 1641; and both the termes thairoff, and this letter, I delyverit to James Murray younger, quho promisit to send it to his sactor John Hog, and caus him wrytt that he hes delyverit it. 23 Junij 1641, Weddinsday. Pacquet cam 23 This day Mungo Murray returnit to Court, and a pacquet sent with him fetters to mf-from" 40 Mr. Alexander, quhairin one to the Erl Lanrek, Secretar, in ansuer of the Erl Lanerk, his rcffavit this famyn day, and schawing him Philpis outrage, quhairof I

L. Panmuir, Erl....., » T-r» i i i i i i Mi of Annandaiil, and hau ane copie. Item, lent to Li. ranmuir, and within his the doubul ot Dean of Winches-Archibald Prymrois instrument, takin 18 Junij, with the copy of my letter to the Erl of Lanerk anent James Philp. Item, letters to the Erl of Annandaill, in ansuer of his reffavit this day. Item, a letter to my sone, and within it one to the Dean of Winchester. Item, the Erl of Annandaill sent a letter to Sir James Balfour, quhilk I gave to Mr. AlexL. Panmuir hU ander Burnet. Item, the L. Panmuir sent letters to the Countes of 1t ten $

Merfchell, to the L. Lour, to John Pilmuir, and Alexander Keyth, quhilk I must fie difpatchit to-morrow, 24 Junij.

Memorandum.—I delyverit, on 24 Junij, to Jolm Stark, servitor to John Peter, a letter to the Countes of Merfchell from me, quhairm is inclofit that off the L. Panmuiris to hir. Item, ane vther letter to John Pilmuir, quhairin is inclosit his awin, with that to the Lord Lour. Item, a letter from the L. of Panmuir to Alexander Keyth, quhilk is all the said John Stark tuik from me in name of Alexander Keyth, and as appointit be him now in his absence in Aberdene to rcffave all letteris concerning the L. Panmuir, and to difpatche the samyn. Dean of Winches-Item, I delyverit a letter from the Dean of Winchester, to Alexander ter-Bowar, vnto Alexander Gordoun of Ardehat, quho promisit to delyver the samyn to him; and als I writ ane letter to Michael Young, the Deanis brother, and thairin inclofit the letter from the Dean to him, quhilk I gaif to Mr. George Noruel to fend to the said Michael.

Pacquett.

25 Junij 1641.

Letteris writtin to the Erl Lanerk and L. Panmuir, anent my convening befoir the Committie this day, and delyuerit to the Lord Lyndsay, quho sent them vnder his cover.

This nycht Sir James Carmichael, Thesaurer Deput, cam from Court. Thesaurer Deput.

26 Junij 1641.

This day, I being defyrit be the Committie of Estates to subscryve the generall band, gaif in my declaratioun, and thai ordanit me to meit with the Erll os Ergyll, the Erl Cassils, and the L. Durie, in the Erll of Ergyllis hous, at 3 efternone.

But I wes warnit be John Douglas, mef, to be at Counsell at 2 efter-His Majestie-s letnone, quhair I mett with Sir James Carmichael, and about 3 hours the £rjterof20,Junijof Ergyll, the Lord Almond, and Erl Southesk cam; quhair being sett, the Thesaurer Deput presentit his Majestie's letter of 20 Junij 1641, quhilk Counsell, 26 Junij. bure that his Majestie had gevin order to Sir James Carmichael to deburse soumes of mony for all thingis neceffarie for his Majestie's provistoun; and this being red,

The Deput producit roll of theis that wer to come with his Majestie, vi3. Lord Duik of Lennox, Lord Marques of Hamiltoun, Erl Mortoun, Erl Lanerk, Erl Holland, Sir Hary Vayne, with his Majestie's domestik servandis.

Item, the Thesaurer Deput declarit that his Majestie wes to tak journey on 5 July, and to be heir on the 10 or 11 July, at sarthest.

Item, ane roll off the officers of his Majestie's hous wes producit, and itThesaurer-Deput. wes thocht that onlie some sevin of them wes neceffar, and the rest mycht stay at home; quhairvpon letter wes appointit to be writtin to the Secretar.

Item, order wes gevin to wrytt for the Erl of Wyntoun, Erl Angus, and Lord Elphinstoun, to be at Counsell on Twysday next.

And word wes fpokin be the Erl of Ergyll for inlarging of Philp, and George, Maister houshold, wes rememberar of it; and I gaif them both thankis. Item, it wes fpokin to haif ane meiting of Exchekker.

Item, this 26 Junij, Mr. Archibald Jonstoun cam home from Londoun, Mr. Archibald and I gat letters from him from my sone Mr. Alexander, daitit 16 Junij, Mysone Mr. Alexand within them the letter of exchange drawin for payment off vc lb sterlingander to the Erl off Stirling, for the place of Maister Wark, quhilk Sir John Vache gatt; and this letter of exchange wes gevin bak be me to my fone Craighall.

28 Junij 1641, Monondday. L. Panmuir. Letteris reffavit from William Hay of Quhitfoum, from the L.-Pan muir, daitit 19 and 20 Junij 1641, and with them 2 letteris to the Countes of Merschell, one to James Murray younger, one to John Pilmuir, and one Erll of Kinghorne. to Alexander Keyth; and in thir he fpeiks anent Erll of Kinghorne.

Item, this day I reffavit letteris from the Countes of Merschel, and in it one to the L. Panmuir, quhilk scho defyris me to keip, if I heir that he is on his journey.

Memorandum.—I delyuerit to John Clerk, doer for Alexander Keyth, on 29 Junij, a letter to the Countes of Merschell, and within it 2 from the L. Panmuir. Item, a letter to Alexander Keyth, and ane vther to John Pilmuir.

30 Junij 1641.

L. Panmuir. This day reffavit 2 pacquetts, one from the L. Panmuir, and within it one to the Countes of Merschell; and als one from the Erll off Annandaill, and within it one to Mungo Murray, (quho past away 24 Junij;) and one to Mr. Alexander Burnet, quhilk I gave him.

1 July 1641, Thursday. Pacquet. Letteris sent to Sir James Galloway, Secretar, vnder the cover of Mr.

James Aikinheid, quhairin to Sir James himself. Item, a pacquet to my fone, and within it to the L. Panmuir, with letteris from the Countes of Merschell, a letter to the Erll of Annandaill, and within it returnit that of Mungo Murrayis.

Item, a pacquet apart to the L. Panmuir, and within it a letter from the Countes of Merschell, and ane vther from Alexander Keyth.

Mr. Robert Craig his sunerallis on Sounday, 4 July 1641, in the Gray Freiris.

8 July 1641, Thursday. Reffavit letters from the Erll of Dunsermling and Lord Loudoun, quho came to Edinburgh from Court 3esternyt, 7 July 1641, vi3. from the L. L0"1 Lowdoun. Panmuir to myself, daitit 29 Junij. Item, to the Countes of Merschell, to panmuir and my the L. Lour, to James Murray, to John Pilmuir. Item, letteris from ', His ressait of my sone Mr. Alexander to myself and his thrie brothers; and I sent his to looft sterling, my eldest fone to Craighall, to quhilk he went this day.

Item, gevin to L. Lour his letter, be John Leuestoun in Edinburgh.

Item, gevin to John Clerk a letter to the Countes of Merschell from me, and within it inclosit one from the L. Panmuir, and als to him one to John Pilmuir.

Item, Mr. George Noruell delyuerit that to James Murray at his hous, becaus he wes at the Conventioun off the Burrows, at Linlithgow.

9 July, Fryday, 1641. Barbara Fleming, dauchter to John Fleming, contractit on John Pen-B. Fleming man, quho wes his awin prenteis, and gevin to the nuris of Alexander Maxwell's dauchter 7 dollors; and thai maryit thairefter on Weddinsday, 4 August 1641.

This 11 July 1641, being Sounday, Mr. Patrik Broun delyverit to me, Pacquet cam on from James Philp, letteris from the Kingis Majestie, daitit 6 July, tbwrtiohowt the Incendiaries. Item, from the Erl Lanerk, the samyn dait. Item, nycht. from the L. Panmuir, and within it to the Countes of Merschell, quhilk I sent to hir Ladyship in one from myself, delyverit to Alexander Keyth. Item, letteris from the Erl of Annandaill, and within them one to Mr. Alexander Burnet, and ane vther to the Lord Maitland; quhilk letteris I delyuerit to Mr. Alexander Burnet. But I red not thir letteris till the morne, being 12 July.

Item, I sent, on 12 July, a pacquet to the Erl Lanerk, quhairin one to Ansuer to the his Majestie, and within it insormatioun anent my ansuers to the Committie, "pacquet off quhilk both I haif an copy. Item, a letter to the Erl Lanerk, andfrom myself to the

,,...,.,,....,... Erl Lanerk, 12 within it the copie of Philpis depohtions, with a copie of my letter writtin July 1641, being to him On 25 Maij. Mononday.

Item, letteris to the L. Panmuir, and within it a reformit Act for the Kirk of Carrestoun, to be signed be his Majestie. Item, the doubill of my informatioun to his Majestic Item, a letter to Mr. Alexander, defyring him, in cace of the L. Panmuir his absence, to reid all, and returne them to me with diligence. Item, a letter to the Erl of Annandaill, in ansuer of his reffavit this day; and all thir putt in ane packett, direct on the bak to the L. Panmuir, and in his abfence to the Erll of Annandaill, and all inclosit in a closit buist to the Erl Lanerk, and went to the Cannogait on Mononday, 12 July, about 4 efternone. Letter from his Item, this 12 day of July, reffavit from the Lord Lowdoun his Majestie's irortiouo/ thV61-er-t0 me o uny» wtn a copie on his Majestie's letters to the Parliament. Commiffioners of Parliament, lefing in thair will to quhat day they wald prorogat the Parliament. Signator of Wat-Memorandum.—Ester I had directit my awin pacquet this day, quhilk went away at 5 hours at nycht, I causit draw vp ane new signatour of Watterheid to Mr. James and his fpous in lysrent, and to Thomas Hope, thair son, and his airs of his bodie; quhilks sail3eing, to Mr. James, his sather, and the heirs of his bodie; quhilkis faieing, to Mr. Alexander, his airs and affignais quhatsomeuer; and I dockittit it, and inclosit it in a letter to Mr. Alexander; and with it sent a letter to Sir James Galloway, Secretar, for paffing of it; and als a letter to Mr. Alexander from his brother Sir Thomas. And all thir, being pacquet vp in a pacquet, wes directit on the bak to my sone Mr. Alexander, and sent to Alexander Keyth, that it may go vnder his couer in Philps pacquet, quhilk wes to go on 13 Julij.

15 Julij 1641.

Parliament, 15 The Parliament mett, and voitit to sit still, notwithstanding off his July 1641 Majestie's letter, but onlie to prepar and not to inact, till 17 August, at quhilk thai expect his Majestie's royall presence.

Quhairvpon I sent an pacquet, quhilk wes stay it on 15 till 16, and on 16 Lanrek. stayit vpon the Lord Lowdoun and Erl Dunsermhngis letteris to his Majestic.

So the pacquet went on Setterday, 17 July, at 10 hours in the morning; and in it to his Majestie, with my accompt. Item, to the Secretar, with a copie off the accompt. Item, to L. Panmuir, and within it from the Countes of Merschel and L. Doun. Item, from Alexander Keyth to him.

Pacquet sent be my self to Erl

Item, my letter to Mr. Alexander, and within it from his brother Sir Thomas; and als letteris to his Majestie from Erl Dunsermling and Lord Lowdoun.

Item, on 16 July, Fryday, reffavit letters from his Majestie, to draw vp aAssemblie 20 July commiffioun to the Erl Weymis to represent his Majestie's perfoun at the Aj£ Sanct Affemblie of Sanclandrois; quhilk I drew vp on a blank sent to me, quhilk I fillit be advyse of the Erl of Southesk and Thesaurer Deput, consorm to his Majestie's letters.

Item, reffavit a letter from Sir James Galloway, quhilk, with the former anent the Affemblie, I ansuerit be wryting to the Lord Secretar, and als be a letter to Sir James Galloway, delyuerit to Mr. James Aikinheid, quho gaiff me the epitaph or epigram of Sir James Carmichael.

22 July 1641.

This day the Exchekker satt, and wes dischargit be warrand of the Estates of Parliament; and befoir it wes dischargit, Mr. John Henrysoun resignit Waterheid and Mynes to the Lo.... the notar Michael Ker.

23 July 1641, Fryday. I wes defyrit to remoue from Parliament, and gaif ansuer as my paper apart proportis.

Item, on that day I wret a letter to Sir James Galloway, in ansuer of his Sir James Galformer, schawing quhat wes done in his buffines of Exchekker, quhilk held lowayon 22 July, at 2 efternone, but wes dischargit be the Parliament immediately; and in the end of my letter I acquaint him with my removing, and Pacquet. defyrit him to signisie the samyn to his Majestie. And this letter I delyuerit to Mr. James Aikinheid, quho sent it in Philps pacquet on 24 July, being Setterday.

27 July 1641, Twysday. This day the Affemblie (quhilk wes translatit from Sanctandrois to Generall AssemEdinburgh) mett at the Gray Freir Kirk, and thair, be pluralitie of voites,bhe8t Edlnbur£hMr. Alexander Henrysoun wes chosin Moderator.

Lord Lowdoun to Item, this day the Lord Lowdoun tuik journey post to Court, about 10 Court, 27 July hourg befo;r none; and sent with him letteris to Erl Lanerk, and within it 1641. '... the forme of my declaratioun, to be gevin in befoir the Estates, anent my removing surth of Parliament, to be schawin to his Majestie; and als acquainting him with the new act made aganis me, to persew theis in the Castell; quhilk I said I wald hardlie eschew. Item, a letter to my sone Mr. Alexander, and within it one to Sir James Galloway to the samyn sense, with a doubill of my said declaratioun. Item, in that to Mr. Alexander, I defyrit him to advertifl me quhen the Lord Saltoun and his vncle ar expected. 28 July 1641, Weddinsday. Mr. John Steuart. This day Mr. John Steuart beheidit at the Mercat Croce of Edinburgh, for his leyis aganis the Erll of Ergyll. 30 July, Fryday.

Delyuerit to Mr. James Aikinheid a letter to Sir James Galloway, anent the breivc of John Duncan, as air to James Duncan of Ratho; and als anent my purpose to re-enter to Parliament, if I be admittit fimplie; and bering this, that if his Majestie come, I haif to mak his Majestie's prerogative royall, anent the officers of Estait, so cleir, that his Majestie cannot want it without his Majestie willinglie consent to quyt it, to quhilk I traist his Majestie will not aggrie.

1 August, Sounday, 1641. Pacquet from This nycht, about 10 hours of nycht, reffavit letteris from Erl Lanerk,

Ju7'i64ilt,t 27 a letter t0 tne OounsoU, quhilk I delyucrit on Mononday befoir 7

Ressavit i August hours, to the Erl of Ergyll. Item, reffavit letters from the L. Panmuir, and with them a letter to the Countes of Merschell, quhilk I inclosit within one from-myself, and gaif to Alexander Keyth, to be sent to hir Ladyship. Item, I gaif one to himself, one to James Murray younger, and one to John Pilmuir, quhilk he promisit to dispatche. Item, I reffavit letteris from the Erll of Annandaill, and with them to Mr. Alexander Burnet, to Lord Mainland, and to the Laird of Lag, quhilk I gaif to Mr. Alexander Burnet.

Item, the Counsell mett at 2 efternone, quhairin wes Ergyll, Galloway, Assurance of his Seyfort, Southesk, Findlater, Elphinstoun, and Advocat; and the letteris from Jjjjjj" JjJjJ the Erl of Lanerk to the Counsell wes red, quhairin he affures the Counsell 1641. that his Majestie wilbe heir on 13 August; and als a list sent of the nobilmen and vtheris to come with his Majestie, and amang them the Prince Palatine.

8 August 1641, Sounday. This day James Lyoun of Auldbar, being at Edinburgh attending the Lyoun Auldbar. Parliament and Generall Affemblie, de-

ceiffit. 9 August 1641, Mononday.

The L. Panmuir cam from Court to Edinburgh, about 8 hours of nycht, L. Panmtdr. and als the Erl of Mortoun; and I mett with them on Weddinsday.

Item, this nycht, at 7 hours at evin, the Affemblie rose; and the nixt is Assemblie. appointit to be at Sanctandrois, on last Weddinsday of July.

Mr. Alexander Henrysoun hes gottin libertie of tranfportatioun from Mr. Alexander Edinburgh, and Mr. William Bennet is ordanit to be transportit from HenryS0Un.

6' r Mr. William Ben
Monymell to Edinburgh. net.
10 August 1641, Twysday.

This nycht William, Erll of Lanerk, Secretar to his Majestie, cam to Edinburgh, and on the morow went to Kynnell, and returnit on Thursday, at nycht.
13 August, Fryday.

This day I mett with him in the bowling-grein, betuix elevin and tuelf Erl Lanerk. hours befoir none.

Item, this nycht certan word cam that his Majestie wes to be in Bervick. Kingis Majestie.

14 August 1641, Setterday. This nycht, about 6 at evin, his Majestie cam to Halyruidhous. 17 August, Twysday. This day his Majestie cam to the Parliament in coche, about 10 hours; and I wes then readmittit to sitt in Parliament, butt not to voitt; aganis quhilk I protestit. 25 August 1641.

Armie returnit. This day the armie returnit, and past to Edinburgh, having liftit and removit from Newcastell on 21 August of befoir. Generall Leslie. Item, 27 August, Generall Leslie cam to Edinburgh, Fryday. Eri Rothes. Item, 28 August 1641, report cam off the Erll of Rothes his decease at

Londoun, quhilk wes muche lamentit.
Erl Lautlerdaill.
1 September 1641, Weddinsday. Memorandum.—Scho borrowit from Mr. James, hir son, for the hous,

Item, payit be the Vicount of Stormonth, on 10 September, ije merkis.

Item, payit be the Erl l of Lauderdaill his promise, in the matter of the holding of Craig j00 merlts, on 17 September 1641; qulrilk I delyuerit to hir for the hous.

Last September 1641, Thursday. This day Hary Hope went to Londoun, and gevin to him, for his mother's dewty of Martimefl 1641, 5 Ib sterling.

Item, this day the Erl of Lowdoun voitit Chancellar.
Lord Lowdoun,
Chancellor.

1 October 1641, Fryday. This day the Lord Lowdoun his gift off the office off Chancellary red, and takin to be confident be the hous; and thairefter, on 2 October, it wes seillit, and the Greit Seill delyuerit to him, and he sworn be the President, at command of his Majestie.

3 October 1641, Sounday. About 9 of nycht, my deir dauchter D. M. Murray, fpous to my sone Craighall, deceifftt in childbirth, scho and the barne in her womb. God in My deir dauchter, mercie pittie me, and my sone and his children, for it is a fore straik. haUfesU. 12 October 1641, Twysday. The rumore brak out of a plott aganis the Marques of Hamiltoun and aganis the , Marquis and Erl the Erl of Ergyll, quhilk fould haif beine actit 3esternycht, being Monon-Ergyll, on li Oc day, 11 October, ather to haif killit them, or to caryit them to the Kingistober 1641 schip, (quhilk wes in the rode, and thence to Londoun; quhairvpon the

Marques, and Erl of Ergyll, with the Erl of Lanerk, went from Edinburgh to Kynnell, and thence to Hamiltoun; and the Parliament examinat

Leutenant Hurrie, quho wes the first divulger, and Capitan Steuart, quho deponit aganis the Erl of Crausuird, Leutenant-Coronell Steuart, and

Coronel Lothian. And thir wer sequestrat be the Parliament, vi3., Hurrie and Captain Steuart, with the Erl of Eglintoun; Erl Crausuird, with James Murray; Coronel Lothian, with John Smyth.
21 October 1641, Thursday.

The Erl of Mar fpak me to haif the rentis off the lordschip of Stirling Erl Mar. afiignit to him in payment of his 50008) sterling, quhilk is dew to him from his Majestie, be contract, for his heretabill offices off the scherifschip of Stirling, chancellarie off the lordschip thairoff, and the bailliery off the Watter of Forth; and offerit to me, for my affistance thairin, a tokin of *jm* merks.

And thairefter, on Thursday, 28 October, being convoying him surth of my 3ett, about halfe 8 in the morning, he said, "I knaw, if 3e fpak his Majestie, and schaw to him the cquitie of it, I will gett it; and I will gif you 100 Ib sterling. "

Item, on Mononday, 1 November, he promisit to gif the 100Bb sterling within 4 dayis.

Item, on Thursday, 4 November, he promisit 150Ib sterling, so sone as his signatour passis the Exchekker; and I challenging his promise of present payment of the 100 Bb, he said, "I wilbe als good as my word; I will giff the 100 Ib sterling immediatlie efter the contract be signit be his Majestie, u and the vther *50* sterling quhen it paffes the Exchekker." But he fpak of 31 3eire' tak.

1 November 1641, Mononday. Mr. Christopher Cokbnrn reportit to me, that the Erl wes content to gitme the deuty of the yeir 1640 or 1641; but himself, on Setterday, 6 November, gaif me the Kingis warrand, and promisit 2000 merks. Item, on 5 November, the Erl of Abercorn promilit 50 dd.

My danchter Anne
Foules.

6 November 1641, Setterday. About 3 eftenone, my dauchter Anne Foules delyverit of a man child, bliffit be the Lord; and gevin to the midwyff j dd. angel. But the bairne wes verie waik, and I defyrit him to be baptizit; quhilk my wyff excusit, that thai durst not tak the bairne surth in the cold air. And it plesit God to keip in his lyse till Sounday, at 7 hours; and I causit him to be baptized be Mr. Andro Ramsay, in the Magdalen Chapell, and he wes namit James. *nto &;ftoS fitys.* And my wyff wes angrie at my greise.

15 November 1641.

Hary Hope. This day my nephew, Hary Hope, cam from Londoun, and he brocht to me ane kist off 38 pund wecht of corfe of cumin at 46f5 the pund; quhilk I payit.

Parliament.

17 November 1641, Weddinsday. The Parliament raid.

Kingis Majestic returne to Ingland, 18 November 1641, Thursday. The Kingis Majestie tuik journey to Ingland. 23 November 1641. The Erlls of Lyndsay and Lanerk this day tuik journey to Court. Item, on 25 November, James Levingstoun went to Court.

Item, this 23 November, my lone Sir Thomas presentit his gift of Justice Generall to the Councell, to gif his oth, quhilk wes deserrit to Twysday nixt, the last November, in refpect the Counsell wes insrequent, the most part being gone to the sunerals of the Erll of Rothes. Item, this day sent a letter to the L. Duik's Grace, to acquaint his Majestie anent the names of Duke Lennox, the Commiffioners of Exchekker.

24 November 1641, Weddinsday.

This day the Lords went to the sunerals of John, Erl of Rothes, performit at Lestie, 25 November 1641, being Thursday.

Item, this day my sono Sir James went to the leid mynes, to tak seising My sone Sir James to himfelf and his fpous in lysrent, and Thomas thair sone in fie. Wandlockheid 25 November 1641, Thursday. This day the sunerals of John, Erl of Rothes, celebrat at Leslie.

1 December, Weddinsday.

A packet wrettin to James Levingstoun, and within it a letter to his Pacquet to my sone Majestie, with a nott anent the mayntenance of the titulars during lyff, tMr iivinmtoun quhairoff I haif the doubills; and this, with a letter to the Erl of Lanerk, and ane vther to William Murray, al l inclosit in a packett direct on the bak to my sone Sir Alexander; and this sent with Dauid Mureheid, quho tuik post this day. My letteris ar all daitit last of November.

Mr. David Muirheid went not quhil l 3 December, and with him also William Murray.

My sone Sir lent to William Murray his signatour of Arbroth, with a letter to him Thomas, Generall thairanent, and anent the oppositioun made to my sone Sir Thomas, OnJusticiar2 December, in his gift of Generall Justiciary and this sent in a pacquet direct from Mr. Thomas Murray, advocat.

Item, sent with him a letter to William Murray, with Sir Robert Gordoun his fignatour for the help of the 2 kirks of Vgstoun and Kynninmound, in Murray.

Memorandum.—The first meiting of the Circuit Courtes, appointit to be Circuit Courts, in ten scherisdomes, is to be the first Twysday of Apryll, in the burgh of Perth.

My sone Sir Thomas to Court, and Packett with him.

11 December 1641, Setterday. This day my sone Sir Thomas tuik journey to Court, and sent with him letters to Mr. Murray and James Vingltoun. Item, one to Sir Alexander his brother, and within it one to Sandsurd. Item, one to the Erl Lanrek, Secretar, anent the Sheriffis and the Commilfioun of the Borderis. Item, to Sir James Galloway, anent the Exchekker. Item, to Sir Richard Graham, anent the Commiffioun of the Borders. 13 December 1641, Mononday. racquet. This day a packet from me to the Erl of Lanerk, sent at the defyre of my Lord Chancellar, be letteris sent to me from Londoun and reffavit this day, and thairin letters from Irland to the Marques of Hamiltoun, quhilk ar inclosit in a letter from myself, in quhilk I entreit his Lordship for my sone Sir Alexander his pensioun. Item, a letter to the Erl of Lanerk. Item, to my sone Sir Alexander, schawing that I haif writtin to the Marques. Item, a letter from the L. Panmuir to John Squyre, Secretar to the Erl of Lanerk, quhilk I haif inclosit in one from myself to him. 16 December 1641, Weddinsday. Robert Lockart. This day Marie Fleming, dauchter to John Fleming, maryit on Robert Lockert. 17 December.

Letteris to Court Letters sent to William Murray of the Bed Chalmer, in anfuer off his and my sones." reffavit 14 December, and within it sent to him letters from his cousing Mr. Thomas Murray, with the signator past his Majestie's hand in his savors of the sew-males of Scone, Strathern, Colbrandspeth, and Galloway, vnder reversioun of vBb sterling. Item, letters to my sone Sir Thomas, and within it the signatour of locality for the fies off the Justice Generall, Clerk, and Deputs. Item, to him from his bedsellow. Item, to my sone Sir Alexander, from me and from my sone Sir James.

All thir direct in a pacquet intrustit to Sir Thomas or Sir Alexander, and sent with Mr. James Primrois.

28 December 1641, Twysday. Reffavit ansuer from the Erll off Lanerk of my pacquet of 13 December. Erl Lanerk. 30 December 1641. *Votum Domino JanctS juratum ab irajbendo cavere, quod quæso Deus* Votum. *gratiqfe perficiat.* 1 Januar 1642, Setterday. *Hodie votum denuo repetitum cavere ab omni ira vel impatientiœi* Votum. *incitamentissuper quo Domini gratiam Juppliciter oravi.* Item, this day, at 2 efternone, I had a heavy brasche off the colick, Brasche of Colick. quhilk vexit me till I vomit all, and gatt rest in my bed from twa till Sounday in the morning, at quhilk I wes delyverit, and rose to the preiching; for quhilk I gif God prayse.

3 Januar 1642, Mononday. This day, as I wes making for reiding off my ordinarie lectwres off the Ane sore fall. Scripture, and colling the candill, and casting the coll surth off the scheiris in the fyre, the schyre quhairin I satt coupit, and I gatt ane heavy sall on my bak to the grund, but my heid wes saiff. Bliffit be the Lord, and God gif me grace to tak thir for warningis, that my Lord is preparing me for my last. 4 Januar 1642, Twysday. This day the Seffioun mett, and all the Lords wer fworne, as chofin be Sessioun. the act of Parliament. 5 Januar 1642, Weddinsday. I sent ane pacquet to the Erl Lanerk, quhairin one to him with the list Pacquet, 8 Jan. of the CommisGoners of Borderis. Item, acquaint him with thair trying of1642me to perfew the incendiaries, and craving to haif his Majestie's expres warrand. Item, letters to James Levingstoun, and in it inclosit Sir Robert Spottifwod his letter to me, testifeing his consent to his brother's signet of the bak band made be the Item, one to my sone Sir

Thomas, schawing him that he is omittit surth of Exchekker, and defyring him to deill with the L. Lyndsay, to gett me his Majestie's warrand to perfew the incendiaries. Item, letters to Sir Alexander from me and his brother Sir James. Item, letters from my Lord Chancellor to Sir Archibald Jonstoun.

Writtin to my fone Sir Thomas ansuer to his former, reffavit on 6 and 10 Januar, and myne, daitit 13 Januar. Item, within it from his bedfellow, and one from Hary to his mother. Thir delyuerit to Archibald Prymrois for the pacquet, 13 Januar 1642, but the pacquet went not till 15 Januar 1642.

15 Januar 1642.

Customes. This day the Customes and Impostis sett to Sir William Dik for fyve 3eiris, for payment off 202,000 merks, and 5000 merks of girfoum; the entrie off the said fyve 3eir tak begining at 1 November 1641.

17 Januar 1642, Mononday. John Fleming. This day, about 5 hours of nycht, John Fleming deceifiit.

Pacquet, 13 Jan. 1642, sent 15th Jan. 1642.

20 Januar 1642, Thursday.

Letters to my sones, Delyuerit to Robert Murray, fone to Jame3 Murray, quho went post, daitit 19 Jan. 1642., ,,. *m* , ,,.',-.,,, _ letters to oir 1 homas and feu: Alexander, and within them one to the Erll of Lanerk, Secretar, anent Incendiaries, quhairof I haif ane copy. Item, letters from my wyff to Sir Thomas, and from Sir James to Sir Alexander.

26 Januar 1642.

Letteris to my gent letters to my fones Sir Thomas and Sir Alexander, daitit 25 Januar, with a letter from my dauchter Helen to hir husband, and delyuerit to Mr. James Aikinheid to putt in his pacquet, quhilk went with a brother off the Register to Court, with the actis of Parliament to his Majestic

Letteris to my sones.

29 January.

Reflavit letters from Sir Thomas, and sent to him ansuer immediatlie, with a letter from his bedsellow, and from his brother James; and thir sent with the Laird of Kinhilt, quhen he went to Court this day, to sollicit for the supplie to Irland.

3 Februar 1642, Twysday. Letteris sent to my fones Sir Thomas and Sir Alexander, from myself, Letteris to Court. Sir James, my dauchter Dame Helen Ra. Item, in myne to Sir Thomas, a letter from L. Panmuir to the Lord Balmerinach. Item, a letter from Hary Hope to his mother. 9 Februar 1642.

Letteris to my fone Sir Thomas, and from his bedsellow. Item, in myne Letters sent with the signatour off the rentis off the Castell of Edinburgh to the Erll of Levin, William Murray with a letter to William Murray to pas it, and in cace off his absence, a letter to the Erl Lanerk; and in both recommends to them my fone Sir James, anent George Foules, for the generells officer of the Mynt-hous. Item, my letter to Sandsurd, and ane uther from his fone to him.

11 Februar 1642, Fryday. Letteris reffavit from my fones Sir Thomas and Sir Alexander, daitit Packett be ane 5 Februar 1642, quhilk I had from a fervand of Sir John Smythe's; and gevin gsf S'r J"hn to him, this day 12 Februar, Setterday, a packet to Sir Thomas, quhairin to himself, with a copie off my declaratioun anent the Incendiaries. Item, ane to him from his bedsellow, one from Craighal, and one from Sir James to my lone Sir Alexander, and to him one from myself. Item, one from me to the Erll of Lanerk, Secretar, and within it a copie of my declaratioun, to be schawin to his Majestie, and his Majestie's plesur thairanent to be reportit to me; and telling his Lordship of my letter thairanent, 20 Januar, sent with Robert Murray, quhairof the pacquet (as I did heir) wes lost. 1 Merche 1642, Twysday. This day I renewit my vow to the Lord, and I wait for the Lord's grace to performe it. 2 Mercke.

Letters sent to my sones Sir Thomas and Sir Alexander, with Sir Dauid Cuningham of Robertland, anent my sone James for the Conehous.

Memorandum.—I wret to Alexander, that I had made Wode agrie with nixt jc Ib sterling for him; and defyrit him to draw it on me, and als to bye the jowells for ane vther jc Ib sterling, and draw it on me.

Item, this day past the licence to Hary for j0 0 stane of wolL quhilk wes tharefter complanit vpon.

5 Merche 1642.

Kri Lanerk. Delyuerit to Mr. Hary Maule the 40 actis quhilk I had from the Erll of

Lanerk quhen his Majestie wes heir, and thairwith ane letter to the ErlL quhairin I expres so muche, and reportis his Majestie's plesur anent the Incendiaries, albeit the dyet be expyrit. L. Murkill. Gevin to William Bruce, portioner of Lyth, the letters of horning, to be exequut *contra* Sir James Sinclair of Murkill. Letters to my sone Ane packet sent to my sone Sir Thomas, with my Lord Montgomerie, Sir Thomas, with quno went post on Fry day the xj Merche 1642, and in it one from me, his 11 Merche 1642. wyff, Alexander Douglas, and my sone Craighall, to himself. Item, a letter from me to my sone Sir Alexander, and with it a letter to the Erll of Lanerk, in ansuer of his Lordship, reffavit 7 Merche, being daitit 3 Merche. Item, a letter from Sandsurd to his sather. Item, a packet from me to the Vicount Stor-Erl of Annandaill, and within it one to his Lordship, from Mr. Alexander month's death. Burnet anent the death of the Vicount of Stormonth.

12 Merche 1642, Setterday. To Sir Thomas my Letteris sent to Sir Thomas, and within it to the Erl of Annandaill, 1642 sehawing him off the warrand past in Counsell for seilling of the charterlust at Scone and Huntingtour. Item, in my letter to Sir Thomas, I told him of the officers to Irland, vi3, 4, sending L. Sinclair, Monro, Home, L. Lawere; 6 regiments by, vi3., one to the Generall, one to Marques of Ergill, one to Erl of Glencarne, one to Erl of Eglintoun, one to the Erl Lyndsay, and the sext to Erl Lothian, Lieutenant-Generall, if he defyre it, &c. This sent with the pacquet of Secret Counsell, by Archibald Prymrois. 17 Merche 1642, Thursday. Letteris sent to my sone Sir Thomas in ansuer off his last, and within Letters to Sir them a letter from his fpous, and als a letter from me to the Erl of Annan-MerctaWi daill, and within it from Mr.

Alexander Burnet. 21 Merche 1642.

The merchand pacquet cam with the Diurnalls from 7 Merche, and with Merchand packet, the declaratioun of the 2 Houffis, sent to his Majestie to Neumarket, and his y1-'81' l Majestie's ansuer thairto, 9 Merche, quhilk beiris a seirsull distractioun betuix his Majestie and the Houffis; the Lord pitie it. And his Majestie at this tyme came to 3ork.

Item, this day befoir nune, being in my Lord Chancellor's ludging, the Marques of Ergyll wes plesit to prorntf, and confirmit with his hand to keip mutual deale, the quhilk wes als welcome to me as it wes vnexpectit, and I tuik it out of my Lord's hands as a pledge of his mercie to me, being so sar grevit of befoir be the nobil man; but within sew dayis I sand a change.

21 Merche 1642, Mononday. Writtin bak ansuer to my sone Sir Thomas, and within it one from his Letteris to my bedsellow; and I writ to him anent Mr John Rollokis defyr, in name offsone 1F Thomasthe Marquis of Ergyll, to bye my sone's comprysing; and said, that albeit I wes ingadgit be promtl5 to Charles Alexander, 3 it I thocht fitt to acquaint him, quhairin I referrit him to God's grace, quhat to mak chose off. Thir letteris gevin to James Murray 3ounger, quho promisit to fend them in the merchand pacquet, quhilk went on Twysday, 22 Merche, at 4 efternoon. *25 Merche, Fryday, 1642.*

Reffavit letteris from my sone, of 17 Merche, with the Diurnall of the Houffis, and als letteris from Sir Alexander, and als from Erll of Annandall, of the samyn dait.

This day my sone Craighal went to Fyff.

26 Merche, Setterday. Thir letteris ansuerit be pacquet to my sone Sir Thomas, and within them to his brother and Erl Annandaill. Item, to him from his bedfellow. Quhilkis letteris went in pacquet by Archibald Prymrois, Clerk of Counsell. 29 Merche 1642, Twysday. MydauchterKerse This day, betuix ane and two efternoon, my dauchter Helen delyverit of chyku"1 f 1"411 a maid chyld, and advertisement gevin therof to my sone Kerf be letters, quhairin one from me, one from his brother James. Item, one from me to Alexander, and another from James to him; and all thir put in packet to my fone Kerf, and delyverit to Mr. James Broun, director of the merchand pacquet, quhilk went this day, about 5 at nycht. 30 Merche 1642, Weddinsday. Harie Hope. My nephew Hary imbarkit for Deep; and gevin to him, for his mother, hir pensioun of fyve Ib sterling, of the first terme 1642; and als gevin to himself fyve doubill angells.

Last of Merche 1642.

Pensioun of 2001b Reffavit from Sir William Dik, (by exchange,) 200 ft) sterling, for my Alexander &c. pensioun of Witfounday and Mertimes 1641, quhairof 100 Ib sterling to my sone Sir Alexander, and the vther 100 Ib sterling to bye jowels to Anne

Foules, and ane cop.

1 Apryll 1642, Fryday. Baptism of my oy This day Sir Thomas' barne baptizit Helene. WitnefP, Sir William Dik, John Morison, Mr. Thomas Nicolsoun, and James Steuart. Memorandum.—Mr. Alexander Henrysoun, *pattiatus*. Mr. Thomas Hen-Item, this day Mr. Thomas Henrysoun tuik post to *Qork,* and sent with with the exchange mm letteris to Sir Thomas and Sir Alexander, my sones, and within Sir of 2ooft sterling. Thomas his letter ane letter of exchange of 200 ft» sterling from Sir William Dik, drawin on Robert Inglis, and in refpect of his absence, on Christian Inglis, his fpous. 2 Apryll 1642, Setterday.

Pacquet went by Archibald Prymrois, quhairin sent letteris to Erl ofPacquet, 2 April Lanerk, to aik ansuer to my last, with one to my sone Alexander, and within1 42it one to Sir Thomas; quhilk both ar to acquaint them with my letteris sent with Mr. Thomas Henrysoun, anent the exchange of 200 Ib sterling.

This nycht, lait, the Erl of Annandaill cam to Edinburgh from Court, Erl Annandaill, and he cam to me on the morow, 3 April, being Sounday, and gave me araonjiTantssir pacquet from my fone Sir Thomas, quhairin letters from himself. Item, Alexander, from his brother Alexander, two to me, one to James, and the contents thairoff wes for a matche; quhilkis letteris I ansuerit on 4 April, being Mononday, and gave the samyn to Mr. Andro Ker, quho patt them in a packet to my Lord of Waristoun, quhairin wes the signatour to the Kirk of 5006 sterling.

9 April 1642, Setterday. Pacquet sent in Archibald Prymrois his pacquet, quhilk went to *ork,* Pacquet. and thairin letteris indorsit to my fones Sir Thomas and Sir Alexander, or ather of them; and thairin direction to Sir Alexander to send the vthcr to Sir Thomas, vi3., from me, from his wyff, from John Arthor, and John Sempill; and I sent to him the copie of the edict anent the ordering of the kirk off Airth. 12 April 1642.

Letters sent to my fone Sir Thomas this Twysday, in ansuer of theis Merchand pacquet reffavit from him be the merchand pacquet 3esterday, being Mononday,t0 Sir T"01"113, xj April. Item, within his one from his bedsellow, and told him of the aduocatioun of Erll of Callendei, Proucst of Falkirk.

Letters sent with William Bruce of Lyth, *alias* Standstell, to the Erl of William Bruce of Cathnes, anent the arrerages of my pensioun, quhairof I have ansuer with *m 'm'* William Bruce, at his returne to the Seffioun; and als sent with him letteris kill, of horning aganis Sir James Sinclar of Murkill, for payment of John Cokburne's money, quhilkis letteris ar rysit in Mr. George Noruell's name, as affigney; and he promisit to returne the samyn exequut aganis him and registrat.

Pacquet to York. Item, the said 12 Apryll, Twysday, a pacquet cam from *ork,* quhairin Eri Ancrum one to me rom my fne Sir Alexander, and I wret to him immediatlie bak, in the pacquet sent be Archibald Prymrois, Clerk of Counfell, quhilk went immediatlie bak this samyn nycht, and in it writtin a letter to the Erl off Ancrum, quho wes newlie returnit to Court, and repoffeflit in his place off the Bedchalmer. Item, sent a letter to Sir Alexander, from his brother Sir James.

Counsell, 13 April 1642.

Letter to Mr. James Sandilands, anent vmquhile

Robert Seytoun.

Pacquet, 13 April 1642.

14 April 1642, 13 Apryll 1642, Weddinsday.

This day the Counsell mett in the Old Seffioun-hous, at 2 efternone.

Item, this day I gaif a letter of myne to Mr. Robert Ferquhar, to send it to Mr. James Sandilands, Profeffor off the Lawis in the Kingis College of Aberdein, anent Robert Seytoun, if a bak band be the officials to him, if he rebell, or if any creditor be joynit with quhom I wold transact.

Item, letteris cam from his Majestie, from Qork, to the Chancellor, expostulating, that one Sir Philip Stapletoun had movit to the Parliament of Ingland, that some had motionat in the Counsell of Scotland, calling in questioun the vnioun and mutuall freindschip of the twa nations; quhilk wes red openly.

Item, ane letter from the Commiffioners, from Londoun, declaring that thai had sent doun one of thair number, vi3., Sir Archibald Johnstoun, to acquaint his Majestie at Qork of thair proceidingis in the Inschekeith and Tamptallon, and from thence to the Counsell, to acquaint them thairwith.

Item, I had letters from both pacquets of £ork and Londoun, vi3., from Londoun be Sir Thomas, and from 3ork be Sir Alexander, quhilk I ansuerit this 13 April.

is April 1642, 15 Apryll 1642, Fryday. with loiTsterting, This day Alexander Narne younger of Sandsurd tuik journey to Court, sent to Sir Thomas, and sent fam a letter to h;8 sather. Item, a pacquet to Sir Thomas. to make vp 1201b _ _ i 1 sterling for joweiis. and within it twentie tuell-pund pieces of gold, to mak vp 120 sterling for the pryce of the jowels, quhilk is coft for my dauchter Anna Hope, and for Anne Foules.

Item, I had letters from Sir Thomas on 15 Apryll, quhilk I ansuerit, and Sir Archibald sent with Mr. Alexander Colvill; and thir I had from Sir Archibald Jonstoun.Jons,oun

Item, this 15 April 1642, I spok the L. of Innes to find one to be myL. Innes, for the deput at Elgin, xj May, for the Justice Air, quhilk he promisit; and I sentSjj"," to him a letter to his hous in Edinburgh, and inclosit thairin ane deputa-May 1642. tioun subscryvit be me, to be fillit vp be suche ane abill perfoun as he sould think fitt.

16 April 1642.

This day, being Settirday, my oy Elizabeth Hope, with hir sather, My oy Elizabeth returnit from the Lady Kynnocher, her mother sister, and cam to Edin-sanctandrois, burgh; and I jraif hir at the first meiting ane Scottis rofnobill. The Lordluhtair »choJwes 6' 6 6 _ _ with the Lady bliffe my barn; and blilht be God, quho by expectatioun hes made hir walk Kynnucher. vprychtlie, without any visibill halt, God mak us thanksull.

Item, this 16 Apryll, sent letters to Sir Thomas, and within them the Mr. Alexander forme off a signatour of the seis to the Justice Generall, Justice Clerk,sixThomas6"31 Justice Deput, and the Deput Clerk, with the vtheris oflficiars, with a signatour blank, to be fillit vp be his hand, and dockettit be me, and subscryvit; and this sent with Mr. Alexander Colvill of Sedan.

18 April 1642, Mononday. This day I gat letteris from the merchand pacquet, from my sone Sir Merchand pacquet. Thomas, and from Sir Alexander. 19 April 1642, Twysday.

This day the Counsell mett anent the traitty of the Irische supplie, and Counsell. satt both foirnone and efternone.

Item, letters sent be the merchand pacquet to Sir Thomas to Londoun, Pacquet to Sir and to Sir Alexander to York, quhairin thair letters quhilk I sent to them Alexander, of 4 Apryll, in the pacquet be Mr. Andro Ker, to Sir Archibald Jonstoun, and quhilk Sir Archibald returnit to me at his coming to Edinburgh, quhilk wes on 16 April, affirming he gatt the pacquet as he wes taking post. Item, I sent to Sir Thomas tua blank formes of pensiounis, dockettit be me and subscryvit, and als the signatour of restoring the Justiciar to the former privileges, quhilk Sir William Elphinstoun gatt signed be his Majestic 23 April 1642, Setterday.

Pacquet. Pacquet sent to my fone Sir Thomas and Sir Alexander, or ather of them; and in Sir Thomas his letter is one from his wyff, with some gold in it, and als the act of Counsell anent habits. This sent with John Perie, fone to Alexander Perrie, quho went post for the Erl of Mortoun.

Exchekker. Item, this day, efter Counsell, the Exchekker satt, and a letter producit from his Majestie, discharging the payment of all pensiones, &c, till first his Majestie did reffaue ane compt of the estait off his Exchekker, how sar the discharge exceids the charge.

Communioun at

Crawmond.

24 Apryl 1642, Sounday. This day communicat at Crawmond kirk, quhair I did consortablie renew my vow to my Lord, and I had his gracious promifl to performe it for me.

25 April, Mononday.

Pacquet. Pacquet sent with Sir James Lockart to my fone Sir Alexander, and within it to Sir Thomas. Item, to Erl Lanerk, anent the letter in savors of John Bellenden, fone to Mr. Adam, styllit thairin Bishop of Aberdein. Item, to Doctor Chalmers. Item, letters from my dauchter Kerf to hir husband, and letters from my fone Sir James to Sir Alexander. And Sir James departit from this on Twysday the 26 off Aprill, and no sooner.

27 April 1642, Weddinsday. Lord Chancellar This day the Lord Chancellor tuik journey to York to his Majestie, pacquet. about tuelff hours in the day; and this samyn day, at 10 hours of nycht, I directit an pacquet to him, quhairin wes a contract betuix his Majestie and him anent the annuity of teinds. Item, ane commiffion for selling thairof. Item, ane gift of the annuity quhill he wes payit of xij011 sterling, and xm fi) sterling, and entres thairoff, all dockettit be me; and als the forme off a contract betuix my Lord and James Levingstoun, with consent of my fone, for his 2000 lb sterling. Item, vther letteris to the Thesaurer Deput, quho went with the Chancellar, quhairin a letter to James Levingstoun, with ane signatour off the rentis of bischopricks to the said James, docketit be me. 1 May 1642, Sounday. 2 May 1642.

Reffavit letteris from Londoun, from my fone Sir Thomas, in the merchand pacquet.

Item, sent with John Comestoun, (quhen my fone Craighal went to My sone Craighall. Couper, for the Erl of Annandaill's tryst,) a letter to Robert Bennet, for precise payment, at Witsounday, 29 May instant, of my dewties, crop 1641.

3 Maij 1642.

Letteris sent with the Kingis Majestie's pacquet to my fone Sir Alexan-Packet to my der to York, quhairin I defyr him to fpeik Sir James Galloway anent thesonesjowells. Item, I advertise him off the L. Lundy his signator, and promilP to him 50 pecis for it. Item, within his to my fone Sir Thomas, in anfuer of his reffavit 2 Maij.

Hodie votum Jancte nuncupatum et jurejurando Jirmatum Domino, Votum. quod prce/lari in perpetuum faxit Dei gratia, 3 Maij 1642. 9 Maij 1642.

Reffavit letteris from Sir Thomas, with a signator for restoring off the Court of Justiciarie to the antient privileges drawin vp be him, and with some deputations for the Justice Courts off Perth and Elgin, quhilk ar to hold on vther, and so comes out of tyme, if thair had beine any neceffitie.

Thir ansuerit immediatlie, and letters sent be John Denholme, half Pacquet sent with brother to James Steuart, to York, to Sir Alexander, in ansuer off bi89May i!ᵀᴹ' reffavit 4 Maij, and within his letteris to Sir Thomas, within quhilk is the signatour of Justiciary dockettit, and a letter from his wyff to him, quhilk my fone Alexander is to fend with one of his awin to Sir Thomas be the said John Denholm, quho gois from York to Londoun.

10 May 1642, Twysday. This day the L. Panmuir, with Corfgray, tuik journey to Court, and I gaif him a letter to William Murray anent Achmuthie, with one to my fone Sir Alexander, and he promiflt to wryt from Court of York to me, anent persuit of Sir William Gray for the patent of fope. 11 May 1642.

William Name. Letteris sent with William Narne to Erl Caithnes, L. Murkill, William Bruce of Lyth, anent my former letters sent with him to the Erll and Murkill. Item, writtin with him to the perfon of Turriff, and Patrik Lesly, Provesl of Aberdein, in savors of William Narn himself.

16 May 1642, Mononday. Pacquettothe This day, about 7 hours of nycht, pacquet sent be me to the Erl of l.il Lanuk. Lanerk, quhairin to himself, with the signator to John Bellenden of 100 lb sterling surth off the rents of the late Bishop of Aberdein. Letteris to L. PanItem, letteris to L. Panmuir, and within them the copie of the act of muir, and to my Parliament anent restoring of horfes and armes, and the names of the Com sone Sir Alexander, ' with signator to miffioners of Teinds. Item, letteris to my fone Sir Alexander, and within them the signator of Lundy, and letters to Erl Ancrum, L. Panmuir, Mr. Levingstoun, and Mr. Murray, for advancing of the samyn. Item, letters from Sir Thomas Erskin, with the signatour of remissioun to his man John Moreis, inclosit in a letter to the L. Panmuir. Item, a letter from Sir Charles to my fone. Item, from Sir James to his brother. Item, from Mr. Donald Mackenzie to Sir Alexander. Item, from Mr. Thomas Henrysoun to Sir Alexander, and als within it letters from me and my dauchter Helene Ra to hir husband Sir Thomas.

L. Lundy.
Remissioun.
Letters to Sir Thomas.

20 Maij.

Letters sent to L. Panmuir, putting him in mynd off the remifsioun sent Letteris sent with to him be Sir Charles, and defyring him, (becaus I vnderstand be Mr.neaMay 1642 Alexander Belsches, at his coming from Londoun, quho came on Twysday,t0 L-Panmuir, Sir 17 May, that he mett Sir Alexander at Doncaster in coche going to LonThomas, doun, with 4 vtheris gentilmen, on Fryday the 13 of Maij,) to call for my letters sent to him, and to direct them to Londoun to him, or keip them till his returne, if he wes to returne; and als inclosit in the L. of Panmuir's pacquet a letter to Sir Alexander, and within it one to Sir Thomas, to be sent to Sir Alexander with the first convenient opportunity; and thir letters sent with young Cathcart, eldest sone to Bryce Sempill. Item, a letter to John Squyre, to the effect foirfaid.

This day report made of the death of worthie Mr. William Scott, minister Mr. William Scott at Couper, quho deceiffit on Thursday the 19 of Maij 1642. deceissit

Last Maij 1642.

Letters to my fone in the merchand pacquet, and to Sir Alexander. Letteris to my sone Item, for Sir Thomas from Mungo Murray. Item, to him from his bed-Sir T00"183, sellow, and from Mr. George Noruell; and I wret to him to haist him home for Falkirk, for the hous bigging be James Murray, and for Mortoun's bans.

1 Junij 1642, Weddinsday. This 1 of Junij the Counsell mett, vpon a petition gevin in 3esterday, to Petitioun off ane suche off the Counsell as mett, be an number off the nobility, gentrie, noMy,ntry, burgesis, and ministeris, defyring that nothing salbe done quhilk mycht pre-burgess, &c. iudge the articles of traitty, or wakning the confidence betuix the twa kingdoms of Scotland and Ingland; and gaiff ansuer thairto, that thai sould haif speciall cair thairoff, and that thai neid not trubill the Counsell with suche supplicatiounis heirefter. 2 Junij 1642, Thursday. This day good Mr. Hary Rollok, minister of Edinburgh, departit this Mr. Harie lyff, betuix 9 and 10 in the morning. deceU$it.

My sone Sir Thomas.

4 Junij 1642.

Mungo Murray returnit to York, and sent with him a letter to my sone Sir Thomas, anent Sir Adam Hepburne bis priority of place.

6 Junij 1642.

Reffavit a letter from Sir Thomas, daitit last Maij, in quhilk he wryttis, that his brother Alexander wes returnit to York.

Item, this ansuerit be the Counsell's pacquet, quhilk went 8 Junij 1642.

11 Junij 1642, Setterday. The Seffioun sat not, becaus it wes the day of prepa-

ratioun to the Communioun.

This day Iffobell Allan, relict of Dauid Alexander, wes buryit, and fcho diet on Fryday, 10 Junij, about 10 hours. Erl Ancrum takin. This day letters writtin to his Majestic and the Commissioners, anent the taking off the Erll off Ancrum be Coronell Monro; and I wret to my sone Sir Thomas.

Communioun.

Issobell Allan deceissit.

12 Junij 1642, Sounday. Communioun. This day I communicat in the Eist Kirk, and gevin to the brod 1 angell and a dolor.

Sir Thomas.

13 Junij.

Letteris to Sir Thomas with Mr. Hary Foulls.

16 Junij.

Sir Alexander. Item, to him and Sir Alexander, quho is now at *Qork,* by Mr. Vmphra Galbrayth, minister at Irland.

Mary Erskin depart! t.

17 June 1642.

This day, being Fryday, about 9 hours in the morning, my deir barne Marie Erskin, (having lyen from 2 Junij in the pockis,) departit at 2 3ieris and half-3eir of aige.

18 Junij.

No Seffioun, becaus of the preparatioun, being Setterday; bot my deir bairn buryit efter the preiching, in the Gray Frier 3ard.

19 Junij 1642, Sounday. This day I did of new communicat in the Eist Kirk, and gevin to the Pastur Communioun. j angell and a dolor, with ane other dollor to my dauchter Anne for the brod. 20 Junij 1642, Mononday. Reffavit letteris from my fone Sir Thomas, from Londoun, be the mer-Packet, chand pacquet, and als from York, from my fone Sir Alexander, be the partit tm3 iyff. Kingis pacquet; and ansuerit the samyn day be Mr. Thomas Murray, quho went to Court to pass the gift of the ward and mariage of the Erl of Athoill, quho deceiffit on Fryday last. 28 Junij 1642, Mononday. Sent in the merchand pacquet to my fone Sir Alexander, and within it Packet, from Sir James and Hew Lyndsay, for the Clerkfchip of the Commiffariat of Sanct Androis. Item, within it from me and my dauchter Kerf to Sir Thomas. 1 July 1642, Fryday.

This day the Marques of Hamiltoun cam to Edinburgh, and als the Lord Marques of

T i o u Hamiltoun, Lord

Lord Saltoun. Saltoun 2 July 1642.

At 8 hours of nycht, my deir oy Thomas Erskin departit this lyff of the Thomas Erskin miffells, having takin seiknes on the Thursday afor the death of his sueit sifter dePartltMarie. The Lord gif me grace to be patient and obedient to his holy will.

3 July 1642, Sounday. My deir barne Thomas Erskin buryit befyd his sister sueit Mary, in the Grey Freirs, foirnent the trie toward the west, quhair my parents ar buryit.

Dream. Item, this nycht, betuix 12 and 1, I dreamit that I wes with one in a wildernes or moffe, and having a ring, that I loffit the diamond being thairin.

Item, about 3 in the morning, advertisement cam that my dauchter Mary wes sick off-her childbirth, quherin I wes muche affrayit, becaus of my dream; but I had my recourfe to the Lord be prayer, and restit on his mercy. 4 July 1642, my And on 4 July 1642, being Mononday, about 3 and 4 efternone, my delyveritof aman dauchter Mary wes saiflie delyverit os ane man child; for quhilk I bliffit child-the Lord. Baptisit John, be Mr. Andro Ramsay, on Twysday, 5 July 1642,

Anne Fouls-m memorie of the Erl of Mar, his guidsir. Item, this nycht, about 8 hours jowell. 0f nyCht, I delyverit to Anne Foules ane jowell or hinger of diamonds, quhilk cost sistie punds sterling, in satistactioun of that qululk I borowit from hir to gif my dauchter Marie.

Packet.

5 July 1642.

Letteris sent in the merchand pacquet to my sone Sir Alexander, and thairin two from Sir James. Item, from me and my dauchter Kerf to Sir Thomas, to be sent to him.

12 July 1642, Twysday.

Ressavit letteris from my sone Sir Thomas, schawing me that the treatie is closit, and that he is on his way to returne; and I sent letteris to Sir Alexander, and within it to Sir Thomas, be merchand pacquet, on Twysday the 12 Merche July.

Hary Hope returnit from France, on Weddinsday the 13 July, 1642 3eiris.

My sone Sir Thomas returnit from London, on Setterday the sextein of Julij 1642, and in good helth; for quhilk I prese the Lord.

Letteris sent to the L. Panmuir, by John Falconer, maister con3ear, on 22 July 1642; and als to my sone Alexander, and within his to Sir James Galloway and Mungo Murray, anent the Deputie of Perth, to Alexander, his brothir.

John Moresoun 27 July 1642, Weddinsday. This day John Moreson, fpous to Margaret Nicolsoun, departit this lyff.

Item, this day the Generall Afiemblie held at Sanct Androis; and the Generall AssemErll of Dumsermling wes Commiffioner, and Mr. Robert Douglas, Moderator.

30 July 1642.

Letter delyverit to Alexander Murray, sear of Annatland, brother to Mungo Murray. Mungo Murray, with ane gift of the Deput Scherifschip of Perth for his lyff, dockettit be me, and sent inclosit in on letter to his brother, quhilk letter Alexander tuik on him to send to his brother, with diligence; and he Mr. Henrie Kinros. cravit powr to mak Deputs, promising to deput Mr. Henry Kinrol5, quhilk I differrit to do, till I sould advertise Mr. Henrie.

1 August 1642, Mononday. This day reffavit letteris from L. Panmuir, from Beverlaw Castell, daitit L. Panmuir. 27 July 1642; and the ansuer thairoff immediatlie writtin, and delyverit to Alexander Keyth. 4 August 1642, Thursday. This day Hew Lyndsay and Elizabeth Anderfoun maryit, and I gaif to Hew Lyndsay. them vc merkis. 9 August 1642, Twysday.

Letteris sent to my sone Sir Alexander, in the merchand pacquet, from My sone Sir Alexme, and my two fones, Sir Thomas and Sir James; and one of myne, quhilk is to be schawin to Sir Thomas Bludder, sather-in-law to Anna Bill.

This day Mr. William Cuningham came and renewit his promitſ to me of Mr. William i-ii i. „ Cuningham. the vc merkis quhilk he promilit. 15 August 1642, Mononday.

I ſpak my sone Craighah, at his return from Fyif, anent the purpose of My sone Craighail. Sir Francis Ruthven; and he ansuerit, that he wes never in any dispositioun for it; and I told him that I had none at all, except to gif him contentment; bot now, finding him so difpoſit, I told him that I wes resoluit never to bring it in hering, becaus I wald not for it all, but truſtit the Lord wald bliſle it.

Item, ſpak him anent his lister Anne, and told him of all occasions; and he promiſit to ſpeik Sir John Murray, &c.

Erl Levin, Lieute-Item, this day reffavit a letter from Knokſergus, from the Erl Levin, from Irland.' Generall; and ansuerit immediatlie.

16 August 1642.

Young Sandfurd. Word cam off the killing of worthie Sandsurd, at Londoun, in ridding off his sonnes in a tumult. Erl AnnandaU. Item, this day sent a letter to the Erl Annandaill, acquainting him with the palling of his 2 signators of ward and nonentrie, for 50 peices.

19 August 1642.

The Counsell rise; and the nixt dyet appointit to be the 21 September 1642.

This day letteris writtin to the L. of Panmuir, in anſuer of his anent the L. of Thorntoun, for his intromiſſion with the annuity.

This day his Majeſtie sett vp his royall standart at Notingham. The

Notſngham Mt" Lord pittie that kingdome, and ſaif his Majeſtie.

Leidhill.

24 August 1642.

This day my sone's dyet wes at the Leidhill, with Langtoun, be viſitatioun of the Lords.

Item, sent letteris to the Erl of Caithnes, and Francis Sinclair of Turbister, his son, anent my penſioun, auchtand for xxi 3eiris, extending to 1050 B, be William Bruce, portioner of Lyth. Mr Walter Bucha-Item, word cam to me this day of the deceit ſ of Mr. Walter Buchanan, minister at Seres,

quho departit on Setterday the 20 of August 1642.

nan deceiſſit. 1 September, Thursday, 1642. 5 September 1642, Mononday. Anne Foules dely-This day my dauchter Anne Foules delyuerit of a dauchter, for quhilk I chyldbaptiſit bliſſe the Lord; and gevin to Jean Cuningham, midwyff, 1 tuelf-pund peice Elizabeths Sep-0f gold. Scho wes happilie delyverit on Mononday, betuix fyve and sex in the morning. 6 September 1642, being Twyſday.

Letteris reffavit from my sone Mr. Alexander, daitit 28 August 1642, My none Sir Alexquhairin he affirmes that he hes not gottin anſuer of his anent his matche, albeit the samyn went in merchand pacquet on 9 August laſt.

Item, this day writtin to him, and cauſit Mr. James Broun wryt to ſork, Anſuer to him. and to Bourtie Mackie, director off the merchand pacquet at Londoun, to mak serche for myne of 9 August, and to delyver it to my ſone. Item, in myne to him, incloſit the douibill off the conditiones of the contract of marriage; and James writt one to him, quhairin is incloſit the copie of my first letter, and directit to my ſone, or, in his absence, to Mr. John Merſchell, in St. Martyne's Lane, at the ſigne of the Croce or at Sir Thomas

Bludder his hous, callit Stanchesurd, 20 myles from Londoun; and to tuiche to my Lord the proviſioun of Seres kirk, and suppley of the presbitrie. Item, to the Erll of Lyndſay.

7 September 1642.

Payit to Alexander Lowis 40 dollors, extending to 162 merkis, quhilk is Thomas Veitche. for Thomas Veitche his annuel-rent of Witfounday and Mertimes 1641, and 2 merks more, quhairof Alexander gaif me acquittance; and he is to send theis 40 dollors to Thomas Veitche to Queinsburgh, and I haif gevin a letter to be sent to him.

13 September, Twyſday. Reffavit from Doctor Hamiltoun a letter from his Majeſtie, and ane vther His Majeſtie's letter. from the Erl of Lanerk, Secretar, for a penſioun of 100 ſc sterling, ſurth of the Bishop of Caithnes; and ansuerit immediatlie, be a letter to the Secretar.

Item, this day mett with William Murray, of the Bedchalmer, anent the William Murray, buffines of Arbroith; and sent letteris to the Erl Lanerk, in anſuer of his reffavit this day, and within them one to L. Panmuir, acquainting him with quhat I had done with Mr. Murray; and ane vther to the Erl of Lanerk, from my ſone Sir Thomas.

17 September 1642, Setterday. My ſone Craighall tuik the sever.

Craighall.

21 September 1642, Weddinsday. Counsdl. The Counsell mett, and report made of the aboliſching of Episcopacie in

Ingland.

22 September 1642.

Thomas Mudie. This day, being Thursday, about 10 hours, Thomas Mudie younger, only sone to Thomas Mudie of Sauchtounhall, deceiffit.

27 September 1642. Letters sent to the Erll of Levin, to Irland, by William Thomfoun. Item, ane anſuer to General Maior Monro of his letter.

Item, this day sent letters to Sir Alexander from myself, with his letter anent the leyne of 1000 merks, writtin in November 1638, quhairby he promiſit, if it wer grantit, never to crave more. Item, a letter from Sir Thomas to him, and ane other from Sir James, all about the 3000 lb sterling; and I defyrit him to send bak to me the letter daitit in November 1638.

28 September 1642, Weddinsday. L. Panmuir. Letter to the L. Panmuir, andwithin it one to Mr. Levingstoun, ac

Mr. Levmgstoun. qUainting ſom the penſioun of 100 lb sterling, ſurth of the Bishoprick of Cathnes, to James Hamiltoun, brother to Doctor Hamiltoun, and servitor to the Marques.

Generall Leslie,

Generall Maior

Monro.

Sir Alexander.

1 October, Setterday, 1642. racquet. This day sent with the pacquet a letter to the L. Panmuir, acquainting him with the closing of the bargan of Arbroith. Commiſſioun for Item, dockettit and delyuerit to the Lord Chancellor a neu commiſſioun, n feu!"8 f Ward for

changing of ward in sew, both of lands haldin off the King and Prince.

Item, delyuerit to his Lordship anc form of letter to the Exchekker, for staying of gifts of the imposts, customs, or lands, or rents of the Croun.

3 October, Mononday, 1642. Mj sone Craighall. This day my fone Craighall first rose from his sever, and putt on his clothes; and the Lord mak him and me thanksull. And it is remarkabill, that the Lord made this sauor of his recoverie to be on 3 October, quhilk day bygain a 3eir his deir bedsellow deceiffit. 4 October 1642.

Reffavit letteris from my fone Sir Alexander, daitit 26 September 1642, Mysone SirAlexand presentlie ansuerit with the merchand pacquet; and befoir the reffaitanderthairoff, I mett with Thomas Dalmahoy, quho told me of my fone's suit of ve sterling, &c, as it is writtin on the bak of the letter writtin to me from my fone Sir Alexander.

10 *Octobris die Luna. Cvbavi ad nonam,Jed per tres horas nulla quies doneesurrexi indutusque votum. vestes et accensa candela legi quatuor capitula Esaiæ a cap. 50 ad 53, et hoc occasione, votum nimeupavi Deo quod faxit Deus persuam gratiam observari et exolvi.* 11 October 1642.

This day, being Twysday, sent be my fone Sir James, to his brother Sir My sone Sir AlexAlexander, ane letter, and within it ane affignatioun to the 2000 % sterling off the annuity of teinds, and his 200 Ib sterling of pensioun.

Item, delyuerit a letter to Hew Tod, direct to the L. Panmuir, and For Mr. Robert inclosit within it the gift of Commiffariat to Mr. Robert Nicolfoun. pinr. '0 " 16 October 1642, Sounday. This day my fone Craighall went to sermoun, and we changit this day craighall. our mourning weidis for my deir dauchter Margaret, and no sooner; and so wore them for a 3eir and 13 dayis.

17 October 1642, Mononday. Reffavit letters from my fone Sir Alexander, daitit at Stanchesurd, 6 and My sone Sir Alex 10 October 1642; ansuerit be the merchand pacquet, on Twysday, 18 Ocandei% tober 1642. z 23 October 1642, Sounday. Communiounin This day communicat In Crawmond kirk, quhair Mr. William Cohan Crawmond. preichit on the Setterday, Mr. William Dalgleische on Sounday befoir none; and Mr. Alexander Henrysoun, *(jpalliatus,')* efter the first tua tables, ministrat the Communioun for *x* tables, and also preichit efternone. 24 October.

My sone Sir Alex-Reffavit from my sone Sir Alexander a letter from Stanchesurd, daitit 16 Payit laoftster-OctODer, anent 150 5) sterling vpliftit from Sir Jolm Smythe. Item, anent ling for him. Thomas Dalmahoy, and anent his matche. And ansuerit immediatlie, be the merchand pacquet, on 25 October 1642. L. Panmuir. Item, letters from the L. of Panmuir, with vthers to Lord Gray, Melgum, and Alexander Keyth, quhilk I sent this day, inclosit in one from me to

Alexander Keyth, quho wes in Angus; and thir directit be John Clerk, servitor to John Peter.

L. Panmuir. And within 2 hours efter, reffavit a new packet from the L. of Panmuir, delyuerit to me be a servand of the Lord Yesteris, and within it one to the Countes of Merschell, and one to Alexander Keyth; and I wret a letter to the Countes, and within it inclosit his; and I wret an other to Alexander Keyth, and inclosit all in a packet, directit on the bak to Alexander Keyth, or in his absence to the Countes of Merschell, and delyverit the samyn to John Clerk, quho hyrit a man to cary the samyn.

Mungo Murray Item, 25 October 1642, Mungo Murray cam to me about 2 efternone, from his Majestie. moyit to *mQ* from Majestie anent Sir William Balfour, Sir John

Meldrum, and vtheris Scottismen quho hes takin armes aganis his Majestie, if thai could be perfewit for treasoun; quhairanent I drew vp, in a paper apart, all quhilk Mungo Murray proponit to me, to quhilk I reserr this. L. Panmuir. Item, I sent a letter to the L. of Panmuir, in ansuer of his reffavit 24 October, quhilk went with a servand os William Murrayis.

Last October 1642.
The pacquet cam, quhilk beiris, that the Kingis armie and.the Parliamentis, led be the Errll of Effex, mett and conflictit, on Sounday, 23 October-Pacquet anent the „11 *n* l battell betuixt the ber; and the report on the victone uncertane. King and Erll

Item, reffavit letteri3 from my fone Sir Alexander, daitit 25 October, sone Sir k,. from Londoun, anent his matche, and sending vp off the band ffor his part of *aader*3000 Ib sterling, quhilk I ansuerit be the merchand pacquet immediatlie.

Memorandum.—I did forgett to insert heir, that on 28 October, being Mem.—His MajesFryday, William Murray of.the Bedchalmer cam to me about 4 at nycht, assUer"hairtoh and repeitit the samyn purpoffes quhilk Mungo fpak to me on 25 October, and thairwith delyuerit to me his Majestie's letter, daitit 16 October, and cravit my ansuer, quhilk I promifit; lykas I wret my ansuer on Setterday, 29 October; but befoir it wes delyuerit to William, the report cam of the conflict betuix his Majestie and the Erl of Effex.

1 November 1642, Twysday. B.

Reffavit, 6 November 1642, letteris from the L. Panmuir, schawing that L. Panmuir. Mr. his signator of Arbroith wes past, with the gift of the Commiffariat of mmariatof" Edinburgh, to my cousing, young Mr. Robert Nicolfoun, and sent with Sir Edinburgh. William Fleming, bot that he hes beine takin be the Erl of Effex his troupes.

8 November, Twysday. This day, (and no sooner,) the merchand pacquet cam, and... 10 November 1642, Thursday. Delyuerit to William Murray of the Bedchalmer my letter to his Majestie, William Murray in ansuer of that I reffavit on 28 October, as als ane pacquet to the L.,for *hh* Majesties » letter. Item L.

Panmuir, quhairin his new fignator off Arbroith. Item, the new gift of Panmuir. Commiffariat of Edinburgh. Item, a fignet of pension to my L. Fotherance, President, with his letter to the Lard, and the letters to the Erlls of
Mortoun and Kynnoull.

11 November 1642.

L. Panmuir. Reffavit letteris from the L. of Panmuir, daitit 5 November, and within a letter to the Countes of MerschelL quhilk I inclosit in one from me to hir Ladylhip, and gave to Alexander Keyth to be sent to hir Ladylhip with diligence.

My sone Alexander Item, a letter from my fone Sir Alexander, and within it the affignatioun tTonoS'ft a" *ofhis* 2000 lb sterling, daitit 22 October 1642. sterling. 16 November 1642.

Pacquet to the L. A pacquet to L. Panmuir, quhilk I tuik bak from William Murray to wrytt over the signator of Commiffariat, in respect that Mr David Falconer had gottin the place of Sir Jherome Lyndsay, and I wret it over blank in the name (?) of vacatioun, and sent it with the lard his awin signator of Arbroith, with the gift to L. Fotherance, and his 3 letters foresaids.

ilary Hope for hU Item, gevin to Hary Hope, for his mother, Mary Neall, hir pensioun of mother. Mertimes 1642, fyve tuelf pund peces of gold. 20 November 1642, Sounday. James Nesmyth's This day Christian Boyd (fpous to James Nesmyth, being bankrupt and incarcerat) departit this lyff. God prepare us. 22 November 1642, Twysday. Pacquet. The merchand pacquet cam, and with it the report off ane vther battell betuix his Majestie and the Erll of Effex for the Parliament, quhairin thair is great slaughter. The lord pitie us. My sone Sir Item, this nycht, at 8 hours at evin, I, with Sir Thomas, Sir Charles and

Sir James, subscryvit the contract of marriage betuix my sone Sir Alexander, and Anna Bell. Item, I wret to Sir Alexander, and sent him the affignatioun to the 2000 8) of annuity off teinds reformit, to be subscryvit, and defyrit him to returne it with letteris to his brother.

26 November.

Newis cam of the vtter overthrow of the Kingis armie be the Parliaments, and of the Kingis flicht.

Last November 1642.

Mr. John Rollok propofit to me anent Cardroffe. Cardrosse.

1 December 1642, Thursday.

This day report cam of a new conflict betuix his Majestie and the Erll of Effex, quhairin thair wes great slauchter; but (praysit be God) it wes not trew.

3 December, Setterday.

Reffavit letteris from my fone Sir Alexander, daitit at London 20 No-Sir Alexander, vember 1642, with letters to his brethir Craighall, Kerf, and Sir James, but none to Cambuskynneth.

This day Mr. George Fyn entered pedagog to my oy Thomas, in place My oy Thomas, of John Lillie.

5 December 1642.

This day Thomas Dalmahoy cam to me and affured me that my fone Sir Mr. Alexander Alexander wes maryit on Anna Bell. maryed.

6 December.

Sent in the merchand pacquet letters to my fone Sir Alexander, quhairin And his contract of is the contract of mariage betuix him and Anna Bell, subscryvit be me, my mamfefone Kerfe, Cambuskynneth, and Watterheid, with the instructions thairanent, and with letters to him from my sones Craighall, Kerfe, and Watterheid.

12 December 1642, Mononday.

This day I told my fone Craighall of his brother, Sir Alexander, his My sone Craigtnariage, and of his defyre to come home, haU

Item, I told him of a motioun made to me be Mr. John Rollok anent Cardrois, quhairvpoun he tuik occasion to speik off promiffes made be me, that the xx00 merks of Hiltonbell fould come to his vse, and that now he finding the contrair is greivit, but he labors to equanimitie, and if he wer putt in certainty he wald rest content of quhat wer my wilL

And I made this ansuer, that I did think ones his defyr wes boundit to the lands in Fyiff and Grantoun, and if that wer preservit to him he had no reffoun to compleane. But seing he preffit me, I told him that I had ingadgit him with the rest off his brethers, Sir Thomas, Sir Charles, and Sir James, for the 2000 lb sterling off the annuitie off teindis to Sir Alexander, quhairof the fourt part wes his hazard.

Item, that I had gevin to James the hous in the Cowgait.

Item, that I intended to bestow the exequutorie on his sister Anne, to the effect scho may be competentlie provydit, of so muche more nor the xxTM merkis to quhilk scho is provydit alreadie.

Item, that I haif gevin to my brother's fone Hary the two houfsi quhilk pertenit to his sather.

And quhen we had fpokin be the fpace of half ane hour, he said, may I wrytt that I sall haif Craighall, Kynninmonth, and Grantoun frie, with this hous quhairin I duell.

I ansuerit, that I do trewlie intend it, and if the Lord fpair me two 3eirs I trust not onlie to leiff it frie but with advantage.

13 December 1642.

This day my Lord Chancellar, Marques of Ergyll, and Thesaurer Deput subscryvit my precept of 100 lb sterling of my pensioun of Mertimes 1642, quhilk I delyuerit to Adam Blair of Lochwod, with ane discharge to him on the reffait thairof, and he tuik it and sent to me be Mr. George Norwell a tikket of rcffait off the precept, with the discharge subscryvit be me subjoynit thairto, and bering to pay the 100 lb sterling, or to giff bak the precept with the discharge to me.

14 December 1642.

Adam Blair of *This* day I mett with Adam Blair in the Exchequer Hous, and gave him

Li Oc h wood bak his tikket, quhilk he reflavit, and I told him that Sir William Dick wold pay me in his discharge, quhilk he promisit to subscryve, being drawin vp.

17 December 1642, Setterday. This day decreit gevin aganis Sir William Gray vpon the declarator of the Saltoun. redemptioun of Saltoun. 18 December, Sounday. Eri Lanerk. 19 December 1642.

Reffavit-from L. Panmuir letteris from Oxsuird, 22 November, reffavitL. Panmuir, L. from Alexander Keyth, quho gatt them from Mr Hary Maull, quho cam in Nk'olsoun companie with the Erll of Lanerk to Edinburgh on Setterday 17 December 1642, and in the letters sent me the gift of pensioun of 200 Bb sterling to the L. Fotherance, President, with the gift of Commiffariat to my cousing, Mr Robert Nicolsoun.

This day good Mr. Nicoll Brown deceiffit. Mr. Nicol Brown.
20 December 1642.

Gevin to the merchand pacquet a letter to my fone Sir Alexander, and to My sone Sir Alex j i. A T» ii i_. r anderandhisspous.
my dauchter Anna JoeU, his ipous.

Item, letteris sent to the L. Panmuir, and within them letters from the L. Panmuir. Lord Fotherance to him, t6 Erl Mortoun, and Erl Kynnoull, and thir letters sent to Mr. Hary Maull, and becaus he wes surth of the way the samyn wes gevin to George Halden.
22 December 1642.

Mr. John Alexander admittit advocat, quho being vnknawin to me befoir Mr. John Alexan that present moment, expreflit his respect in geving me publiklie thanks. der'advocat.
28 December 1642.

Mr. William Cuningham renewit his promis of the vc merkis, and promilsitMr-William Cun ingham.
to pay it betuix and Candelmes nixt. *Item-, 29 Merche* 1643 *renewit with oth to pay at Witsounday.* Item, this day, efter the Commiffioun, the Erl of Southesk and John Fal-Mr-Counyear and my sone. coner, Mr. Coun3ear, with my sone Sir Jaines, anent the fies and dewis of the copper coyne, quhair, efter long reffoning, it wes clofit thus, that if my sone could prove that at any time in Mr. Briottis tyme both silver and copper wes working in the Cowiehous in any one month, then the Mr. aggreit to *i* pay the fies for the copper als well as for the silver, and if vtherwais my sone did quyt the samyn.
Januar 1643, Sounday A. Robert Corsell. 7 Januar 1643, Setterday, the caus betuuc Robert Corfell and Robert Durie decernit be submiffioun to the haill Lords, quho ordanit Robert Dury to pay to Robert Corfell his haill foumes with the annuelis thairof.
11 Januar 1643.

L. Panmuir. Letteris sent to the L. of Panmuir, in ansuer of his of 29 December, anent .... voitis rycht but fpeikis none. Erll of Annandaiii. Item, letters to the Erl of Annandaill anent the Lord Nepar.

13 Januar 1643, Fryday. Mr. Thomas Rig. The contract of manage subseryvit betuix Mr. Thomas Rig and Anna Dundas, dauchter to George Dundas of that Ilk. 17 Januar 1643.

Sir Alex-Letter sent to my sone Sir Alexander, defyring to know how his wyff is in helth, in respect he wrett in his last that scho wes diseasit. Item, to send me the duplicat of the contract subseryvit be hir and hir freinds, and for money I defyrit him to draw on me for a quarter of the annuitie contenit in the contract of mariage, payabill 20 dayis after Candelmes, 60 lb sterling, and to draw it on me or Sir William Dick, and I sould sie it payit.
Erl Laoerk.
William Murray.
23 Januar 1643, Mononday.
The Erl of Lanerk and William Murray tuik journey to Court.
24 Januar, Twysday.

Sent a letter to Sir Alexander and his spous be the merchand pacquet, Sir Alexander and quhairby I promise to sie thair monyis imployit quhen thai send them. hls 8pus 28 Januar 1643, Setterday. Reffavit letters from L. Panmuir, daitit at Oxford, 7 Januar, and from L. Panmuir and my fone Sir Alexander, daitit at Londoun, 22 Januar 1643. MysoneAlexander.
1 Februar 1643, Weddinsday. This day Hary Lord Ker deceiffit. Lord Ken-.

Item, this day the Lord Chancellor beguid his journey to Ingland. Lord Chancellor.
2 Februar 1643. bes renewit his pr him in the Councell, contra Mr George Leslie.

This day Mr William Forbes renewit his promise of 25 dollors for affifting Mr. William For 3 Februar 1643.

This day John Seytoun of Manie renewit his promifl of 50 pieces for L. Many, affifting him in his persuit aganis L. M'Lean, (?) and James Keyth, servitor to John Dunlop, wes present, and he promisit to satisfie Doctor Chalmer.

This day Thomas Erll of Kelly deceiffit. Erl Kelly.
15 Februar 1643, Weddinsday. This nycht, about 9 hours at evin, a fyre in the thak houlP at the sutt ofFyre quenchit,

the close, quhilk brunt twa of the vppermost of the thak houffi, but blissit be God quho in mercie quenchit the fyre.
16 Februar 1643.

Contract of mariage betuix Mr. John Home, minister of Lesmahago, and Isobel Hope. Iffobel Hope, my neice.
21 Februar 1643.

Letters sent be the merchand pacquet to my sone Sir Alexander, from me My sone Sir Alexand my sones Sir Thomas and Sir James, for his journey to be haistenit. ander 2A

Contracts of Saltoun.
Jame3 Murray.
24 Fcbruar 164.3, Fryday.

This day decreit gevin ordaning the contractis of Saltoun to be cancellit, and accordingly canccllit in prefence off the Lords.

Item, this day my letteris found ordorlie proccidit aganis James Murray for closing vp his dores and windows.
Quean.
25 Februar 1643.
This day report cam of the Quean hir landing in England within 14 mylles to Hull, and that the Erll of Newcastell being occasionally neir the part of hir landing, sent 2000 hori5 for hir convoy, and causit the foote armie to follow.
Fast.
26 Februar, Sounday. This a solemn sast, and Thursday 2 Merche.
Cessatioun from armes.
27 Februar 1643.

This day being Mononday, report cam off the ceffatioun from armes, eoncludit betuix his Majestic and the Parliament, to begin on 4 Merche, and to continow to the 24 of Merche.
Marques of Hamiltoun.
1 Merche, Weddinsday.
3 Merche, Fryday, the Marque of Hamiltoun went to Court.
4 Merche 1643, Setterday. Act for voluntar This day the act passed for voluntar lone of 2000 lb sterling, more or less, tneIrisSe Irrnk sor suPP15e off the armie in Mand, quhairin I wes gevin vp for 200 lb sterling. 6 Merche 1643.
Lord Chancellor. Letters sent to my Lord Chancellor, anent the proceidingis in the cornItem, Erl Lanerk. mittie off teindis, and to the Erll of Lanerk anent

the ischearie, with my objectionis and Langtoune's ansueris.

8 Merche 1643.

James Allisoun for James Allisoun fpak me anent the stopping off the re-ediseing of the thak the thak liousis. housjP

Item, 9 Merche 1643, Thursday, Iffobel Hope maryit on Mr John Home, Isobel Hope, minister of Lesmahago, and gevin to hir 10 doubill peices.

15 Merche 1643.

Gevin to Wm. Bruce letteris to Francis Sinclair of Northfield, for his effairs Francis Sinclair of with his sather, the Erl of Caithnes, quho deceiffit, being 83 3eiris of age, in Northfieldthe beginning of Merche.

Item, gevin to him letteris of treafoun aganis Sir James Sinclair of Murk-William Bruce, kill, to be exequut to the 15 of Junij nixt, and if John Innes Murkils scr-and siJamefl''' vand, quho is laitlie come to toun, gif satisfactioun, I am to wryt to William Sinclair of Murkill. befoir the 15 of Apryll, to caus him stay the vsing of the letters.

24 Merche 1643, Fryday. At 7 in the morning good Mr. Adam Colt, my regent and minister at Mr Adam Colt

T n J-/TV deceeissit.

Inueresk, deceeiht.

1 April, Setterday, 1643. 3 April 1643, a berar went with letters from the Commiffions of Perth to Pacquett thair Commiffioners, and I sent a letter to the L. Chancellar, quhilk wes delyverit to my L. Chancellar.

Item, I delyverit to Archibald Prymrois, in his pacquet to the Erl Lanerk, Michael Fraser. a letter to the L. of Panmuir, and within it a gift to Michael Fraser, off the wardan of Cun3iehous.

10 April 1643, Mononday. Betuix xi and xij hours, Archibald Hamiltoun, officer, and the Dean of Discharge off the Gild, dischargit the workers at the thak housitf pertening to Mr. John and fof my ylw Robert Gihnour to work, lykas, immediatlie thairefter my sone Sir James as hereto perfonally inhibit the workmen to work any more, with certisicatioun the samyn salbe demolischit, notar, Michael Fraser, witnei5, Mr. Robert Lumsden, reider in Edinburgh, and James Drysdaill, my steuart Gregor. A nott wes drawin vp, quhilk is subscryvit be the notar and witnel?. 25 April 1643, Twysday. My sone Sir Alex. This day, about 5 at nycht, my sone Sir Alexander, with his fpous, Anna anderandhisspous. t(j Edinburgh

Item, this day I wes witnefl to ane barne of the Lord Balgonies, callit Agnes.

Lord Chancellar.

Sir Alexander.

1 May 1643, Mononday. 6 May 1643, Setterday, this nycht at 9 hours at evin, the Erl Lowdoun, Chancellar, returnit from Ingland, and he reportit that the toun of Redding wes takin in be the Parliament. King of France May, quhilk is in France 14 May 1643, Lues 13 King of France deciefsit, and Lues 14 his sone succedit, the Quean Mother Regent. 12 May 1643, Thursday. This day a meiting off the Counfell, Commiffioners of Perth, and of Com

Conventioun of

Estates. moun Burthingis, quhairin wes concludit a Conventioun of estates, to be holdin on 22 Junij nixt.

Item, this day mett anent my sone Sir Alexander, the perfyting off the conditiounes off his contract of mariage, and resoluit that he sould move William Inglis of his bedfellow to subscryve the contractis, and to accept our band for hir joynter ceiss!t.t0Un de on? B) sterling, to be made vp of ouris and hiris, and if scho mak ony seru pill, in that cace Sir Alexander to gif bak the contractis to me. MydauchterAnne Item, movit anent Anne, all my sones being present, and Cambuskynneth, and efter long debait I gave way for Mr. William Scott, he getting presently 10s1 merks of rent and 5000 merks of saitye, in rent ester his satheris deceafl, but this being proponit wes not acceptit, and so it left. _..,, Item, my sone Sir Alexander, efter the meiting diffoluit, cam to me about

Sir Alexander *my J 0* one. 7 hours at nycht, and gaif me bak the contract of mariage, quhilk I patt in my blak cabinet, in the midmest of the twa black sohotells, quhilk are in the middis thaiross.

Item, I gave to him, in part of payment off his duty till Witsonday nixt, 15 doubill peices of gold, quhilk he gave to his babie to keip hir purl5, and I gave hir besoir to keip hir purfl 1 quadrupill pistoll, 1 old rosnobill, and 1 doubill dowcatt.

28 May, Sounday.

Communicat at Cramond, quhair I renewit my vow to the Lord, and had Communioun at this paffage, I will not leive ye comfortles, John 14, 18, for my teffara, andCrawmondefternone Mr. Alexander Henrysoun, on Ps. 119, 173, Lett thy hand help me, for I haif chosin thai preceptis.

1 Junij 1643, Thursday. This day the Counsell mett, quhair his Majestie's letter wes red, with his His Majesties dedeclaratioune to manteine the actis for religioun and liberties off the king-0 aratloundom, and of the last actis of Parliament, and it ordanit to be publiscb.it, and letteris of thanks writtin to his Majestic for the samyn. 8 Junij 1643.

Cautioun for John Ewing, for keiping off the planting of Carbiston vncutl Sir Charlis and till 28 July, and than to appeir perfonally befoir the Counsell, and the 4 of Jlm EwingJuly appointit for surveying the fruit treis. L. Elphinstoun for him, and for my fone Mr. John Rollok.

Memorandum.—23 *Junij* 1643, *this prorogat be the Act of feffioun to* 1 *January* 1644.

12 Junij 1643, Mononday.

This day my fone Sir Charles went to Leyth to tak his journey to France, SirCharles-joumey with the Erll of Hadingtoun and William Erskine, his brother german. t0 France

Memorandum.—On 11 of Junij 1643, Sounday wes a publik sast, and Fast and fyre. thairefter on Weddinsday, being 14 Junij, at quhilk thair wes a fyre the tyme 0 Nonas'" off the exhortatioune befoir the preiching beguid, quhilk interruptit neir hand 3 quarters of an hour. The fyre wes in the ludging in the foir gait south, nixt Niddries Wynd on the eist, but bliffit be God it wes quicklie quenschit, and immediatlie thairefter a noyse wes made off ane other fyre about John Morisoun's close, on the north fyd off the gait, quhilk brocht greit seir, and the peopill did so violentlie preys out of the College Kirk, that the stair off ane loft brak, and cruschit many, quhairof 2 dyet.

15 Junij 1643.

Mr. w. Cunning-This day Mr. William Cuningham renewit his promitf of vc merks, and addit to pay annuell for it and the principal betuix and Lambmes nbrt.

19 Junij 1643. Lady Cardrois deceiffit Mononday. 22 Junij 1643.

This day the Conrentioun os estates, indictit be the Counsell without his Majestie's warrand, mett and satt till 26 August 1643, being Setterday, on quhilk it raise, leving a committie till the Parliament.

In the nycht preceding this 22 Junij, efter 12 hours of nycht, and about 2 or 3 in the morning, I fell in 2 dreamis, be one I dreymit that all nycht coveringis on my heid wer sallen off, and I focht and sand them all, and seftinit them on againe, except the reid cloth quhilk I vse upon it. Item, efter I awok I sell a sleiping, and dreymit of new that I wes at a manage, and wes cled in satinis, but does not remember quhois mariage it wes, and quhen I awok agane I callit on the name of the Lord and promisit subniiffioun to his holie will; quhatever his Majestie fould appoint for me or myne, the Lord make me readie.

23 Junij 1643. Coronell Mathcfoun deceiffit.

Item, this day, be warrand from the estates, the Erll of Carnweth chargit to enter his perfon in ward within the Tolbuyth off Edinburgh within 12 hours, vnder the payne of 1000 fi).

24 Junij 1643.

A woond dreame. This nycht I thocht that a tooth (quhilk wes loose) sell out of my gumes, and that I tuik it in my hand and keipit, thinking to haif sett it in agane, and it seymed to me so reall that quhil I awakit I thocht it reallie trew, and could scarcely beleve it to be otherwais quhen I had awakit. Thir repetit dreams portendis some calamitie to me or myne; but I haif reffoluit to sub ham.

Lady Cardros.
Conventioun.
Dream.
Dream.

Coronell Mathesoun.
Erl Carnwath.
mitt myself to my good Lord, and to adore his providence; and the Lord give me his grace to bear it patientlie. 25 Junij, Sounday.

At nycht I dreamit that quhil I wes pulling on my left buit both the A 3 dreamc. tungis of it brak. *This fell out recdlie on 26 September thairefler, being Tvoyfday morning. God prepare me. The Lord prepare me, for I luik certainly to suffering in fuche way as my Lord plejfis.* 28 Junij 1643, Weddinsday. At nycht dreamit thair wes lottis castin in a number to vndergo some Dreame 4. burding, quhilk I do forget quhat it wes, and I fred-quhat this is I know not. But I wait on the Lord.

1 July 1643, Setterday. My dauchter L. Cambulkynneth delyverit of a man chyld about 7 hours My dauchter Lady in the morning, being Setterday, for quhilk I bliffe the Lord. Cambuskynneth % e .. . delyvered of a man
Item, with this the Lord gave a bliffing in the nicht befoir hir delyverie, chyld, &c. ffor the lycht stair of my sone Sir James, his studie tuik fyir, quhilk wes espyit be the smok arrysing, and it being efpyed, wes easilie quenchit, and sua the Lord hes vouchaffit a doubill mercie.

The 4 of July of July 1643, Twysday.

The barne baptiffit Charles be Mr. William Colvin; witnefl, Erll of Buchan, Baptisit Charles. Scottiscraig, and my four fones, with my self, quho held up the babe and namit him Charles, from his sather being absent in France.

In the eist kirk I tuik the holy communion on 23 July 1643, and in the Commnntonn in Gray Freir Kirk on 30 of July. Edinburgh.

17 July 1643, Mononday. This day, at 8 in the morning, my sone Sir Alexander tuik journey to My sone Sir AlexCourt with William Murray, and gave to him 50 lb sterling. andcr 25 July 1643.

Hary for in Gevin to Hary Hope to send to his mother, for hir pensioun of Witsoun mother. _ _ day 1643, 5 tuelf pund peices of gold. James Murray This day James Murray and his fone cam to my chamber, about 6 at elder and younger, nycht, and in presence of Mr. John Skene and Mr. John Rollok, pat them selfis in the will of me, and my fone Craighall being present, anent thair entrie and windowis.

4 dreame fulfillit. 31 Juty 1643, being Mononday. 1 August 1643, Twysday. Commissionaris to This day, efter the preiching, the Erl of Lanerk cam to me and gaif me sembbegtin Majestie's letter anent the Commiffionrie to the Affemblie, quhilk made August 1643 at me astonischit. The Lord direct me in it. .dmbu gb. Item, immcdiatlie ester reiding of his Majestie's instructiounes, I directit a letter to his Majestie, schewing the impoffibility off the last article, daitit 1 August 1643.

Assemblie. Item, on 2 August, being Weddinsday, the Affemblie mett efter preiching, quhair Mr. Alexander Henrysoun wes chosin Moderator, and I wrett a fecund letter to his Majestie, daitit 2 August 1643, and both wer sent away on Weddinsday, the 2 of August, and no soner.

8 August 1643, Twysday. My deir fone Kerfl tuik his distemper, the Lord cure him, and lay doun on Thursday the 10 of August. Packet to his Ma-Item, on the 11 of August, Fryday, directit be me (in respect of the Erll ALmbHe. of Lanerk his absence) a pacquet to Sir Eduard Nicolas, Secretar to his Majestie for Ingland, quhairin a letter to his Majestie, and within it the Journell of the Affemblie, and als a part the copies of the purpois exhibit be the Inglische Commiffioners.

Item, a pacquet from my dauehter Anna to hir husband Sir Alexander, and ane vther from Sir James to him, and directit to him on the bak.

Item, a letter to Sir Edward Nicolas, Secretar, from me, defyring him to delyver theis to his Majestie, and to haist me ane ansuer thairof, and of my former, writtin 2 August, and als defyring him to delyver the vther pacquet to my sone Sir Alexander.

Item, at 5 hours at nycht sent a letter to Mr. Hary Maull, praying him, if the Erl of Lanerk cam this nycht, to caus send my pacquet, or oppen it and direct one of his awin, provyding he did direct it this nycht, and if he can not, that he wald concur with my servand to sie myne directit.

Memorandum.—The Erll of Lanerk cam to me about 6 at nycht, and I Erll Lanerk. schew to him the paper quhilk I wes to give in anent the sending of Ministers to the meiting of the divines in Ingland, quhilk he allowit, except that he wald haif addit thir words, "andif vtherwais I be thir presents disaffent," &c.

Item, I gave him the copies of the 4 papers, producit be the Inglische Commiffionares, quhilk he promisit to returno to me to-morrow.

Item, he promisit to gett me the extract off the last act, quhilk is the conclusioun off the Seffioun of Parliament in Junij 1640.

15 August 1643.

Letter writtin to his Majestie, with the new propositioun red in Affemblie, To his Majestie. 15 August 1643, and the copie off that quhilk wes producit to the conventioun on 14 August preceding. Item, the procedingis in Affemblie from Packet. 11 August to 15 of August. Item, a letter to Sir Edward Nicolas, Secretar, all inclosit in ane buist, with a letter to the Erl of Lanerk, quho wes at Innerwick, to dispatche the samyn efter reiding, and to close with his awin stamp the haill sent, and directit on the bak to the Erl of Lanerk, to be delyverit to him at Innerweik, ones this 15 August 1643.

Item, this day Mr John Sinclair, sone to Stevinstoun, deceiffit. Mr. John Sinclar.

17 August 1643.

The Countes of Home tuik journey to Bervick, and thair takkis schip to Countes off Home. Yarmouth, neir to quhilk the lady hir mother remaynes.

Item, letteris direct to his Majestie quhairin the procedingis of the As-Letteris to hi semblie on 16 and 17 August, with my declaratioun anent the new Covenant. Maiestle 3B

Item, the last declaratioun be the Inglische Parliament, and the remonstrances be the Ingbs Commiffioners to the Affemblie, and all thir put vp in a pacquet of paper, with a letter to Sir Edward Nicolas, Secretar, and sent to the Erl of Lanerk, quho wes at Edinburgh, and with a letter.to his Lordlhip for expeding the samyn to his Majestie with diligence.

Assemblie closit.
Lctterig to his
Majestie.
My first and 2 dreams.
My deir sonc Sir Thomas.
23 August 1643, deceissit.

19 August 1643, Setterday. The Affemblie closit, and the nixt appointit to meit the last Weddinsday of May 1644.

Item, letteris fent to his Majestie this nycht, at 7 hours of nycht, and with it the procedingis in Affembly on 18 and 19 dayis of August, and als the prentit proclamatioun be act of conventioun, daitit 18 August 1643, and proclamit 19 August 1643. Item, letter to Sir Edward Nicolas, Secretar, all inclosit in a paper pacquet to him, and sent with a letter to the Erl of Lanerk, quho wes this nycht at Edinburgh, and within my letter to Ids Lordstup the doubill of the forsaid proclamatioun, praying his Lordship to difpatche my letters to his Majestie.

This 19 August 1643 the saittis of seiknes increscit on my deir sone Sir Thomas, quhilk he tuik first on Thursday the 10 of August, butwes four or fyve dayis befoir very sad and melancholious. The Lord pittie and fpair him, if it be his holy will, and the Lord give me ane humbill and contentit fpirit.

My deir sone departit on 23 August 1643, being Weddinsday, a litill befoir 9 hours of nycht. The Lord comfort me and his poore bedfellow, and supplie hir and my wants, and blifs5 his deir children.

25 August 1643..

Buryed. My deir sone wes buryet in the Graysreris, on the west fyd thairof, imme diatlie vnder the erectit tombes. Vow. This day I vowit to my Lord, humilitie, patience, abstinence, sobrietie, and not to eat but one kynd of meit at denner, and not above 2 drinks of wyne.

The Lord gif me grace to performe it.

30 August 1643, being Weddinsday.

This day Thomas Hatcher, one of the Inglische Commiffioners, with Mr. L. Maitland, Mr. Philip Ney, one off the Inglische divines, with the L. Maitland, Mr..Alex-uaMr""7" ander Henrysoun, and Mr. George Gillefpie, ministeris of Edinburgh, com-George Giiiespie, miffioners from our Generall Affemblie, tuik journey be sea to Londoun, toLomjoun_ y vrge the new Covenant to be concludit in Parliament.

Item, this samyn day the Countes of Home tuik journey in the samyn Countes of Home, schip with the forfaids Commillioners, for 3armouth, to meit thairabout with the lady hir mother, quhois place is within some 7 myles to annouth.

Letters sent to my fone Sir Alexander for the place of Seffioun to his My sone Sir James for the place of Sessioun. brother Sir James, with a letter to his Majestie, and one to William Murray, and with it a letter from Sir James; and the gift thairwith drawin vp, 24 August 1643, but not sent. 1 September 1643, Fryday. This nycht, about 6 hours at evin, my letters went post to Innerweik, for Packet for it to Sir to be sent to Sir Alexander, anent the place. 2 September 1643.

Sir Alexander Clerk, Prouest of Edinburgh, deceiffit of 2 dayis seiknes. Sir Alexander
Clerk deceissit.

4 September 1643.

Aggriet with Mr. George Lychtbody to catechise my samilly on Sounday Mr. George Lychtefternone, Mononday, and Weddinsday; and promisit to him for a 3eir 100bodiemerkis, quhairof gevin him in hand 5 dollors, quhilk is 20 merks.

Reffavit from Francis Van Hoff ane barrell of Malvesie, and ane vther of Francis Van Hoff. reid sack wyne.

5 September 1643, Twysday. The Committie appointit be the Conventioun to ordor the posture off the Committie for levying so"1 futt kingdome rose, and thai haif appointit 3000 sutt and 400 horfl to be levyit, ami 4m norss and hes nominat coronels in ilk scherisdom to follow surth this levey, and to mak report on 27 September instant; and that, in the meantyme, any neceffitie occur,

hes appointit the Lord Balmerinach or Lord Waristoun to advertise the Committie to meit sooner. And the charges for levying off this number off men is to come from the Parliament off Ingland. Sir Alexander Item, this day Sir Alexander Clerk, Prouest, buryet in the tomb off raiUs!61"6 Gilbert Prentice, his sather-in-law.

Item, this nycht resolvit not to vrge more in the way off, &c, butt to wait vpon the Lord, &c. *But 26 September; item, 19 October; item, 3 November; 10 November to 5 December; and now to 1 Januar.* bar 1643.

8 September 1643.

For my oy Thomas Gevin to my sone Craighall the precept of sesing, vnder the Quarter hall6 ff CnUg" Seill, vpon the last instrument off the baronies of Craighall, Kynninmonth, Carffes, Hiltarvet, and Grantoun, to him and me in lysrent, and to his sone Thomas, my oy, in fie, to tak seising thairvpon quhen he gois over to Craighall, quhilk he intends within 8 dayis.

11 September 1643, Mononday. My nephew Hary My nephew Hary went to Leyth for to saill to Bourdeaux; and I gave him ten lb sterling of gold, by ten tuelf-pund peices; and he defyrit me to caus pay the compt at Mertimes to Robert Murray. to Bourdeaux. 14 September 1643, Thursday. Seasing to ray oy Seising gevin to my oy Thomas vpon the fie of Craighall, &c, and Granrhomas. toun. Baillie Peter Rollok of Piltoun, actornay; my sone Craighall, for his sone Thomas. Notaris, John Louwstoun, and Robert Hamiltoun, servitor to Craighall. Witnes, Mr. William Dalgleish, minister; Bryce Wallace, servitor to my son; Thomas Jonstoun, servitor to Piltoun; and Robert Tait, gardner of Grantoun. Seising takin betuix hours at nycht. 26 September 1643, Twysday. 3 dreame accom-In the morning both the taggis of my left buit (quhill I wes pulling it pUschit. on my alone brack. qullilk *i* deceit 0f Def0ir, *25* Junij 1643.

Item, this day my sueit babe John Erlkin begoud to be seik of a dcfluc tion, and thair wes a cauter putt in his neck, be advyse off Doctor Arnott; My oy John but he peynit and peynit still to the 5 of October 1643, being Weddinsday,Kr8kin deP8rtitat 6 in the morning; at quhilk tyme he departit.

I being ernest in prayer with my Lord for the barne, on Twysday the 4 October, ather in mercie to spair him, or to ease him of his payne, for he wes heavilie paynit; at nycht I went to bed, and about 12 hours of nycht 1 had this dreame, that I thocht I had loffit 3 peice of gold, and one greit one, and wes buffie seiking to haif them agane; and it wes told me that I fould haif them again, and gatt them all except the greit peice, quhilk I in my dream schew to my wyff, and scho said that wald be had; and this I told to none, for my wyff wes not with me, but attending the barn.

13 October 1643.

This day the Covenant subscryvit and fworne folemely in the Eistmost Covenant, 13 Kirk of St. Jells, be the Committie of the Conventioun and the Committie October 1643of the Generall Affembly, efter Mr. Robert Douglas had preichit on Item sworn be the 2 Chron. xv. 12; and efter him Mr. Merschell, the Inglische minister, fpakNovember", to that samyn end publikly, being fitting with the Inglische Commiffioners, quho satt under the reideris dask; and the nobilmen satt foiranent the minister, at the fyd of ane tabill coverit with greyn; and all the perfones off the Committie, both of Estait and Affembly, satt at the tuo endis of the tabill, in a traverfe tabill both south and north.

And I being thair, renewit my vow, in presence off the Lord, to adhere Sworne and vowit to his blhUt trewth, aganis papistrie, hyerarchie, and all breaches thairoff, me the Lord*contra omnes mortales;* but I scrupillit at that part of the Covenant, to sueir to mayntene the privilegis of the Parliament of Ingland, becaus I, as ane subject of Scotland, cannot be tyet to mayntene, or sueir to mayntene, the Parliament of another kingdome, and liberties thairoff.

Item, this day word cam to the Erll of Annandaill off the death of Lady Lady Sophia Sophia Murray, his sister, quho diet at Londoun on 12 or 13 off September MurTay deceissit. 1643.

Item, on 14 day of October 1643, being Setterday, about 12 hours, I My hatch of tuik ane heavie brasche, quhairof I lay all Setterday and Sounday, and'

Doctor Kincaid and William Castelhall waitit on me theis two dayis; and on Mononday I began to be somehow recoverit, for quhilk I pryf 1 the Lord, albeit I did tak death to myself; and I humblie pray the Lord to mak thi3 prolonging off my lyff a Miffing to me, and to the good of the publik, and the glorie of my Lord.

Gevin to Doctor Kincaid, for his 2 dayis attendance, 2 doubill angells; and as to William Castelhall, he is to giff in his accompt.

23 October, Mononday. Sir Lues Stewart. Word cam that Sir Lues Stewart had gottin the places of Justice-Generall and Seffioun, quhilk wer my deir sone?s. *But it wes not trew.*

About this tyme we hard that Mareschall Haircourt cam from the King of France to Ingland, to mediat betuix the Kingis Majestie and the Parliament.

Item, thairefter Monseur Boiffiebon cam to Scotland, to deill with the Estates off Scotland not to assist the Parliament againis the Kingis Maiestie.

Mareschall Haircourt and
Monseur Boyssibon.
Duk Harailtoun.

1 November 1643, Weddinsday. This day reportit that the Marques of Hamiltoun wes made Duk Hamiltoun.

Covenant sworne in counsell.

Duk Hamiltoun.

2 November 1643, Thursday.

The Covenant suorne be all the Counsell present, quhairof I haif ane note apart, and quhat wes ansuerit to me be the Marquis of Ergyll, quhen I defyrit my scrupill to be clerit. Item, suorne be the Seffioun on Twysday, 14 November thairefter, quhairin I repeittit my fcrupill.

Item, this day the patent of dukedom to the Marques of Hamiltoun and the airs maill of his body, quhilks saibjeing, to his dauchters, the eldest in the first place.

My sone-s contract of marriage.
3 November 1643, Fryday. This day my sone's contract of mariage with the Lady Curriehill fubscryvit, at quhilk I could not be present. 11 November 1643..

This day I repeitit the resolutioun of 5 September, with a promise not to Memorandum, alter till 25 November instant; but on 20 November I now renewit, *cum voto,* till 5 December.

My dauchter Lady Kerf wes happilie delyuerit of a man child, posthume, Lady Kerss delion Sounday, 12 November 1643; baptizit Johne, on Weddinsday the 15 ujlof B man November 1643.

23 November 1643.

Alexander Barbour, sone-in-law to good Mr. John Rig, deceiffit. Alexander Bar bour.

27 November 1643.

Sent letteris to the Erll of Lanerk, Secretar, and within the draucht of a Pacquet anent warrand from his Majestie sot payment to me of 1680 5) sterling, for my y!dtowamie for attendance of 18 day is of the indurance of the Affemblie. Item, letter to the commission of Mr. Murray for that samyn end, and within his a doubill of the warrand. semblie.'11 AS Item, a letter to my fone Sir Alexander..

All thir in a pacquet to the Erll of Lanerk, and inclofit in ane pacquet, with a letter, to the Erl of Dumfries, quho is at Doncaster, to caus delyver the samyn to the Secretar; quhilk pacquet, direct to the Erl of Dumfries, I delyverit to James Creichtoun, his brother, on 27 November 1643, quho told me of the occasioun, and promisit to caus delyver the samyn saiflie to his brother.

Memorandum.—Thir not sent to Erl of Dumfries, but delyuerit to Sir William Bellenden, to be convoyit with him, and this to Thomas Robertsoun, quho sent the samyn to Sir William, with my letter to Seffurd.

1 December 1643, Fryday. 5 December 1643, Twysday. Sir John Hamiltoun of Prestoun, being 85 3eiris of age, having come in L. Prestoun. helth from Prestoun to Edinburgh, on 2 December, tuik suddane seiknes, and deit in the Cannogait. 7 December 1643, Thursday. Cwighall maryed, This nycht my sone Craighall maryet with Dame Rachell Speir, Lady Currihill, *quod fælix faujlumquesit.* 21 December 1643, Thursday. Sir Alexander. At 11 at nycht, my sone Sir Alexander returnit from Londoun be sea, and landit at Saltprestoun. 22 December 1643, Fryday. Anent the rysing This day from the Committie of Estates thrie cam to the Seffioun, vi3., Erl Lauderdaill, L. Wauchtoun, and Coronel Hamiltoun, Generall of the Artail3earie, and gave in a recommendatioun to the Lords of Seffioun anent the intermiffioun of the Seffioun for a tyme, in respect of the expeditioun of the armie to Ingland; quhilk being red, wes voitit, and thocht fitt that jointly the Counsell, Committie, and Seffioun sould meitt, and resolve thairanent.

On 23 December And thai mett at 4 efternone, in the Counsellious of Edinburgh, quhair it wes resolvit that the Seffioun sould ryse the morne at 12 hours, being Setterday, and sitt doun on Twysday the 16 day of Januar 1644. to 16 of Januar. 25 December 1643, Mononday. Prorogatioun Vow. Prorogat my intentioun to 20 Januar 1644. 27 December 1643. This prorogatioun resolvit this day in a solemne vow, to quhilk I humblie crave the affistance of Godis grace. 30 December 1643.

My daueheter Anne This day, being Setterday, betuix 6 and 7 in the morning, my dauchter Fouie, demerit, Dame Anna *YouUx,* (with Godis bliffing,) saiffie delyverit of ane maid child, and gevin to Jean Cuningham, midwyff, j doubill angell.

1 Januar 1644, Mononday. 2 Januar 1644, Twysday. This day my worthie cousing, William Rig off A thernie, departit, at his Worthie Athemie hous of Athernie, having takin bed on Sounday of befoir, and deit on the 11 on Fryday 3 day; and this wes reportit to me be Mr. John Skene, his brother-in-law,12 Januar.

on Thursday the 4 off Januar 1644, at 10 in the morning. The Lord prepare me; for this, nixt to my deirest fone, is ane heavie strok.

8 Januar 1644, Mononday.

Generall Leslie, his Excellence, cam to my chamber about 6 at nycht, E. Levin, Generali. and tuik his leve of me, being to begin his journey in Ingland on the morow, being Twysday.

Item, this day gevin to the foiours of Craighall, quho gois vnder Capitan Moffet, ilk of them thair collors of blue and jellow silk ribbeins, quhilk cost 4 merks.

Item, to them to drink amang them, j angell.

On 7 of Januar 1644, being Sounday, and on 10 thairof, being Wed-Solemn fast for the dinsday, wes solemn sast, for succefl to the armie pasting in Ingland.

11 Januar 1644.

This day renewit my vow to the Lord, and addit to it, not to kyth any Vow renewit to the impatience againis any injuries offerit to me, but to pour them surth befoir Lordthe Lord.

Item, 11 Januar 1644, the report cam from Ingland, that the Duk Duk Hamiitoun Hamiltoun, and his brother the Erll of Lanerk, wes committit be the King XoMrGeorge in Oxsurd or Wodstok, and that sundrie pointis of treasoun wer laid to thair Lychtbodie 5 charge; and the auld challenge off the Lord Ochiltre and Lord Raa aganis him renewit and walknit.

12 Januar 1644, Fryday. This day, about 11 hours, the Marques of Ergyll tuik journey to Ingland, Marques of Ergyii and wes this nycht in Broxmouth, with his cousinges the Lady Ker. t0 lD8,and 9 C

Sessioun mett 16 Jamiar, and thairefter prorogat to the first of Februar.

16 Januar 1644.

This day the Seffioun mett, and some cauffis wes callit, and witneffes reffavit and examinat, and namelie, in the actioun of reductioun off the Lord Ochiltry his rycht off the Lord Saltoune's landes, perfewit in name of Sir Archibald Steuart off Blakhall, quhairto wes alledgit aganis the witness, that *perdiderunt tejlimonium,* being examinat of befoir be the Kingis Commiffioner, quhilk wes repellit.

Butt befoir 12 hours the Chancellar movit to the Lords, be order from the Committee of the Conventioun, that the Seffioun mycht be 3H prorogat to the first of Februar, becaus the regimenttis and levies wer not 3U compleittit in the seuerall scherisdomes; and it wes delayit till efternone, at 6 hours, quhair the Committee mett in the Laich Counselhous, with 8 of the Counsell and 10 off the Seffioun, and the Committee wes not sull, being only 4; and thair it wes votit and concludit the Seffioun to be prorogat to the first of Februar, but longer prorogatioun.

17 Januar 1644.

Sessioun rase. This day, being Weddinsday, the Seffioun mett, and satt quhil tuell hours; and the prorogatioun to first of Februar wes proclamit at the mercat croce of Edinburgh, at tuelff, to the sirst of Februar.

Promise to
5 Februar.
20 Januar 1644, Setterday. Prorogat the promise made 5 December to 15 Februar, and if convenientlie, to the last thairof; *keipit till 14 Februar. Item, thairefter till 24 Februar. Item, to 4 Merche. Item, to 15 Merche.* 25 Januar 1644.

Conventioun. The Conventioun of Estates mett, and satt till the 2 of Februar, at quhilk thai rase.

Sessioun.
1 Februar 1644, Thursday. This day the Seffioun satt doun. 2 Februar.

The Conventioun ordanit ane excyse to be raisit off all meit, drink, goodis, Conventioun. and geir, quhilk is thocht to extend ilk moneth to 2000 lb sterling; and this to indure till the returne of the armie from Ingland, quhilk past surth of Bervick on day of Januar 1644, and is now befoir Neucastell.

Item, the Conventioun ordanit 200 0 lb sterling to be presentlie borrowit from all perfouns having moneyis, and that vpon sufficient security, till the excyse come in; and gaif power to the Committee to force all monyet persones to len the samyn.

Item, this day the Conventioun rose.
16 February, Fryday. This day worthie Mr. John Ker, minister at Prestoun, deceiffit. The Mr. John Ker Lord prepare me, for we wer off one age. 1 Merche 1644.

The first or 2 Merche our armie past the riuer of Tyne, about Hexfpeth, Annie pest Tyne. above Rystoun and Neuburne serne.
3 Merche 1644.

Hary Hope landit at Bruntiland; and in that schip, or some vther, wes Hary Hope realfo the Countes of Home and the Erll of Lanerk. The Lord be thankitturnit home. for Hary his saiff returne.
4 Merche 1644.

Coft for my sone Sir Alexander his great coatche for 40 ft) sterling, Cost the great quhilk is in Scottis money 720 merks sterling; and the great coche is puttcoatchein the hall of the Castell of Edinburgh, to be keipit.
15 and 16 Merche 1644. On 15 Merche the Erl of Caffills maryet on Lady Ker. Erl cassills. 16 Merche, *Votum solemniter renovatum Domino cum in preparatione Petroceliam. itineris ad Petroceliam.* 29 Merche 1644, Fryday. Hope, sone to Sir James, d son to Sir James,", e, .. ". deceissit. Item, buryet on Setterday, 30 Merclic; ms father being at the Leidhill.
—, —j —j

Thomas Hope, My dcir oy, Thomas Hope, sono to Sir James, departit this lyff.
son to Sir James, 1 April 1644, Mononday. Marques of Ergyll. The Marques of Ergyll cam from the armie (quhilk wes lyand at Sunderland) to Edinburgh, to attend the Conventioun, quhilk wes to meit 10 of Apryll. 5 April 1644.
To Francis Sin-Sent to Francis Sinclair of Northfeild the ansuer off his letter, quhilk I ckirof Northfleld,gatt from William Narne on first of ApryU, sehawing how I wes not

£t letter-sent ue
William Bruce, ansuerit of that money quhilk he directit William to get from Sir George portioner of Leyth. Hamiltoun, and thairfoir intretit him to fend the writtis or band quhairvpon that mony is dew, that I may caus perfew; and als intreting him to pay, at Witfounday 1644, the soumc of j00 merks, on payment quhairof I wald quyt the remainder, quhilk extends in haill to 1800 merks, vtherwais wald perfew him vpon his letter. John Clerk feit. Item, this day my wiff feit John Clerk, in place of the boy John Dempstar, to attend me; and my sone Sir Alexander tuik Dempstar to him.
8 Apryll 1644.

To Craighall. Sent my bookis to Craighall, being of purpose to go thither myfelf; and my wyff and samily Avent to Craighall on 9 April.

Mem.—Dream. Memorandum.— This nycht a dream occurrit quhilk carry is some sear with it; but I wait on the Lord. It wes, that the rod quhairwith I walk with wes brokin in peices, and nothing left of it but the siluer head.
10 April 1644.

Conventioun. This day the Conventioun of Estates mett.
14 April 1644.

This day, being Sounday, Mr. John Adamsoun, in the Eist Kirk, be warrand of ane act off the Commiffioners of the Generall Affemblie, of dait Summar excomthe 12 Aprill, (quhilk wes publiklie red,) did, be reiding the prayer conMubof Huntly, tenit in the psalmebook, excommunicat George, Marquis of Huntley; Alex-&cander Irwing younger of Drum; Robert Irwing, his brother; Sir John Gordoun of Haddo; Robert Hay, his servand; William Seatoun of Schethin; William Innes of Tippertie; and Mr. James Kennedy, fervand to the Marques of Huntley, be summar excommunicatioun, for thair notorious coming in arm es aganis the Covenant.

Memorandum.—Mr. John Paip younger wes excommunicat be the said Mr. John on the Sabboth-day preceiding, being 7 April 1644.

This nycht word cam that 8000 Inglischemen wes come within the west Inglischemen in i i A oi,i 5 the west bordour.

bordor ot Scotland. 17 April 1644, Weddinsday. I went to Craighall, and left Thomas Betoun, masoun, at the mending off I went to Craighal. the chymnois, and harling off the south wall of my duelling-hous; and als ItaWU af defyrit my sone Sir James to imploy him to big the west dyik off the middyik. 3ard, and to alter the stair thairof to the west, and als to big ane stabill at the end of the laich 3ard. 1 May 1644, Weddinsday. Being at Craighall, I gatt letteris from my sone Sir James, on Thursday My sone Sir the 9 of May, that my sone Sir Charles cam home from France on Twysday?harl5? returmt ' J J from France. the sevint of May; and that the Countes of Mar, his mother, had takin a deidlie brasche; quhairvpon immediatlie I went surth of Craighall, about 8 in the morning, and cam to Bruntiland about xij hours, and wes at Leyth ane quarter efter one. 11 May 1644.

This day, being Setterday, bet uix 11 hours and 12 befoir none, Dame Countes of Mar Marie Steuart, Countes of Mar, deceiffit in my hous in the Cowgait, andt,ecelsSlt the dyet of hir Ladyship's soneralls is appointit to be on Thursday come 8 dayis, the 23 May, at Alloway.

Retumit to Craig-Item, I returnit to Craighall on Mononday the 13 May 1644; and on Ti'vuotoj 22 Weddinsday, 22 May, I went to Alloway, to the suneralls off the Countes May-of Mar, being 20 hors in trayne, quhair my charges wer 96 Ib; and returnit to Craighall on Setterday, 25 Maij. To Edinburgh, Item, on 28 May I went to Edinburgh, being writtin for be the Conven2» May. tioun to attend the Parliament.

29 Maij 1644, Weddinsday. Geoeral Assembly. The General Affemblie at Edinburgh, quhair no Commiffioner from his Majestie, and Mr. James Bonar chosin Moderator. 30 May, Thursday.

Dream. In the nycht thairof following it, I dreamit that my dauchter Anne wes clothit with a new garment of schyning taffaties, and we cam ryding togither to ane hous quhair wes sett at tabill ane number of perfones, and amang them on, vi3., vmquhill Mr. John Nicolsoun: my maister, said, "Weilcome, Mr. Thomas;" and I went to ane vpper rowme, quhilk I obfervit to be repairit, and castin in ane vther frame nor had I fein it the day befoir, and wonderit how it could be so sone done in one nycht's space. The Lord saif my dcir dauchter, and prepare me to obey and submitt myself to my Lord's will.

31 May 1644, Fryday. Thomas Veitche Alexander Lowis rcportit to me, that Thomas Veitche, my sisteris sone, wes deid, 17 December last, in Dantisk, and had left behind him his wyff and 2 boyes. The Lord mak me ready.

Item, I reffavit heiranent a letter from Conneinilbrig.

1 Junij 1644, Setterday. Parliament.

4 Junij 1644. The Parliament holdin at Edinburgh, quhairin wes 14 erlls, 6 lords, and Erl Lauderdaill chosin President.

Item, this nycht, about 8 of nycht, the Generall Affemblie diffoluit, and General! Assemthe nixt wes appointit at Edinburgh, the last Thursday of May 1645. 5 Junij 1644.

To Mr. George Lychtbody, 5 dollors. Mr-G-Lychtbody.

7 Junij.

To Anne my dauchter, to pay for a velvet caffikin too myself, 80 B). Velvet cassikin. Item, to hir, for ane saidill, 50 dollors, *inde* 200 merks.

11 Junij 1644, Twysday. Word cam of my Lord Durie's death, quhilk I wische may be sals; and, L. Durie deceissit. however, the Lord prepare me. 24 Junij 1644.

A letter from Mr. Thomas Sandilands, daitit at Abirdein, 15 Junij 1644, Mr. James Sandiquhilk wes reffavit from the post of Abirdein on Mononday, 24 Junij 1644;10"18 decei88itand it beris, that his sather Mr. James deceiffit 7 Junij 1644, being Fryday.

1-July 1644, Mononday. This day wes the battell at £ork, betuix Prince Rupert for the King, Battell at York, and the Generall of the Scottis armie, the Erll of Levin, afljstit with Sir LoMeratounThomas Fairsax and Lord Manchester; quhair our armie, be the bliffing of Muir within 4 God, wes victorious, and Prince Rupert desaitit; and the Marques 0fmyles to or Neucastell and Generall King, quho wer beseagit in £ork, (to quhilk thai fled efter the conflict at Bowdounhil befyd Sunderland, quhilk wes fochin on 24 and 25 Merche 1644,) having fortit forth of £ork to affist Prince Rupert, quho came for thair releiff, both fled surth off the toun, and went be fea.

Item, this wes first reportit on Sounday, 7 July, quhilk wes the first lasting day, quhilk I keipit at Cramond, and thairefter confirmit on Thursday the xj of July, being the second sasting day.

Item, I cam to Edinburgh on Friday the 12 of July, quhair I hard a report of a conflict betuix the Kingis Majellie and Sir William Waller, quhairin Sir William prevaillit.

Item, returnit to Grantoun on Setterday, 13 July, and abaid thair till Mononday, 22 July, on quhilk (being fent for be the Committee of Estates) I cam to Edinburgh and abaid. L. Haddo exequut. Memorandum.—On Fryday the 19 July 1644, Sir Jolm Gordon of Haddo, and John Logie, fone to Mr. Andro Logie, minister, ane off the North capitanes, wes exequut and beheidit at the mercat croce of Edinburgh, be fentence of the Parliament, for the Northern rebellion.

24 July 1644, Weddinsday. This day the suncralls off the Lord Durie celebrat at the kirk of Scony, at quhilk I could not be present, being deteynit be the Parliament.

Erl Crausurd.

Erl Lyndsay declarit Erl Crausurd, and he nominat also be the estates High Thcsaurer.

25 July 1644, Fryday. Erl of Craufurd, General Ruthven, Erl off Forth, General King, and Lord Ythen forfalt, and thair armes rivin at the mercat croce; and the Erl of Lyndsey declarit Erll of Crausurd, in refpect he wes provydit be the Kingis Majeftie's patent to the erldome, sailbjing off Lodouik, Erl of Crausurd, and the airs maill off his body, quhilks saucet be his forfaltor. Item, the said Erl of Lyndsay, be act of the Estates, is chosin Heigh Tbesaurer of Scotland. 30 July 1644, Twysday. Sara Hope, This day, betuix 2 and 3 in the morning, Sara, dauchter to my fone Sir daughter to my T sone Sir James, JamCS, deceiillt. deeeissit. Memorandum.—The Parliament rose on Mononday, 29 July 1644; and

Parliament pro- rogat to 7 Januar prorogat it to the first Tysday of Januar 1645.

Item, in the mean tyme, a Committee from the Parliament to ane number off the Estates, and by them to vtheris not being off the Estates, to dispose and ordor publik effairs.

1 August 1644, Thursday. This day, being Thursday, I went to Craighall, with my sone and his To CraighaU. wyff, and remaynit thair till Fryday, 26 October.

On 1 September, being Sounday, wes the conflict at Perth, quhair our Conflict at Perth, pepill wes inhumanelie dcsait be the Irische.

Item, on 13 September 1644, Aberdein wes takin be the Irische, and Abenieine takin. our forces desaittit.

Item, on 19 October 1644, Setterday, Neucastell wes takin be our armie Neucasteii takin. thair.

November 1644, Fryday.
1 November.
Dreamit that I tuik out one of my schaft toothes with my awin hand. Dream. The Lord prepare me.
2 November 1644.

Lent to my sone Craighall 4 tomes os the Hebrew Bibill, of Rotus Hebrew Bibil. Stephanus characteris, vi3., ane tome contening Genesis, Exodus, and Leviticus; 2, contening Numers and Deuteronomie; 3, contening the Psalmis, Proverbis, &c.; 4, contening the 12 Small Prophets. *Item, thairefter the tome of Jq/ua, Judgis, and Samuell; but this last he gaif bak, and took for it that volum of the Greit Prophets, 21 Januar 1645.*

7 November 1644.

Dreamit that I wes at the mariage of my sone Sir Alexander with my Dream, dauchter Anna Foules; a folische dream. But I nather trust nor fear them, but waites on God, and observes or notes the samyn, that I may compare them with Providence, as the Lord sall pleis to mak the event appeir.

9 November 1644, dyet Nidrj to 22 November. Nidrj. Item, 23 November 1644 to 7 December inclusive, HJtt TDJ t D

December, Sounday.

3 December 1644, Nidrie, to 10 thairoff.

Item, from that to 20.

Item, this nycht, being Tuysday, the Erll of Levin, Generall off our armie quhilk went to Ingland, returnit to Edinburgh from Neucastell.

General Ruthven, sometyme Erl of Forth, departit, be wounds reffavit at the seild of Newbury. The report went thus, but he is not dead. *n»pi,.* This day report come of ane meteor sein at Londoun, on 19 day of

November, being Twysday, and the birthday off King Charles, V13., thrie fonnes feine in the morning, (efter the son© wes aboue the horyzon half ane hour,) one be east the body of the fonne, ane other bewest the body of the fonne, so bright as thai could not be lookit on, and above the fone itself ane rainbow, with the bak thairof to the fone, and the hornis of it toward the north pole, or neir our zenith; and this apparitioun did continew sull two hours. This portendis strange and feirsull events. The Lord mak us readie.

13 December 1644, Fryday. Marques of Ei-gyll. The Marques of Ergyll, with the L. of Nidrie, and Mr. Mungo Law, minister, and Archibald Sidserff, took journey to Ergyll, to labor ffor releif of Mr. James Hamiltoun, minister, surth of prison. 22 December 1644.

Mr. John Skein Good Mr. John Skeine deceiffit, being Sounday, at 6 hours of nycht.

deceissit. rrll x, 1 he JLord prepare me. 24 December 1644, Twysday. Nidrie and Jephilla to 1 Januar 1646.

David Gourlay deceissit.

25 December 1644. Good Dauid Gourlay departit, at his hous in Prestounpannis, about 8 hours of nycht. ; 31 December 1644, Nidrie, to 10 Januar 1645. To Mr. George Lychtbodie, 10 dolloris. 1 Januar 1645, Weddinsday. 1 Januar, Gad-Nu, *TTRV* Psalm cxxxviii. 8; i. Genesis. 7 Januar 1645.

Tbe Parliament sett doun, being Twysday. Parliament.

8 Januar 1645, Weddinsday.

The Lords of Seffioun sat doun in the Old Seffioun Hous, and reffavit Sessioun satt. Mr. George Gibsoun, Clerk of the Bills, in place of good Mr. John Skene; and satt also 9 Januar, and

quhilk day I obtenit decreit off the Lords, 9th. allowing the alienatioun of Dalders to the Erl of Callendar; but the Parlia-Decreit f D"Mer8, ment this day voitit that the Seffioun sould be prorogat to Junij.

Item, this day the Parliament voitit the rysing of the Seffioun to the first Sessioun rysit. of Junij nixt.

10 Januar 1645, Fryday. This day my sone Sir Alexander tuik journey to Londoun, and went to My sone Sir Hadingtoun, and from thence, or Beruick, wes to tak post. ingknd '' 18 Januar, being Setterday. At 4 hours in the morning, John, Erl of Lauderdaill, being President of Tne Eri of Lauthe Parliament, deceiffit. He wes borne in May 1593.

Item, Erl Crausurd chosin President of Parliament in his place. President.

Item, report cam this day, that the Archbishop of Canterburie, William B. of Canterburfe
r, r headit in the Tour.

Laud, wes condemned be both Houffis of Parliament, and that samyn day the Service-book abolifchit be both Houffis, quhilk wes on 7 Januar 1645; and he exequut and headit in the Tour, on 10 Januar 1645.

22 Januar 1645.

The Generall Affemblie, quhilk wes extraordinarlie indictit be the Kirk,

Generall Assem-wes oppenit this day, and satt doun (efter a publik sast and preiching befoir 22 JaarbUrgh none and efternone) about 4 hours at nycht. Had no Commiffioner from 1645; dissoluit, his Maiestie: and Mr. James Bonar, quho wes Moderator at the last 13 Februar 1645,..

Thursday; and the Affemblie, preichit in the Eist Kirk on 1 John i. 3; and Mr. Robert DIXt jdy i646TP0" Douglas, efternone, on Esai lxii. 6; and thair-wes also preiching in all the vther kirks of Edinburgh. Mr. Robert Douglas chosin Moderator.

Mr. Robert Nicolsoun deceissit. ErU of Carrik.

L. Lawcris.

28 Januar 1645.

This day, being Twysday, good Mr. Robert Nicolsoun deceiffit, betuix ellevin and tuelff hour of the day.

Item, this 28 January 1645, the Erll of Carrik buryet in the Abbey kirk.

Item, about this tyme Sir James Campbell of Laweris, sather to John, Erll of Lowdoun, Chancellar, deceiffit, at his awin place of Laweris.

1 Februar 1645, Setterday. Directorie.

3 Februar 1645, this day the directorie of divin worfchip, quhilk wes ag greit on betuix the Affemblie of divines and the Commiffioners off the Kirk of Scotland at Londoun, wes past, and allowit in the Generall Affemblie convenit at Edinburgh. 6 Februar 1645.

My dauchter Anna Foules delyverit, and baptized Robert that day 8 dayis.

8 Februar 1645.

This day being Setterday, in the morning word cam off a desait gevin be

Anne Foules delyverit of a man chyld, Robert.

Defait at Loch oCandlemas day, tne Insche and the Erl Montroitf to that part of our armie quhilk wes led be the 2 1645.

Februar the L. of Auchinbreck in Lochquhaber. God be mercisul to us.

Thairefter the word cam that this conflict wes focht on Sounday, 2 Februar 1645, and that the haul bodie of our armie wes thair, and the Marques of Ergyll in perfoun, and that thair weB killit and takin off our armie ane thousand and fyve hundredth men, and that the L. Auchinbrek wes ather slane or takin, and the Marques fled to Inverara. The Lord be mercisul to this poore kirk and kingdome, for this is ane sad and heavy llrok.

Item, tllis day, about 4 hours eftennone, Thomas, Erll of Hadingtoun, Erf Hadingtoun deceaffit of a dwyning aithik disease. deceissit.

13 Februar 1645.

The Marques of Ergyll cam to Edinburgh. Marques of Ergyll.

13 Februar 1645, Thursday.

The barne of Sir James and Anna Foules, his fpous, baptisit Robert, witMy oy Robert neffes Lord Dal3ell, Lord Humbie, Robert Nicolfoun, Commiffar RobertbaptlsltHepburne, Robert Foules, Robert Lockart.

The Affemblie rose, and the nixt appointit to be at Edinburgh in July GenerallAssemblie 1646, reserving *pro re nata* to appoint soner. rysm 14 Februar 1645.

The Countes of Kinghorne fpok me anent hir brother.

15 Februar 1645, Setterday.

Thomas, Erll of Hadingtoun, buryit in the Abbey of Halyruidhous. The Erl of Hadingtoun buryit.

27 Februar 1645.

Mr. James Weymes, Commiffar of St Androis, deceilfit, and to him sue-Commissar of St cedit Mr. William Bruce of Balquharge. Androis eceissit.

1 Merche 1645, Setterday. ny? M cept.

5 Martij. OB 3 Merche 1645,

Word cam of a conflict betuix the Lord Fairsax for the Parliament, and Conflict at York, Sir Marmaduk Langley for the Kingis Majestie, neir *&ork,* quhairin theLord Fw ". Kingis Majestie prevaillit, and the armie off the Lord Fairsax for the Parliament wer routit.

7 Merche, Fryday.

Packet sent with Gevin to Mr. George Gillefpie apacquet of letteris to my sone Sir Charles, Mr George Gilles-quhairin to himself and Sir Alexander from me, my dauchter, his spous, the babie Sir James. Item, from the Erl Mar to Sir Charles. Item, from Lady Brochtoun and Thomas Robertfoun to the Lord Cardros. Item, from me two to the Lord Chancellar.

8 Merche, Setterday.

Parliament rose.; The Parliament rose at 10 hours of nycht, and continewit to the second Twysday of July, quhilk is 8 July.

17 Merche 1645.

Lord Waristoun. Delyverit a packett of letteris from me, my dauchter Marie, and Anna Bell, and from Sir James to Sir Charles Areskin my sone Sir Alexander, to my Lord Waristoun, quho wes to ryd post to-morow.

21 Merche 1645, Fryday. My dauchter Marie About 2 hours efter midnycht my dauchter Marie saiflie delyverit of a ch/ lcT"1 s 8 man cnykl. Bleffit be the Lord, quho laidis us daylie with benefits. 22 Merche, Setterday. Fyre. This nycht, about 8 hours at nycht, I wes standing at the syd off my chamberboord, reiding the Commiffioun of Parliament, gevin to the Committee thairoff, and my bak toward the southmest off the two candells, and suddenlie my ruff tuik fyre, and brak surth in ane low, quhilk I preislit to quench, but could not, quhairvpon I cuist my gown from me, and ran down the bak paffage crying for help, but gat none till I cam to the hall, quhair the servandis cam surth, and specially the steuart James Twysdaill, and glafpitt the low in his handis, and tuik my ruff from my craig, and so freed me off my seir, ffor quhilk I pray the Lord to mak me thanksull, for it wes a greit mercie. 25 Merche 1645, Twysday,

This day my oy baptizit James, witneffes James Erl Buchan, James HaBaptisme of my oy miltoun, brother to the Erll of Hadingtoun, Sir James my sone, and James Steuart, Mr Mungo Law, minister.

Item, this day a packett gevin to Mr. James Brown, to go in the mer-Pacquet to my chand pacquet, and in it letteris to my sone Sir Charles, and within it the slrexander articles off the contract anent my dauchter Anne, quhairof I haif a doubill. Item, to him from Sir James. Item, from me and my dauchter Anna Bell, and my sone Sir James to Sir Alexander, and the packet is direct on the bak to Sir Charles or Sir Alexander.

Item, 27 Merche, letteris to my fones Sir Charles and Sir Alexander, de-Letteris to my lyverit be me to Captain James Cuningham. sones

Item, this day report cam from Craighall that the myne of Callcnge wes CoM fund at the wrocht to the coill, and that the coill wes sund sex foot at the levell, but wold CaUendrawin be sund 8 sutt thick thairefter, and that the costs earis ar sallin to work doun from Balding burne.

a sink, quhilk will be the longer in working, becaus the mettell of it is all querrell. 1 Apryll, Twysday. 1645, I Leviticus. 1 April 1645, Letteris gevin to the merchand pacquet, from me and my Pacquet. dauchter Anna Bell, to my fones Sir Charles and Sir Alexander.

Item, this day Kelfo, with the hail houffes, cornes, barnis, banards, Kelso brant, brunt be fyre, causit be a clinging off ane of the houses thairoff quhilk wes insectit with the plaig.

6 April 1645.

My oy Helene deceiffit at the Kerf this day, being Sounday, betuix 7 The death of and 8 of nycht, and wes buryet in the buriall-place of Falkirk on Twysday Helene my oythe 8 of Apryll.

8 Apryll 1645..

This day, rysing to go to the kirk, I tuik ane stronge fitt off the gravell, Fitt of the gravell. Pacquet.

Dundie assaultit but relevit.

quhilk forcit me to lye doun and keip bed till 3 efternone; but then it plesit the Lord to ease me.

Item, this 8 Apryll my letteris gevin to Mr. Andro Ker, to be sent in the publik pacquet, quhairin to Sir Charles, with ane warrand from the Committee to come home. Item, to him from his bedsellow. Item, to Sir Alexander from me and his wyff. Item, one from Mr. John Rollok to Sir Charles. Item, one from me to Mr. Thomas Henrysoun. Item, one to my Lord Chancellar anent Mr Levingstoun for arreisting.

Memorandum—on 4 Apryll, being Fryday, the Irishes affaultit Dundie, and gatt entrie in the toun, but wer repulsit be the valor of the citizenis, and be the help of Coronell Hurrie, quho cam in a happie tyme for the tounis releeff.

Hary Hope and his motheris comptis.

Anent the buriall of my oy Heleine in Larber Kirk.

9 Apryll 1645.

Payit to Hary Hope his compt, presentit to me be him 15 November 1644, extending to 786 lb 19½ 8d, quhairin ther is ane article for a suit of hangingis, to my fone Sir Alexander 10 lb sterling, and ane vther for his motheris pensioun of Mertimet f 1644 and Witfounday nixt 1645, extending to 10 lb sterling per annum.

Item, this day my fone Craighall reported to me that yesterday, 8 April, the minister and feflioun of Falkirk resusit to suffer the barne Heleine to be buryet in my sone's buriall-place inFalkirk, quhairvpon he tuik instruments in the hands of Mr. James Aikinheid of Donypace, notar, quho kyndlie offerit himself to that dewtie, and went with them a mile sarder to the kirk of Lerber and

buryit the barne. The minister resusit without consent of the Seffion; the Seffioun being convenit resusit, and the Erll of Calendar his baillie, namit Alexander Livingstoun, resusit, and one John Monteith promisit affistance to my fone, but wes the cheiff opposer, and my fone offerit to burie in that place quhilk wes knawin to be my sones, and not in that part yairoff quhilk is claimit be Claffincarie, and surther my fone offerit to gif band to pay 1TM merks if ather the kirk or my Lord Callendor sould find it vnlawsull.

15 April 1645, Twysday. This day letteris from Londoun and Newcastell, daitit from Londoun, Pacquett to Sir from Sir Charles and Sir Alexander on 8 and 9 April, and Newcastell from Chrl' *fJ?"'* r ander, Lord W ans

Mr. Thomas Henderfoun 13 April, and sent this day to Mr. Thomas Hen-toun.

rifoun be Mr. James Brown in the merchand pacquet, and within his to the Erl of Callender and Mr. Andro Ofwell anent the outrage at Falkirk 8

April last.

Item, sent be Mr. Andro Ker a pacquet direct on the bak to my Lord To my Lord ChanWaristoun, quhairin one to himself, and within it to my Lord Chancellor, tell-anSue'r 0f my it ing his Lordship of the mariage of his dauchter Lady Jean, quhilk wes cele-?net James . Leuingstoun, and brat this day about 6 at nycht in the Kirk of Halyruidhous be Mr. John schawing that Neva, minister at Lowdon, and requyring his Lordship's affistance to haif dachr asfthis libertie to my fone Sir Charles to come home. Item, ane pacquett direct to day maryit. Sir Charles, and within it from me, from his wyff, from my fone Craighall. Item, to Sir Alexander, and to him from his babie, all thir inclosit in the pacquet to my Lord Waristoun, with order to give them to Sir Charles, if he be thair; but if both he and Sir Alexander be gone, to keip befyd himself till he have occaffioun to return them to me.

Item, this day the laureation off the masters wes at the College of Edin-Laureation, ... » », «. «,, 1.,,, T Thomas Veitch, burgh, in reipect ot the leir ot the plaig, and amang them wes Laureat

Walter Rollok. Thomas Veitche, my god fone, and Walter Rollok, fone to Mr. John Rollok.

21 Apryll 1645.

This day good Thomas Maccaula buryet. Thomas Maccauia.

Item, this day letteris from Londoun, vi3., from my sones Sir Charles and Pacquet-2i April Sir Alexander, and als from my Lord Cardros, but none from the Lord Chancellor.

Item, letteris from Mr. Thomas Henrysoun from Neucastell, but no ansuer from the Erl of Calendar or Mr. Andro Ofwell. Thir ansuerit be letteris to my Lord Waristoun, and within them one to my Lord Chancellar, craving ansuer anent Mr. Levingstoun.

E 28 April 1645, Mononday. Pacquet. Letteris reffavit fiirth of my Lord Balmerinach his pacquet, daitit from my fone Sir Charles to me and his bedfellow, schawing that he wes to tak post on the morow homeward, being 23 April, and letteris from Sir Alexander to his babie, bearing that Lord Cardrois, Sir Charles, and he wes to tak post on the morow, the letteris daitit at Londoun 22 April 1645. 30 Apryll 1645.

James Small. This day on James Small of 68 3eirs, ordanit to be hangit at the croce of Edinburgh, for carying of letteris to and from the Erll of Montrois, quhilk wes done on first of May.

1 May 1645, Thursday. Hebrew lection. This day beguid at the 4 of Numbers in the Hebrew lectioun. My sones Sir Alex-This nycht, about 7 hours at evin, my fones Sir Charles and Sir Alexander "hariecamfrom 03,111 Londoun, and this day cam from Bervick, about 7 at nycht, and Londoun. in thair companie the Lord Cardrois. n«(£lw/tOf.........a 6 May 1645, being Twysday. My sone Sir Alex-The buffines betuix my fone Sir Alexander and Mr. Levingstoun, efter Levingstoun thrie monethis trubill, and als money changes as thair is weikis, wes endit a88reit-and subscryvit, V15., ane affignatioun be him to my sone, and ane discharge be my sone Sir Alexander, with consent of me and my sone Sir James, of all that we may crave of him, ather be the Kingis Majestie's warrand or be the first affignatioun, or be the

claus in the submiffioun, or vtherwais quhatsomever. Pacquet 6 May Item, this nycht sent letteris to my Lord Waristoun, and within it one to my Lord Chancellar, acquainting his Lordship with the aggriement made betuix my sone Sir Alexander and Mr. Levingstoun, and humblie intreating my Lord to pay at Witsounday to my sone the arreragis of 480& sterling, to quhilk my fone is affignit. Thir letteris putt in the pacquet from my fone Sir Charles to the Commiffioner at Londoun. 7 May 1645.

The Counsell satt, quhair act paffit that proclamatioun sould be made for Seffioun. sitting doun of the seffioun on 3 Junij nixt, and the nixt counsell dyet wes appointit to be on xxi of May.

12 May 1645.

A dauchter of Sir William Grayis departit off the plaig, quhilk put us all Sir W. Gray, in greit fear.

This day a letter wiittin to Mr. Thomas Henrysoun, and delyuerit to Leutenant-Coronell Scott off the Erll of Buccleuchis regiment, in ansuer of one gevin me.

13 May 1645, Twysday, Letter gevin to Mr. Andro Ker, to be sent to my Lord Waristoun, crav-Lord Waristoun. ing bak my letteris to Sir Charles and his nephew, sent 21 April, and ane ansuer of myne to my Lord Chancellar, sent (inclosit in myne to my Lord Waristoun) to my Lord Chancellar anent 480fl) sterling to my sone Sir Alexander. 14 May 1645, Weddinsday.

Sent (with Mr. Archibald Law, wryter in Sir William Scottis chalmer, Francis Sinclair of quho gois to Caithnes be sea) to Francis Sinclair of Northfield, the ansuer of his letter reffavit be me on 6 May, and with it inclosit ane affignatioun to 100 lb., as a part off the band off 2395 1b 4si, maid to him be John Denholm, quhilk band Mr Archibald Law left with me, and I patt it in the schottill of my black cabinet in my studie.

This day the Erl of Lothian sent Mark Caffe of Cokpen to me, with theErl Lothian, dispositioun of the sew-maill of Watterheid to my sone Sir James, and the discharge of the sew-maills of the 3 part of Southfyd, with ane letter from my Lord sull of courtesie, quhilk I ansuerit instantlie with Cokpen.

15 May 1645, Thursday. This day a general! bruit come of a bloodie conflict betuix Montrois and

Conflict in Murray Maior Hurrey, neir to Spynie in Murray, quhairin wes greit slauchter on and Hurrie. both fyQes But Montrois kepis the fieldis, and Hurrey fled to the Castell of

Spynie. The Lord be mercisul to us. At Audieme Mure Butt immediatlie we hard be letters from the Lord Fraser to the Lord m Murray. Balmerinache, and from Sir James Melvill to his sather-in-law, Mr. Robert

Ferquhar, prouest of Abirdein, that Hurrey keipis the seild, and Montrois fled to the hillis; and that it wes fochtin in a mure neir Aulderne, on Fryday, 9 Maij, be the space of tuelff hours.

20 May 1645, Twysday. L. Laweris killit. The certainty cam off the conflict, quhilk wes worfe nor the fiıst report, and litill trew of the second, and the more lamentabill that the worthie Lord of Laweris wes killit in that conflict. Pftckett. This day letteris sent to Mr. Thomas Henrysoun, and within his to the

Erl of Calendar anent the decreit gevin aganis the Erll of Errollis cautioneris on 15 May, and stay it till this day, quhilk I gave to Mr. Andro Ker. L. Warriston. Item, a letter to my Lord Waristoun, anent my Lord Chancellar his ansuer.

INDEX.

INDEX.

Abercorn, Earl of, 41, 154.
Aberdeen, 29, 144, 209.
, Bishop of, 37.
, College of, 55.
  Abernethy, the Jesuit, 76.
, James, 118.
, Mr John, (Bishop of Caithness,) 82.
  Aboyne, Lord, 100.
  Acheson, Sir Archibald, 6.
, Sir Patrick, 80.
  Adamsoun, Mr James, 35.
, Mr John, (minister,) 204.
   Aghan, Alexander, (in Ireland,) 49.
   Ahannay, Mr James, 8.
   Aikenhead, Mr James, 132, 149, 150, 158.
, (of Donypace, Notar,) 216.
   Aird, Mr John, 75.
   Airdes, Viscount of, 77.
   Airth, Countess of, 4., Kirk of, 163.
) Earl of, 12, 13, 21,104,114,116,130, 137,139,141.
   Alder stoun, 18.
   Alexander, Lord, 8, 9,10,12,14,15, 17, 21,
51, 53, 65, 67, 69, 71, 72.
, Alexander, 5,34.
, Anthony, 8, 16, 17.
, Charles, 161.
, umquhile David, 59, 170.
, Hary 12, 17, 20, 21, 26, 29, 31, 35, 52, 69.
, Mr John, 183.
   Algeo, Peter, 58.
   Allan, Isobell, 170.
, Jonet, 59.
, Robert, 17.
   Allartoun, 120.
   Allison, James, 186.
   Alloway, 205, 206.
   Almond, the Lord, 74.
   Amsterdam, 65, 73.
   Ancrum, Earl of, 4, 5, 12, 14,18,19,21,26,
28, 40, 44, 48, 49, 62, 66,168,170.
   Andersoun, Andro, 97.
, Elizabeth, 173.
   Angus, Earl of, 51, 86, 138, 142, 145.
   Annand, Lord, 113.
   Annandale, Earl of, 3, 8, 14, 15, 17, 18, 19,
20, 31, 32, 33, 35, 36, 41, 44, 52, 62, 66, 68, 69, 84, 86, 120, 127, 129, 132,136, 137, 144, 146, 148, 160, 161, 163, 174, 184, 197.
, Countess of, 52, 66.
   Anstruther, Sir William, 58.
   Arbroith, 34, 59,175,176,179.
   Ardoch, the Goodman of, 50.
   Argyll, Earl of, 90,102,105, 115, 138, 140,
142, 143, 145, 150, 151, 153, 198, 201, 204, 213.
, Marquis of, 160, 161,182.
   Arnott, James, 63, 66, 68.
, Doctor, 197.
   Arthur, John, 163.
   Arundell, Earl of, 93.
   Auchinbreck, Laird of, 212.
   Auchterhous, the Lord, 85.

Aulderne, 220.
Awmonthe, Lord, (Lieutenant-General,) 142.
Aytoun, James, (mason,) 28, 30., Mr David, 114,
Babethan, Laird of, 17, 22.
Balcanquill, Mr Robert, 37.
—, D, 126.
Balcomie, Lord, 90.
of Balquharge, Mr William, 213.
of Lyth, William, 163, 168.
Baldingburne, 215.
Balfour, Sir James, 144.
, Sir William, 5, 57, 178.
, Doctor, 116.
Baillie, Doctor, 7, 13, 14.
, Sir Gideon, 119.
, Sir James, 15.
Balgone, 33.
Balgonie, Lord, 188.
Ballincreif, 27.
Balmaketly, Barony of, 79, 82.
Balmaver, 56.
Balmeno, 56.
Balmerinoch, Lord, 9,11,15,16,17, 21, 66,
196, 218, 220.
Banff, Lord, 20, 96.
Bankis, Mr, 32.
Barclay, Mr Robert, 3.
Barbor in Kirkcaldy, William, 60.
Barbour, Alexander, 199,
Barrie, 9.
Bass, The Lord and Lady, 60.
Beatson of Cardon, David, 9.
Belheavin, Viscount, 28.
Bell, Anna, 173, 180, 181, 183, 188, 214,
215.
Bellenden, Mr Adam, (Bishop of Aberdeen,)
82, 166.
, John, 36, 166, 168.
, Sir William, 199.
, Mr William, 26.
Belsches, Mr Alexander, 21, 113, 169.
Bennet, Mr G., (minister,) 23, 24, 27, 123.
, Mr James, 48.
, Thomas, 25.
, Mr Robert, 48, 112, 123, 167.
, Mr William, 151.
Berridaill, Master of, 106
Berwick, 3, 86, 89, 98,102,151,193,
211,
218.
Betaun, Thomas, (mason,) 205.
Beverlaw Castle, 173.
Binning, Lord, 36.
Blair, Laird of, 1.02.
of Lochwood, Adam, 102, 182.
Blacater, Laird of, 97.
Bladder, Sir Thomas, 173, 175.
Boissiebon, Monsieur, 198.
Bonar, Mr James, (minister,) 206, 212.
Borders, the, 11.
Borrowmure, the, 88.
Borthuik, Mr Eleazer, 27, 32, 40, 44, 54.
, Lady, 35.
Bourdeaux, 196.
Bowdounhill beside Sunderland, 207.
Bowse, Ninian, 107.
Boyd, Lord, 122.
, Christian, 180.
, James, 57.
Brechin, 9, 14, 30, 34, 43, 49, 54.
, Bailliery of, 36, 38, 125.
, Bishop of, 16, 27, 33, 45, 54, 57, 82.
Brechin-muir, Marches of, 55.
Briot, Monsieur, 5, 184.
Brochtoun, Lady, 214.
Broghe, Lord, 93.
Brown, Mr James, 162,175, 215, 217.
, Mr Nicoll, 53, 183.
, Mr Patrick, 147.
Broxmouth, 15, 201.
Bruce, Alexander, 38.
, George, 91.
, of Balquharge, William, 213.
, William, 160, 174, 187.
Buccleuch, Earl of, 5, 219.
Buchan, Earl of, 4, 11, 24, 113, 191, 215.
Buchanan, Mr Walter, (minister of Seres,)
174.
Burgleish, Earl, 21.
Burley, the Lord, 122,137.
Burnet, Mr Alexander, 42, 76, 94, 127.
, Gawin, 48.
, Mr Robert, 35, 36.
, William, 71, 72,109,129,132,135, 136, 144, 146, 151, 160,161.
Burntisland, 55, 106, 120, 203, 205.
Butter, William, 55.

Caddell, Laird of, 35, 56.
Caithness, Bishop of, 6, 175.
, Earl of, 122, 163, 174, 187.
Calis 40 65.
Callendar, Earl of, 163, 211, 216, 217, 220.
Callenge, Myne of, 215.
Cambuskynneth, 104, 118, 181.
, The Lady, 135,191.
Campbell, Archibald, 23, 53.
, Colin, (tutor of Calder,) 105.
of Lawers, Sir James, 212.
, Mr Neil, (Bishop of the Yles,) 82.
Canterbury, Archbishop of, (William Laud,)
13, 15, 19, 21, 46, 58, 59, 61, 63, 211.
Capringtoun, Laird of, 41, 91.
Carbistoun, 189.
Cardross, 12, 181.
, Lord, 190, 214, 217, 218.
Carloungie, 14.
Carmichael, Sir James, 11, 12, 14, 15, 16,
23, 25, 48, 49, 145, 149.
Carmyllie, Newtoun of, 49.
Carnoch, Laird of, 4.
Carnwath, Earl of, 190.
Carrestoun, Kirk of, 147.
Carrick, Earl of, 212.
Carstairs, John, 85.
Cass of Cockpen, Mark, 12, 219.
Cassillis, Earl of, 145, 203-
Castelhall, William, 198.
Chalmers, Doctor, 4, 10, 22, 87, 166.
, Mr William, 76.
Cheislie, Mr John, (minister,) 24.
Classincarrie, 216.
Clerk, Alexander, 14.
, Sir Alexander, (provost of Edinburgh,) 195, 196.
, John, 46, 52, 53, 63, 66, 146, 147, 178, 204.
Cockburn, Mr Christopher, 154.
, Mr John, 47, 163.
Colace, Mr William, 106.
Colbranspeth, 156.
Coldenknowis, 4, 6, 12.
College Kirk, The, 189.
Colvill, Mr Alexander, 106, 165., John Lord, 10.
, Mr William, (minister,) 27,178, 191.
Colt, Mr Adam, (minister at Inveresk, 187.
Comestoun, John, 167.
Comming, Mr George, (merchand at

Doles,)
114.
   Conneinisbrtg, 206.
Cook, Mr Patrick, 35.
Corsell, Robert, 184.
Corsgray, Laird of, 168.
Cossinis, Laird of, 133.
Couper, 167-
   Crafurd, Earl of, 105, 153, 208, 211.,
David, 123.
   Crafurd, Patrick, 123.
Craig, Mr John, 112., Mr Robert, 10, 146.
   Crlighall", 10, 20, 22, 24, 65, 66, 72, 77,100,
104, 116, 120, 196, 205, 206, 209. *Vide Petrocella.*
, The Laird of, 79, 88, 90, 91,141, 146, 152, 161, 175, 176,182, 196.
   Craigs, Barony of, 79.
   Cragyvar, Laird of, 4, 40, 41,44, 45, 68, 76,
113.
   Craill, Town of, 22.
Cranstoun, Lord, 46, 90, 92,
Cranstounriddell, 28, 50, 90.
Crawmond Kirk, 27, 30, 60, 166, 178, 189,
207.
   Creich, Laird of, 55, 62.
Creichtoun, James, 199.
Crichton, Lord, 62.
Cunnaquhy, 85.
   Cunningham, Sir Adam, 90, 101. of Auchinhervie, Sir David, 61, 63, 65, 71, 73, 85, 116, 121.
of Robertland, Sir David, 160.
, Captain James, 215.
, Jean, 105, 135, 174, 200.
, Mr William, 91,112, 173, 183, 190.
   Curriehill, the Lady, 198, 200.
   Dalders, 211.
Dalgleish, Mr David, 57.
, Mr William, (minister,) 178,196.
   Dalkeith, 67, 70, 72, 87, 88, 100., Lord, 31.
   Dalmahoy, Thomas, 13, 177, 178, 181.
Dalzell, the Lord, 74, 76, 82, 93, 109, 213.
, Master of, 27, 23, 32, 33, 34, 35,38.
, John, 31.
, Sir Robert, 42.
   Dantisk, 206.

Davidsoun, Doctor, 3, 44.
of Blackstoun, Sir Alexander, 121.
, Mr Robert, 45, 48.
, Mr Samuel, 121.
   Dempster, John, 204.
Denholm, John, 167, 219.
Denmiln, Laird of, 41.
Dernway, 76.
Dick, Mr David, 103.
, Mr John, 39, 59.
, Sir William, 158, 162, 182, 184.
2 F
   Dick, William, 141, 143.
Dicksoun, John, 137.
, Patrick, 3.
   Diep, 50, 79,127, 162.
Dirltoun, 12, 113., 104.
, Admiralty of, 113.
   Doncastes, 169, 199.
Do nypace, Master of, 31.
Douglas, Marquess of, 3.
, Alexander, 160.
, Colonel, 55.
James, (callit Nikstikks,) 131,-
, Sir James, 103.
, John, 142, 145.
, Mr Robert, 173, 197, 212.
, W illiam, 131, 134.
   Doun, Lord, 9, 10, 148.
Dresdan, Battle of, 59.
Drummond, Mr Andro, (minister at Panbryd,) 30.
, Mr Hary, 12, 19.
   Dry burgh, 104.
Drysdaill, James, 187.
Dumbarro, Laird of, 32.
Dumbarton, 88, 119.
, Castle of, 119.
   Dumfries, Earl of, 20, 199.
Dunbar, 94, 98.
, Commonty of, 28, 29.
Dunblane, Dishop of,
   Duncan, James, (postmaster of the Cannogait,) 132, 133.
of Ratho, James, 150.
, John, 150.
   Dundas of that Ilk, George, 184.
, Anna, 184.
   Dundee, 66, 79, 216.
   Dunfermling, Earl of, 101, 110, 118, 146,
148, 173.
Dunglas, 119.
Dunlop, John, 185.
Dunsyre, Sir Thomas, 59.

Durham, 94.
, Mr John, (minister,) 104.
   Dury, the Lord, 35, 79, 88, 90, 91,102,145,
207, 208.
, Robert, 184.
   D wo, Laird of, 70.
Dyn, John, 85.
   Edyar, Elizabeth, 53., George, 53.
   Edyar of Weddcrlie, John, 53.
of Newtoun, Richart, 53.
   Edinburgh, Bishop of, 6, 19, 36.
, Castle of, 87, 93, 99,119.
, College of, 217.
, Dean of, 64.
., Tolbooth of, 190.
   Eglinton, Earl of, 153.
Eistbank, Lord, 90, 92.
Elgin, 165, 167.
   Elphinstoun, Lord, 90, 138, 145, 151,189.
, Mr William, 28, 36, 48, 50.
, Sir William, 15, 166.
   Ernock, Laird of, 28, 49.
Erroll, Earl of, 220.
Erskine, Colonel, 94, 95.
, Lord, 102.
, Alexander, 85.
——, Colonel Alexander, 119.
, Charles, 84, 85, 94.
, Sir Charles, 214.
, John, 50, 196.
, John, 85.
, Mary, 170,171.
, Sir Thomas, 168.
, Thomas, 171.
, Mr William, 85, 189.
   Essex, Earl of, 179, 181.
Ewing, John, 189.
   Fairfax, the Lord, 213.
, Sir Thomas, 207.
   Falconer, Mr David, 15, 180.
, John, (Maister Conyear,) 172, 184.
Falkirk, 169, 215.
Falkland, 121.
Farquhar, Mr Robert, 164.
Farquharson, Donald, 96.
, Mr James, 17, 18.
   Fennick of Meldin, Sir William, 121.
Ferquhar, Mr Robert, (provost of Aberdeen,) 220.
Fetteresso, 31.
Findlater, Earl of, 151.
Finlay, Mr James, 82.
Fithy, Mr Henry, 104.

Fleming, The Lady, 21.
, Barbara, 147.
, John, 147, 156, 158.
, Marie, 135,156.
, Robert, 137.
, Sir William, 179.
Flescher, Sir Andro, 37, 139.
Flescher, Sir George, 6, 8.
Forbes, Master of, 96.
, Mr William, 112, 185.
Forman, Thomas, 25.
Forth, Water of, 153., Earl of, 210.
Fotherance, Lord, 90, 92, 101, 179, 183.
Foulden, 99.
Foulis, Anna, 69, 85, 128, 154, 162, 165,
172, 174, 200, 209, 212.
, George, 159.
, Mr Hary, 170.
, Mr Robert, 69, 213.
France, 38, 45, 189.
, Louis XIII, King of, 188.
, XIV., 188.
Fraser, the Lord, 220.
, Michael, 187.
Freir, William, 48.
Frendracht, the Laird of, 39, 57, 76.
Frithy, Mr Hary, 40, 131.
Fyff, 24,161, 182.
, David, 49.
, Henry, 49.
Fyn, Mr George, (Pedagog,) 181.
Gaitgirth, Laird of, 102.
Galbraith, Mr Umphra, (minister in Ireland,) 170.
Galloway, 156.
, Earl of, 90, 151.
, Sir James, (Secretary,) 129, 133, 140, 146, 148, 149,150, 156,167,172.
Garnock, 25.
Gibson, Mr George, 211.
Gicht, Young Laird of, 32.
Gillespie, Mr George, (minister,) 195, 214.
Gilliroy, Laird of, 40, 41, 44.
Gilmuir, (Gilmour,) Mr John, 73, 76, 187.
, Robert, 187.
Glasgow, 80.
, Kirk of, 82.
Glass, Patrick, 41.
Glencairn, Earl of, 160.
Glenco, 44.

Goddice, Charles, 31.
Gogar, Laird of, 119.
Gordoun of Ardchat, Alexander, 144.
, Mr James, 3, 6, 9,14, 17, 18, 20, 31, 33, 34, 36, 41, 45, 47, 49, 61, 65, 67, 70, 73, 80, 87, 111.
of Haddo, Sir John, 205, 298.
, Sir John, 30.
Gordoun, Mr Robert, 6, 16, 32, 34, 39, 48,
53, 54, 57, 93, 95, 101, 113, 155.
, Mr William, 37.
Gourlay, David, 123, 210.
, Janet, 48.
, Thomas, 123.
Graham, Mr, (Inglishman,) 85., Captain, 19.
, Mr George, (Bishop of Orkney,) 82.
, Sir Richard, 156.
Granger, Mr Arthour, (schoolmaster of Ar-
broath,) 38.
Grant, James, 42, 43,116.
Grantoun, 42, 136, 182,196, 208.
, Wester, 67.
Gray, Lord, 84, 178.
, Sir William, 168, 183, 219.
, William, 128.
Gravfrier Kirk, 149, 171, 191.
Guthrie, Mr John, (Bishop of Murray,) 82.
Hadden, (Halden,) George, 47, 55, 79, 114,
126, 183.
Haddo, Lord, 96.
Hadingtoun, 98, 211.
, Thomas, Earl of, 58, 61, 100, 119, 189, 213, 215.
Haig, Mr William, 11.
Hair court, Mareschall, 198.
Halhill, Laird of, 55.
Halkerstoun, younger, Lord, 100.
Haltoun, 34, 56.
Hamilton, 81, 131, 153.
, Duke of, 198, 201.
, Marquis of, 5, 7, 9, 10, 11, 13, 15, 17,18,34,38, 45,47—57, 72, 74—94,
99, 122,145, 153, 156,171, 176, 186.,
Colonel, (general of artillery,) 200.
, Sir James, 18, 100.
of Prestoun, Sir John, 199.
of Orbistoun, John, 19, 24, 25, 34,

48, 71.
, Archibald, 187.
, Sir William, 41.
, James, 176, 210, 215.
, Sir George, 204.
, Doctor, 175, 176.
, Robert, 196.
Hatcher, Mr Thomas, 195.
Hay of Quhitsoun, 146., Mr Alexander, 113.
Hay of Smeithfield, Sir James, 106.
, Sir John, 10, 31, 87, 93.
, Robert, 205.
Hendersoun, Mr Alexander, (minister,) 82,
97, 103, 111, 149, 151, 162, 178, 189, 192, 195.
, Mr John, 149.
, Mr Thomas, 30,162,163,168, 216, 217, 219, 220.
Hepburn, Colonel, 21.
, Mr Adam, 93.
j-, Sir Adam, 170.
, Mr Alexander, 29, 30.
, Commissar Robert, 213.
Hexspeth, 203.
Hilltarvet,ll, 12,196.
Hiltonbell, 181.
Hoff, Francis Van, 195.
Hog, John, 144.
Holland, Earl of, 97, 145.
Hollanders, the, 108.
Holyroodhouse, 74, 81, 82, 151, 213, 217.
Home, Countess of, 10, 37, 39, 41, 87, 108,
193, 203.
, Earl of, 108.
, G., 12.
, Mark, 118.
of Manderstoun, Sir Alexander, 21, 36, 42, 48, 54, 62, 78, 79, 108. of Threip-
dailly, Sir Alexander, 27, 36,
42, 48, 54, 62, 78, 79, 108., Mr John, (minister of Lesnrahago,)
185, 187.
Hope, Alexander, (Sir Alexander,) 6, 7, 13,
14, 19, 21, 24, 33, 35, 38, 40, 41, 42, 44, 48, 53, 54, 56, 63, 75, 102,114,121, 141, 156—185, 188-218.
, Elizabeth, 165.
, George, 25, 41, 56.
, Hary, 7, 23, 39, 40, 50, 65, 73, 88, 106, 138, 152, 180, 185, 196.

, Isobell, 185, 187.
, James, (Sir James,) 3, 7, 18, 23, 38, 39, 40, 48, 52, 54, 63, 68, 69, 85,106,113,
114, 121, 129. 132—177—185—208.
, John, 23, 85.
, Sir John, 14, 18, 40, 42, 44, 54, 58, 65, 68, 69.
, Mary, 24, 42, 53, 84, 85, 93,172, 214.
, Robert, 6, 11, 12, 14, 39.
, Sara, 208.
, Sir Thomas, (younger,) 3, 13, 14, 18, 28, 44, 54, 58, 65, 68, 69, 93, 106, 113, 117__157—177—185.
   Hope, Thomas, 23, 54, 85.
, William, 5.
   Hull, 186.
Humbie, 54.
, Lord, 212.
   Huntingtower, 160.
Huntly, Marquis of, 21.
., Anne (Anna,) 93, 165.
, Charles, (Sir Charles,) 96, 106—218.
, George Marquis of, 73, 76, 93, 108, 205.
, Margaret, 100, 177.
   Hurrie, Colonel, 216.
, Lieutenant, 153.
, Major, 220.
   Inchaffray, 5.
Inehkeith, 164.
Inchmahomo, Priory of, 104.
Inglis, Christian, 162.
, John, (skinner,) 28.
, Robert, 141, 143, 162.
   Inglistoun, Laird of, 119.
Innerpeffer, Lord, 89, 90, 92, 107.
, 37.
   Innes, Laird of, 46, 165.
, John, 187.
— of Tippertie, William, 205.
Innerteill, Laird of, 79, 88, 90.
Inner weik, 113,193.
   Irving, younger of Drum, Alexander, 205.
, Robert, 205.
   Innerury, 96.
Inverara, 212.
   Jamesoun, Thomas, 27.
, Mr William, (painter,) 75, 76.
   Jedburgh, 55.
   Johnstoun, Mr Alexander, 109.
, Mr Archibald, 97, 106, 145.
, Thomas, 196.

Ker, Mr Andro, 163, 165, 215, 217, 219,
220.
, Hary Lord, 185.
, Mr John, 58, 203.
, The Lady, 201, 203.
, Sir Mark! 81.
of Mersingtoun, Thomas, 53.
, Michael, 149.
   Keir, Mr Richard, 123.
Kellie, Thomas, Earl of, 185.
, Sir Archibald, 158, 164, 165.
   Kelso,215.
Kempis, Thomas, 39.
Kennedy, Mr James, 205.
Kerse, The, 77.
, Laird of, 192.
, Lady, 199.
   Keyth, Alexander, 113, 114, 117, 126, 128,
129, 134, 136, 138, 139, 140, 144, 146, 147,148, 150, 173,178,180.
, James, 185.
, 134.
   Kilmarnock, 122.
   Kincaid, Doctor, 198.
   King, General, 207.
   Kinghorn, Countess of, 112, 126, 213.
, Earl of, 118, 126, 128, 131, 139, 140, 146.
   Kinhilt, Laird of, 159.
   Kinloch, Francis, 63, 109.
   Kinneir, Laurence, 56.
   Kinnoull, Earl of, 37, 74,100,110,179,183.
   Kinross, Mr Henry, 173.
   Kintyre, 23.
, Earl of, 126.
   Knockfergus, 174.
   Kylismuir, Gentlemen of, 8.
   Kynetlis, Laird of, 141.
   Kynnell, 151, 153.
   Kynninmonth, 11, 14, 20, 24, 46, 104, 155,
182,196.
   Kynnocher, The Lady, 165.
   Lamingtoun, Laird of, 122, 124, 127, 129,
130.
   Lanerk, Earl of, (Secretary,) *passim*.
Langley, Sir Marmaduk, 213.
Langtoun, Laird of, 186.
„ 174.
   Lauder, Mr John, 35.

Lauderdale, Earl of, 9,10,21, 35, 37, 39, 41,
82, 90, 100, 107, 152, 200, 206.
Law, Mr James, 4, 29.
, Mr Mungo, (minister,) 210.
, Mr Archibald, 219.
   Lawers, Laird of, 160, 220.
Lawsoun, Mr John, 20.
Layng, Mr John, 26.
Ledingtoun, 13, 14.
Leith, 98, 189.
   Lennox, The, 44.
, Duke of, 112, 145.
   Leslie, General, 92, 97, 152, 201.
, The Lord, 118.
, Mr George, 185.
, Sir James, 25, 26.
, Patrick, (provost of Aberdeen,) 168.
, 155.
   Lerber, Kirk of, 216.
   Lermonth, Mr Andro, 26.
, John, 139.
   Lethnot, lands of, 43.
   Leven, Earl of, 159, 174, 176, 207, 210.
   Levingston, James, 3, 4, 6,13,15,17, 21, 27,
28, 32, 33, 39, 48, 51, 58, 60, 68, 75, 81, 92, 102, 104, 107, 109, 113, 132.
of Kynnaird, Sir James, 114.
, Alexander, 216.
, John, 147.
   Ley, Laird of, 23.
   Leyis, Lands of, 79-
   Libertoun, 24.
   Liddes, Thomas, 54.
   Lillie, John, (pedagog,) 181.
   Linlithgow, 66, 67, 147.
   Loch, Peter, 50.
   Lochmaben, 132.
   Lochquhaber, 212.
   Lockhart, Allan, 9,11.
, Sir James, 6, 7,10,16,19, 22,27, 38, 41, 166.
, Robert, 156, 213.
   Logie, Mr Andro, (minister,) 208.
, John, 208.
   London, 3, 33, 120.
   Lorne, The Lord, 3,19,20, 21,23, 44,56, 71.
Lothian, Colonel, 153.
——, Earl of, (Lieutenant-general,) 12,
14, 66, 101, 161, 219., Mr John, 30.
   Loudoun, Lord, 90, 91, 101, 110,

138, 146,
148, 152,188, 212.
Lour, Laird of, 144,147.
——, Lands of, 79.
   Loustoun, John, (notary,) 196.
   Lowis, Alexander, 7, 25.
   Lowmonds, The, 32.
   Lowrie, Alexander, 23.
   Ludquharn, Laird of, 11, 96.
   Lumsden, Mr Robert, (reider in Edinburgh,)
187.
   Lundy, Laird of, 167, 168.
Luthriemuir, Gentlemen of, 43.
Lychtbody, Mr George, 195, 207, 211.
Lyndsay, Colonel, 72.
——, Lord, 18, 90, 97,113, 145, 154.
——, Mr Alexander, (Bishop of DunkelcL)
82.
——,Mr David, (Bishopof Edinburgh,) 82.
of Kynnettles, David, 133,134.
——, Hew, 97, 109, 171,173.
——, Sir James, 171.
——, Sir Jherome, 180.
——, Mr John, 29.
——, Mr Patrick, 9,16, 20, 31, 33, 56.
——, Patrick, 106.
   Lyne, Andro, 77.
Lyon of Auldbar, James, 151.
——Anna, 4.
   Maccaula, Thomas, 217.
Mackenzie, Mr Donald, 168.
Mackie, Bourtie, 175.
Macmorran, John, 4.
M'Brair, Mr, 31.
M'CalL David, 59,105, 107.
——, Katharine, 107.
M'Fathrik, Neil, 41.
M'Gie, Mr John, 58.
M'Jockies, The, 60.
Magdalan Chaple, the, 154.
Maitland, Lord and Lady, 10, 82, 136, 247,
150, 195.
Manchester, Lord, 207.
Mar, Countess of, 25, 57, 85, 87, 102, 112,
113, 124,129,134, 205, 206., Earl of, 12,17, 24,64,66,69, 90,153,
172, 214.
   Marischall, Countess of, 95, 98, 111, 114,
121, 123, 125, 128, 130, 133, 136,137,
139, 141, 143, 146,148, 150,178,180.
——, The Earl of, 31, 36,139.

Marjoribanks, Mr Andro, 44.
Matheson, Colonel, 190.
Maule, Henry, 84, 128, 131, 134, 137, 143,
183, 193.
——, Jeane, 80.
——, John, 21.
——, Patrick, 26.
——, Robert, 128, 130.
   Maxwell, Captain, 4.
——, Alexander, 135.
——, James, 12, 32, 36, 38, 55, 56, 104.
——, Mr John, (Bishop of Ross,) 82.
——, Mr, 113.
   Maxwell, Richard, 26.
——, Thomas, 14, 20, 30, 35, 36, 39, 42, 44, 63, 86, 127, 129, 135, 137.
May, The licht of, 38.
Meldrum, Laird of, 86.
——, Sir John, 178.
   ——, John, 4.
   Melgum, Laird of, 178.
Melvill, Lord, 24, 26.
————, Sir James, 220.
Menmuir, Lands of, 43.
Merschell, Mr John, 175, 197.
Michell, William, 45.
Mickle, Mr Andro, 30.
Milmay, Sir Hary, 102, 103.
Minthous, Master of the, 43.
Moffet, Captain, 201.
Moir of Stentoun, Mr John, 41.
Moneky, 19, 25, 104.
Monro, Colonel, 53, 107.
——, General-Major, 176.
——, David, 122.
   Monteith, John, 216.
   Montrose, Earl of, 92, 101, 120, 140, 212,
218, 219.
——, 130.
   Monymale, 151.
More, John, 95.
Morison, John, 162, 172.
s Closs, 189.
   Morphie, Laird of, 37, 56. 58.
   Mortoun, Earl of, 16, 24, 31, 40, 64, 69,131,
145, 150, 166, 179, 183.
Mo watt, Charles, 4, 11, 24, 25.
Mowbray, 110.
——, Mr William, 35.
   Mudie of Sauchtonhall, Thomas, 176.
——, William, 130.
   Muir, Sir John, 80.

——, Mistres, 80.
   Muirhead, David, 4.
,, 39, 155.
   Murkill, Laird of, 168.
   Murray, the Earl of, 10, 37, 39, 41, 76, 90,
108.
——, Alexander, (fear of Annatland,) 173.
——, David, 111.
——, James, 14, 20, 40, 46, 58, 65, 117, 118, 119, 134, 139, 143, 146, 147, 150, 153, 158, 161, 169, 186, 192.
——, Sir James, 16, 50.
——, Sir John, 64, 173.
——, John, 20, 64, 85.
   Murray.Mungo, 6, 48,63,121,144,146,169, 170, 173, 178.
——, D. Margaret, 68, 152.
——, Sir Patrick, 27, 51.
——, Patrick, 5, 131.
——, Robert, 158, 159, 196.
——, Lady Sophia, 197.
——, Mr Thomas, 26, 155, 156, 171.
——, Sir William, 4.
——, William, 7, 12, 30, 83, 155, 159, 168, 175, 179, 180, 191,195.
Muschet, (servitor to the Earl of Airth,) 106.
Musselburgh, 72.
Mynto Steuart, Laird, 37.
   Norie, Mr Robert, (Bishop of Brechin,) 37.
Norvell, Mr George, 13, 102, 114, 144, 147,
163,169, 182.
Notingham, 174.
Nuck, 15.
   Ochiltree, Lord, 201, 202.
   Oliphant, Mr John, 59.
——, Patrick Lord, 103.
   Orleans, 48, 54.
Oswell, Mr Andro,217.
Oxenfurd, Lord, 131.
Oxford, 185, 201.
   Paip, Mr John, 205.
Palatine, Prince, 53.
Panbryd, 25, 38.
Panmuir, Lord, *passim.*
Paris, 52.
Park, John, 85.
Paterson, John, 30.
Patoun, James, 130.
——, William, 57.
   Peacock, George, 51.

Pembroke, Earl of, 49-
Pencaitland, 57.
Penman, John, 147.
Persoun, Mr David, 33.
Perth, Earl of, 90.
, Burgh of, 155, 167, 209-
　Peter, John, 178.
Petrocella, (i.e. Craighall,) 123, 203.
　Phillorth, Lord, 85,101
　Philp, James, 117, 122, 123, 125, 126, 133, 135, 137, 138, 140, 141, 142, 149.
Piggot, John, 115.
　Pilmuir, John, 4, 5, 6, 20, 34, 41, 42, 44, 49, 57, 68, 85, 114, 126, 130, 133, 137, 139, 144,147-
　　Pirrie, Alexander, 7, 28, 166.
　　——, John, 166.
　　Pitcairn, Andro, 11, 62, 65.
., Arthur, 11.
　　Pitscotty-Eister, 112.
　　Pitsligo, Tutor of, 95, 101, 102.
　　Poppill, 73.
　　Portland, Earl of, (treasurer,) 5.
Possill, 20.
　　Potterrow, The, 93.
　　Prentice, Gilbert, 196.
Prestoun, 199-
　　Prestoungrange, Laird of, 46, 119.
Prestounpans, 210.
　　Prymrois, Archibald, 142, 144,158,161,162, 164,187.
, James, 21, 23, 29,43, 94, 96, 113, 114, 156.
　　Queensberry, Earl of, 29, 41.
Queensferry, toun of, 31, 52, 78.
　Queinsburgh, 175.
　　Quhytfurd, Mr Walter, (Bishop of Brechin,) 22, 82.
Quhythall, 86.
Quhythill, Lord, 14, 35.
Quhytlaw, Patrick, 58.
Quodquhoun, 24.
　Raa, Lord, 95, 201.
, James, 30, (minister at Marykirk,) 39.
, John, 20.
, Dame Heleine, 67, 159, 168.
　Ramsay, Mr Andro, (minister,) 5, 51, 69, 85, 154, 172.
, Sir Robert, 19.
　Register, The Lord, 4, 18, 23, 58.

Reidhous, Sir John of, 58, 119-
　Ridpeth, Captain, 116.
　Rig of Athernie, William, 201.
Alisoun, (spouse of Mr John Skene,) 129.
, Mr John, 31, 199-
, Mr Thomas, 184.
　Ripon, 120.
　Robertsoun, Mr James, 40.
, Thomas, 199, 214.
　Rollok, Mr Hary, (minister of Edinburgh,) 169-
, Mr John, 85, 161, 181, 189, 192, 216, 217.
of Piltoun, Peter, 196.
, Walter, 217.
　Roo, Mr, 101.
　Ross, Bishop of, 13, 15, 22, 46., The Lady, 33.
　Rothes, Earl of, 9, 35, 90, 91, 97, 101, 112, 124, 129, 152, 155.
Rouen, 6.
　Roxburgh, Countess of, 21.
, Earl of, 13, 15, 17, 35, 51, 54, 66, 67, 72, 84, 95, 139-
　Roy, John, 51.
　Rupert, Prince, 207.
　Ruthven, General, 99, 116, 119, 210.
, Sir Francis, 173.
　Rystoun, 203.
　Rytounfurd, 119-
　Saltoun, 183, 186.
, Lord, 113, 117, 118, 121, 122, 126 171, 202.
　Saltprestoun, 200.
　Samuelston, The Lady, 20, 73.
　Sanctandrois, 12, 14, 149, 173.
, Archbishop of, 12.
　Sandfurd, Laird of, 8. See *Nairn.*
　Sandilands, Lieut. Colonel, 219-
, Mr James, (professor in Aberdeen,) 164.
, Mr Thomas, 207.
, Mr William, 137, (minister at Couper,) 169, 188.
, Sir William, 219-
　Sayis, Lord, 93.
　Scone, 50, 69, 156, 160.
　Scott, Sir John, 55.
, Patrick, 113.
　Scottistarbet, the Laird of, 19, 88, 90.
　Scottiscraig, Laird of, 129, 191.
　Scrimgeor, Hew, 12.

, Mr Henry, 50.
　Seaforth, Earl of, 151.
　Seatoun of Schethin, William, 205.
　Sempill, Bryce, 169.
, John, 29, 38, 42, 67, 70, 79, 163.
　Seres Kirk, 175.
Scytoun, 135.
, David, 57.
, Lady Grissell, 35.
of Barnis, Sir John, 56.
——— of Mania, John, 185.
, Robert, 164.
of Marry, William, 86.
　Sidserff, Archbald, 210.
　Sinclair of Northfield, Francis, 187, 204,219.
of Turbister, Francis, 174.
, G, 122.
of.Murkill. Sir James, 95, 160, 163, 168, 187.
　Skene of Halyards, Mr Andro, 76.
, Mr John, 111, 192, 201, 210.
　Skynner, Mr Laurence, (minister of Navar,) 43, 54.
Small, James, 218.
Smyth, Mr John, 91, 114, 153.
　Smyth, Sir John, 159, 17 8.
　Souter, David, 56, 130.
　Southesk, Earl of, 46, 58, 90, 102, 104, 107, 142, 151, 183.
Southsyd, 219.
Speir, Dame Rachell, 200.
Spottiswood, Mr John, (late Chancellor,) 118., Sir Robert, (President,) 9, 87, 157.
　Spynie in Murray, 220.
　Squyre, John, 132, 156, 169.
Stanchefurd, 175, 178.
Stapleton, Sir Philip, 164.
Stenton, Kirk of, 35, 36, 42, 43.
Steuart, Captain, 153.
of Blantyre, Captain, 113.
, Lieut.-Colonel, 153.
, Alexander, 103, 109, 116, 121.
, Archibald, 138.J
of Blackhall, Sir Archibald, 102,202.
, Donald, 60.
, James, 66, 68, 162, 167, 215.
, Sir James, 14.
, John. 42, 46, 150.
, Sir Lues, 57, 73, 76, 108, 126, 196.
, Dame Marie, (Countes of Mar,) 205.
, Walter, 112, 117.

, Captain Walter, 113.
, Sir William, 4.
Stevinsoun, Mr Andro, 35.
Stirling, Earl of, (Secretary,) 3, 4, 6, 7, 8, 9, 10, 14, 15, 16, 17, 18, 9,*ptusim.*
, George, 50.
, Kirk of, 102.
Stormonth, Viscount, 14, 152, 160.
St radian, Patrick, 15.
Straffurd, Thomas Earl of, (deputie of Ireland,) 136.
Strathern, 13, 156.
Stratoun, Arthour, 95.
Struther, Mr William, 128.
Sueden, King of, 77-
Suedens, the, 59.
Sunderland, 204.
Sutherland, Earl of, 105.
Sydserf, Mr Thomas, (Bishop of Galloway,) 82. 86.
Tait, Robert, 196.
Tamptallon, 164.
Taverner, Mr, 49-
Thomson, William, 176.
Thorntoun, Laird of, 16, 174.
Tod, Hew, 177.
Torphichen, 19.
Traquair, Earl of, 3, 7, 8, 12, 15, 19, *passim.*
Tullibardin, Earl of, 50.
Tullibody, 104.
Tullycultry, 4, 32.
TurrifF, the Person of, 168.
Twysdaill, James, 214.
Tyne, the, 119, 203.
Ugstoun, Kirk of, 155.
Vache, Sir John, 88, 146.
Vayne, Sir Henry, 145.
Vdward, Mr Nathaniel, 15, 24.
Vetche, John, (younger of Dawik,) 52.
, Thomas, 175, 206, 217.
Volusenus, Florentius, 37.
Wallace of Auchans, 35.
, Bryce, 196.
, Robert, 101.
Waller, Sir William, 208.
Waristoun, Lord, 196, 214, 217, 219, 220.
Waterheid, 219.
, Laird of, 181.
, Mynes of, 104, 130.
Wauchope, William, 98.
Wauchtoun, Lord, 67, 200.
Wedderburn, Laird of, 42.
, Mr James, (bishop of Dumblane,) 82.
Wemyss, Earl of, 149.
, Mr James, (Commissar of St Androis, 213.
Wigton, Earl of, 90,
Wilkie, John, 98.
Wilson, Mr James, 118.
Winchester, Dean of, 5, 12, 14, 16, 30, 50, 62, 133, 137, 141, 144.
Windsor, 16, 47-
Winram, Mr George, 34.
Wintoun, Earl of, 31, 142, 145.
Wod, Patrick, 8, 14, 42, 62, 64, 65, 71, 73, 83.
Wodstok, 201.
Woodhall, Lord, 90.
Wriglisworth, Richard, 114.
2g
Yarmouth, 193, 195.
Ylaw, 32, 35, 54, 55, 56, 105, 112.
Yester, Lord, 35, 178.
York, 84, 89, 93, 161, 162, 164, 166, 167, 207, 213.
Young, Alexander, (skynner in Elgin,) 95.
of Downachar, Sergeant David, 133. , Doctor John, (Dean of Winchester,) 133. , Michael, 144.